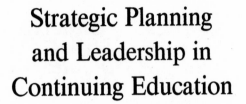

Strategic Planning
and Leadership in
Continuing Education

*Enhancing Organizational
Vitality, Responsiveness,
and Identity*

❖ ❖ ❖

Robert G. Simerly
and Associates

✥   ✥   ✥

Strategic Planning and Leadership in Continuing Education

Jossey-Bass Publishers

San Francisco

STRATEGIC PLANNING AND LEADERSHIP IN CONTINUING EDUCATION
Enhancing Organizational Vitality, Responsiveness, and Identity
by Robert G. Simerly and Associates

Copyright © 1987 by: Jossey-Bass Inc., Publishers
                       350 Sansome Street
                       San Francisco, California 94104

Library of Congress Cataloging-in-Publication Data

Simerly, Robert.
  Strategic planning and leadership in continuing
education.

  (The Jossey-Bass higher education series)
  Bibliography: p. 215
  Includes index.
  1. Continuing education—Administration.
2. Strategic planning. I. Title. II. Series.
LC5225.A34S55   1987   374   86-27382
ISBN 1-55542-034-6 (alk. paper)

Manufactured in the United States of America

JACKET DESIGN BY WILLI BAUM

HB Printing   10 9 8 7 6 5 4 3

FIRST EDITION
    First printing: March 1977
    Second printing: December 1989

Code 8703

✛ ✛ ✛

The Jossey-Bass
Higher Education Series

Consulting Editor
Adult and Continuing Education

Alan B. Knox
University of Wisconsin at Madison

✦ ✦ ✦

Contents

Preface   xi

The Authors   xix

Part One: An Overview of Strategic Planning

1. Why Continuing Education Leaders
    Must Plan Strategically   1
    Robert G. Simerly

2. The Strategic Planning Process: Seven Essential Steps   12
    Robert G. Simerly

3. The Leader's Role in Strategic Planning   31
    John W. Schmidt

4. How to Conduct an Internal Diagnosis of a
    Continuing Education Organization   51
    Robert G. Simerly

    **Part Two: Putting Strategic Planning to Work in
    Continuing Education Organizations**

5. Matching Programmatic Emphases to the Parent
    Organization's Values   71
    Michael J. Offerman

6. Building an Effective Organizational Culture: How to Be
    Community-Oriented in a Traditional Institution   87
    Terrence E. Deal

ix

7. Managing the Tensions That Go
    With the Planning Process   103
    Francis M. Trusty

8. Linking Continuing Education to Community and
    Economic Development   125
    Gordon H. Mueller

9. Developing a Strategic Marketing Plan   149
    Mary Lindenstein Walshok

10. Using Evaluation to Monitor Plans and Assess Results   168
    Margaret E. Holt

Part Three: Challenges for Continuing Education Leaders

11. From Marginality to Mainstream: Strategies for
    Increasing Internal Support for Continuing Education   185
    James C. Votruba

12. Achieving Success in Strategic Planning: A Practical
    Road Map for Continuing Education Leaders   202
    Robert G. Simerly

    References   215

    Name Index   237

    Subject Index   242

❖ ❖ ❖

Preface

Continuing education makes substantial contributions to the gross national product, provides opportunities for adults to engage in lifelong learning, which is important to enhancing the quality of their lives, and offers ways for people and organizations to engage in self-renewal. Although everyone acknowledges the need for continuing education, it is frequently viewed as marginal to the central mission of the organization providing it. *Strategic Planning and Leadership in Continuing Education* demonstrates how continuing education practitioners can improve their effectiveness as leaders and can address the following three important issues:

- How to develop strategic plans that will help the parent organization realize that continuing education should be an integral part of its own central mission.
- How to use strategic planning to encourage the type of self-renewal that is important in maintaining organizational vitality, growth, and adaptivity to change.
- How to make strategic planning an integral part of staff training and development in order to encourage all staff to participate in setting and achieving organizational goals.

Strategic planning and effective leadership are linked together in a symbiotic relationship in which each enhances the other. Developing successful strategies for profiting from this symbiosis involves engaging in systems analysis and environmental scanning as a way of gathering reliable data about how the continuing education organization is perceived by its important constituencies. This is a central theme developed throughout the book.

xi

Who Should Read This Book

Strategic Planning and Leadership in Continuing Education is written by practitioners for other practitioners who seek effective ways of building bridges between the continuing education unit and the parent organization. All of the creative approaches to strategic planning and leadership discussed here are already being used in daily practice in some of our most successful continuing education organizations. Thus, this book does not simply present an idealized version of what continuing education organizations might become. Instead, the authors provide practical ideas, suggestions, and guidelines for professional practice as well as case studies that illustrate the principles being discussed. All of the authors have been instrumental in linking theory and practice in their institutions. They all emphasize the importance of developing both a strong conceptual basis for leadership and a cohesive team spirit that is capable of fostering cooperation with the parent organization as well as with the many constituencies served by continuing education. Thus, this book is designed to assist all continuing education professionals who are charged with developing and maintaining dynamic, responsive organizations.

Overview of the Contents

Part One of the book provides an overview of strategic planning. In Chapter One, Robert G. Simerly offers a comprehensive definition of strategic planning and links it to effective leadership. This chapter analyzes why many traditional forms of organizational leadership and planning are no longer adequate for today's sophisticated, high-performance organizations. The underlying theme of the chapter is that today's effective continuing education leader should be a behavioral scientist who is continually seeking new and effective ways to develop strategies that will ensure the health and productivity of the organization.

Chapter Two, also by Robert G. Simerly, deals with the process of strategic planning. Because strategic planning gives everyone in the organization a chance to participate in decision making, anomie, the loss of personal power and the resultant feeling of disenfranchisement, is virtually eliminated. Seven specific steps in the strategic planning process are identified, and examples are given to illustrate the relationship between each step and the overall concept. In addition, ten issues that should be considered when implementing strategic planning programs are identified and discussed.

Chapter Three, by John W. Schmidt, shows practical ways of applying strategic planning concepts from the behavioral sciences to a continuing education organization. Schmidt provides a useful historical analysis of change in higher education as a basis for demonstrating that the various publics demanding changes today are simply fulfilling the historical role of American society in influencing educational policy. He analyzes various hindrances to strategic planning and offers suggestions on how to overcome these. Practical methods for engaging in environmental scanning, a theme that recurs throughout the book, are emphasized. Lastly, the author shows how strategic decisions can be linked effectively to program planning.

Chapter Four, by Robert G. Simerly, illustrates how a management audit can be used to conduct an effective internal diagnosis of a continuing education organization. This important aspect of strategic planning enables leaders to develop a process for constantly reevaluating their organizations and thus increasing their accountability to the many publics they serve. An integral part of strategic planning involves finding the balance between maintenance and change. Case studies illustrate how this can be done.

Part Two considers processes important in implementing strategic planning. In Chapter Five, Michael J. Offerman analyzes the importance of values clarification, an initial step in strategic planning, and demonstrates how the leader's approach to this aspect influences continuing education programming in important ways. He stresses that continuing education programming is most successful when it is infused with the guiding values of the parent organization. Nine interrelated programming values that contribute to organizational integrity are identified and discussed.

Chapter Six, by Terrence E. Deal, addresses the following important issues: (1) How can continuing education leaders shape both the identity and the image of their organizations? (2) How can conflict between the cultures of traditional programs and those of continuing education programs within the same institution be managed? (3) What specific leadership strategies should be considered in building culture and tradition under nontraditional conditions? Deal provides useful advice on building nontraditional cultures in response to community needs without undermining traditional programs and the organizational culture on which they are based. The theme of the chapter is that effective leaders can actively shape the identity of their organization by reinforcing its system of values and beliefs.

In Chapter Seven, Francis M. Trusty explores the conflicts generated by strategic planning. His thesis is that eliminating the conflict would be dysfunctional because it would diminish the energy needed to achieve change. Therefore, continuing education leaders need to acquire the necessary skills to manage conflict effectively rather than expend energy in attempting to eliminate it. He identifies effective conflict-management skills, including the development of win-win strategies.

Chapter Eight links continuing education to the development of the community and of the economy. Here, Gordon H. Mueller argues that continuing education's marginal position can only be overcome through the active participation of its leaders in systematically planning the academic future of our colleges and universities. His conceptual framework considers three broad areas of linkage between these organizations and the constituencies they serve: (1) joint research, (2) technology transfer and entrepreneurial assistance, and (3) human resource development (education and training).

In Chapter Nine, Mary Lindenstein Walshok emphasizes that successful marketing involves clearly understanding the needs of the publics, constituencies, and interest groups who legitimately make claims on the institution for services. The institution must be responsive to these publics and must be able to provide programs designed to meet their specific needs.

Chapter Ten, by Margaret E. Holt, develops the theme that the mastery of the design, implementation, interpretation, and use of evaluations is one of the primary tools of superior leaders. She provides an in-depth analysis of the following three major ideas: (1) how to match the organization's culture and needs to an evaluation plan, (2) how evaluation can assist in strategic scanning and planning, and (3) how evaluation can bring visibility to the leader's vision. The theme of the chapter is that by monitoring four key environments in a continuing education organization (external, institutional, structural, and cultural), a leader is better equipped to develop planning strategies. This, in turn, helps to increase accountability.

Part Three looks toward the future and suggests ways of integrating strategic planning and effective leadership. In Chapter Eleven, James C. Votruba identifies practical ways in which continuing education activities can be linked to the essential priorities of the parent organization in order to achieve acceptance and support. In addition, he explores how continuing education leaders can help create a sense of organizational vision and how this can lead to an improvement in the organization's ability to respond creatively to the threats and opportunities that confront the parent organization.

Chapter Twelve, by Robert G. Simerly, summarizes the book's major themes and ideas. In the future, some roles in continuing education will be redefined in order to accommodate the changing demands of the next decade. This chapter discusses the competencies required of future continuing education leaders and recaps the twelve important issues that will affect the future of continuing education.

Acknowledgments

Many people have helped me with this book. A special thanks goes to Alan B. Knox, professor of adult education at the University of Wisconsin at Madison and consulting editor for Jossey-Bass books on continuing education. As a result of his suggestions for revisions, this manuscript has become stronger and more coherent. He has been a major force in shaping the literature of continuing education, and I have benefited from his insights and assistance.

In addition, I wish to thank the authors who have contributed to this book. All of them took valuable time from their busy
schedules to put into writing the lessons they have learned from
striving to become successful leaders. Their practical expertise is
the result of engaging in the personal introspection required of
effective leaders in highly complex organizations.

I completed this manuscript while serving as head of the
Office of Conferences and Institutes at the University of Illinois at
Urbana-Champaign. A special word of thanks goes to the secretar-
ial staff there for their help with the typing and editorial work. I
particularly wish to thank Sue Overmyer and Lynn Padilla, our
word processing experts, who patiently provided several revised
drafts of the chapters. A special thank you also goes to Eileen
Goodchild, my secretary at the University of Illinois, who worked
with me as a partner in editing the manuscript. In addition, she
willingly assumed important administrative duties so that I could
have the time to devote to the many tasks associated with this
manuscript.

Jean Deichman, director of graphic design in the Office of
Conferences and Institutes at the University of Illinois at Urbana-
Champaign, has contributed many of the charts, figures, and
diagrams found in this book. I am grateful for her ability to
translate complex thoughts into coherent graphic designs that
assist in explaining ideas.

An important part of the thought behind this manuscript is
a result of the team efforts generated by all of the people who work
in the Office of Conferences and Institutes. This administrative
team was headed by program directors Carolyn Carson, Roy
Roper, and Craig Weidemann. Through daily interaction with
this team of dedicated, professional experts, I have learned much
about the complexities of today's high-performance continuing
education organizations.

I also wish to thank three colleagues in continuing education at the University of Illinois at Urbana-Champaign who were
particularly helpful to me and my work. Charles Kozoll, associate
director of continuing education and public service, provided
intellectual support and encouragement for my many writing
projects. I value his advice, suggestions, and friendship. In

addition, I am grateful to Dennis Dahl, director of continuing education and public service and associate vice-chancellor for academic affairs. His model of warm, supportive leadership was of value to all of us at the university. I am grateful to him for his professional and personal friendship. In addition, I wish to thank Robert Bender, assistant vice-president for academic affairs at the University of Illinois. His vision of systems approaches to continuing education is always helpful. As a friend and professional colleague he has influenced my thinking in important ways. In addition, I wish to thank my new colleagues—the staff in the Division of Continuing Studies at the University of Nebraska at Lincoln. Their encouragement and support is always appreciated.

And lastly I wish to thank my wife, Coby Bunch. I am grateful for her personal and professional support throughout this project. All drafts of the manuscript have benefited from her expertise in the behavioral sciences. Her comments on and insights into the dynamics of modern organizations have significantly affected my thinking and writing.

Lincoln, Nebraska   Robert G. Simerly
January 1987

✤   ✤   ✤

The Authors

Robert G. Simerly is dean of continuing studies and professor of vocational and adult education at the University of Nebraska at Lincoln. Until recently he was head of the Office of Conferences and Institutes in the Office of Continuing Education and Public Service at the University of Illinois at Urbana-Champaign. He has held teaching and administrative positions in both the United States and Europe. Simerly received his B.S. degree (1961) in education, his M.A. degree (1963) in liberal arts, and his Ed.D degree (1973) in educational leadership, all from the University of Tennessee at Knoxville. He is particularly concerned with helping people in organizations find ways of increasing the effectiveness of their leadership. In addition to having written many articles related to this topic, Simerly also wrote the book *Successful Budgeting for Conferences and Institutes.*

Terrence E. Deal taught at Harvard University before becoming professor of education at Peabody College of Vanderbilt University, where he teaches symbolism in organizations and organizational theory and behavior. For several years he has studied the roles of myth, ritual and ceremony, and symbols in organizational settings. This research led to the book, *Corporate Cultures: The Rites and Rituals of Corporate Life,* which he coauthored with Allan Kennedy. In addition, Deal has coauthored six other books and has written numerous articles and papers. He consults internationally with both business and nonprofit organizations. He is also on the faculty of the Institute for the Management of Lifelong Learning that is held each summer at Harvard University. Deal holds a B.A. degree (1961) from Laverne College in history, an M.A. degree (1966) from California State University at

Los Angeles in educational administration, and a Ph.D. degree (1970) from Stanford University in educational administration and sociology.

Margaret E. Holt is an assistant professor of adult education at the University of Georgia and an associate of the Charles F. Kettering Foundation. She is an editorial advisor to *The National Forum* (Phi Kappa Phi journal), associate editor of *Innovative Higher Education,* and a member of the editorial board for *Continuum,* the journal of the National University Continuing Education Association. She received her B.A. degree (1969) from Ohio Northern University in English, and her M.Ed. (1975) and Ed.D. (1979) degrees from the University of Georgia in adult education.

Gordon H. Mueller is dean of Metropolitan College and professor of European history at the University of New Orleans, where he administers the continuing education program, off-campus centers, and international study programs. His professional and research interests involve an exploration of the future of educational change, higher education administration and leadership, and the university of the twenty-first century. He is a graduate of Harvard's Institute for Educational Management (1984) and a recipient of Austria's Distinguished Cross of Honor for Science and Art (1979). Mueller has studied at the universities of Zurich, Vienna, and Berlin. He holds a B.A. degree (1961) from Stetson University and M.A. (1963) and Ph.D. (1970) degrees in European history from the University of North Carolina at Chapel Hill.

Michael J. Offerman is director of continuing education and outreach at the University of Wisconsin at Stevens Point. He received his B.A. degree (1970) from the University of Iowa in history, his M.S. degree (1979) from the University of Wisconsin at Milwaukee in educational leadership, and his Ed.D. degree (1985) from Northern Illinois University in adult continuing education.

John W. Schmidt is professor of speech and dean of General Extension, University of Wisconsin Extension. He works with the twenty-six institutions in the University of Wisconsin system. His statewide responsibilities include developing a statewide long-range plan, determining program priorities and goals, reviewing annual program plans for each institution, and allocating resources to support the long-range and annual plans. He received his B.A. degree (1956) from Illinois College in history and his M.A. degree (1961) from Bradley University and his Ph.D. degree (1969) from the University of Minnesota in speech.

Francis M. Trusty is professor of educational leadership at the University of Tennessee at Knoxville. He also serves as executive director of the Administrator/Supervisor Evaluation Program in the Tennessee Career Ladder Program. He is a distinguished professor of the National Academy of School Executives, recipient of a Danforth Foundation fellowship and of the Quill E. Cope Award for Outstanding Teaching, and editor of *Administering Human Resources: A Behavioral Approach to Educational Administration.* He received his B.S. degree (1949) from Oregon State College in education, his M.S. degree (1955) from the University of Oregon in education, and his Ed.D. degree (1960) from Stanford University in educational administration.

James C. Votruba is professor of education and dean of the School of General Studies and Professional Education at the State University of New York at Binghamton. For the past decade he has been both an administrator and scholar in the general area of continuing higher education. From 1980 to 1983 he was a Kellogg Foundation National Fellow studying leadership in adult education and innovation in a variety of international settings. He received his B.A. degree (1968) in political science, his M.A. degree (1970) in sociology, and his Ph.D. degree (1974) in higher education, all from Michigan State University.

Mary Lindenstein Walshok is the associate vice-chancellor for extended studies and public service and associate adjunct professor in the Department of Sociology at the University of California at San Diego. She is also a Kellogg Fellow involved in researching issues related to science, technology, and educational policy. She received her B.A. degree (1964) from Claremont College, her M.A. degree (1966) from the University of Indiana, and her Ph.D. degree (1969) from the University of Indiana, all in sociology.

❖ ❖ ❖

Strategic Planning and Leadership in Continuing Education

Enhancing Organizational Vitality, Responsiveness, and Identity

✤ 1 ✤

Why Continuing Education Leaders Must Plan Strategically

ROBERT G. SIMERLY

Continuing education organizations exist to achieve goals. In any organization that seeks to achieve goals, groups of people cooperate in the complex task of organizing activities. It is through this cooperative work effort that organizations define activities, develop and implement plans of actions, and evaluate their successes and failures. Planning and effective leadership are central to such work. At a time when the national consciousness of the need for organizational excellence has never been higher, a central issue has become how to integrate effective planning into leadership activities. Accomplishing this can enable organizations constantly to renew themselves through defining new directions for the future (Peters and Waterman, 1982; Peters and Austin, 1985; Tannenbaum and Associates, 1985). This book analyzes ways to use strategic planning for strengthening leadership in the large and diverse field of continuing education.

Strategic planning is a process that gives attention to (1) designing, (2) implementing, and (3) monitoring plans for improving organizational decision making. There are many approaches and methods that are helpful in thinking through this process. However, a review of the literature suggests that strategic planning is most effective when it incorporates the following activities:

1. Conducting a management audit to determine the strengths and weaknesses of the organization
2. Clarifying the important organizational values so that they can be used as a foundation upon which to build planning activities

3. Involving a wide variety of staff and important constituencies in creating a mission statement to guide the organization
4. Establishing goals and objectives to be achieved to fulfill the mission
5. Creating an action plan for implementing goals and objectives
6. Conducting a reality test to determine the availability of resources required to achieve goals and objectives and modifying plans as necessary
7. Designing a feedback system that allows constant modification of strategic plans in order to respond to changing conditions in the internal and external environment

A detailed discussion of steps in this strategic planning process and how to use it for creating long-range plans is found in Chapter Two. Subsequent chapters further illustrate the many complex aspects of the relationship between strategic planning and effective leadership. Throughout, this book addresses the following important relationships between strategic planning and effective continuing education leadership:

1. The skills required of continuing education leaders to engage their organizations in effective strategic planning
2. The impact organizational culture has on strategic planning and leadership
3. The important dynamics that groups experience and how understanding these can help leaders develop more effective plans and strategies
4. The use of systems analysis and environmental scanning as an integral part of strategic planning and effective leadership
5. The importance of using strategic planning as a vehicle to help all organizational members create successful leadership strategies for themselves

Strategic planning should be a part of every leader's repertoire of skills (Craig, 1978; Steiner, 1979; Pfeiffer, Goodstein, and Nolan, 1985). Strategic planning is most effective when it becomes an integral part of the fabric of daily work life rather than being viewed as a separate activity. It then becomes possible to use strategic planning principles as a basis for all organizational activities. For example, it can become a guiding principle for the management of human resources (Odiorne, 1981). It can be effective in developing plans for introducing change (Quinn, 1980; Tichy, 1983; Kirkpatrick, 1985). And it can become an integral part of developing overarching patterns of organizational success (Steiner and Miner, 1982; Kaufman and Stone, 1983; Cameron and Whetten, 1983; Pennings and Associates, 1985).

Literature from the social sciences has enlarged our perspectives on improving leadership, and there has recently been an increased emphasis on using systems approaches to strengthen leadership. Such approaches have a common theme: strategic planning and leadership are such interrelated concepts that it is difficult to speak about one without considering the other (Cohen and Cohen, 1984; Argyris, Putnam, and Smith, 1985; Bennis, Benne, and Chin, 1985; Pennings and Associates, 1985). As a nation in search of excellence, we are finding new and improved ways to help individual managers think about developing strategies for becoming more successful in their jobs (Argyris and Schön, 1978; Bolman and Deal, 1984; Cleveland, 1985; Bellman, 1986; Beck and Hillmer, 1986).

Basic Questions for Strategic Planners

This book synthesizes research on leadership and strategic planning from the social sciences and merges it with very practical ideas that continuing education leaders can use to enhance their effectiveness. This is a practical book for professionals. As such, it does not attempt to provide prescriptive solutions for complex leadership and planning issues. Rather it invites introspection on the part of leaders—introspection directed toward improving their own leadership effectiveness as a first step in developing strategies for improving overall organizational leadership. The book explores in depth the previously mentioned five issues related to strengthening leadership through strategic planning.

1. What skills are required of continuing education leaders to engage their organizations in effective strategic planning?

Complexity, diversity, ambiguity, and decentralization are the watchwords in today's organizations. Leaders have to cope with increased complexity. They have to deal with increased diversity in terms of the public they serve. They must deal with increased levels of ambiguity and uncertainty in daily problem solving and decision making. Many traditional styles of leadership are proving to be ineffective for coping with such increased complexity (Boyatzis, 1982; Kanter, 1983; Fiedler and Chemers, 1984; Geneen and Moscow, 1984; Drucker, 1985; Srivastva and Associates, 1986).

Bradford and Cohen (1984) provide us with an excellent analysis of why traditional models of leadership are often ineffective in today's organizations. Such models are based on heroic views of leadership. In heroic leadership models the leader is viewed as an expert—a technician who can skillfully carry out all the important jobs in his or her unit. It is the leader's job to mobilize technical expertise and to act as a conductor to get work done. Today, however, most organizations demand more sophisticated approaches to leadership because of the increasingly complex tasks that must be accomplished in order to achieve increasingly complex goals.

Today's leader can be most effective when acting as a developer of human resources within the organization. This involves giving attention to four basic tasks: (1) building a team in which responsibility for success is equally shared, (2) giving attention to the continuous development of team members' individual skills, (3) creating consensus for a common organizational vision, and (4) encouraging staff to integrate strategic planning into all aspects of their daily decision making (Bradford and Cohen, 1984).

Strategic planning involves challenging individuals and groups to achieve excellence in all their activities. An analysis of the Bradford and Cohen research shows that when leaders in high-performance organizations are asked what challenges them, they consistently mention two basic things. First, they emphasize that the job itself must be challenging. Second, they say that they rarely see their bosses. Across all managerial levels, the degree of satisfaction experienced by subordinates tends to be in direct proportion to the degree that their bosses let them alone. Thus older, heroic models of leadership that emphasize the technical expertise of the leader who serves as a conductor for subordinates, in much the same way as an orchestra conductor leads an orchestra, rely on metaphors and actions that are inappropriate in today's sophisticated, high-performance organizations. Leaders in the future will need to concentrate more on becoming developers of people. They will need to concentrate on coaching and counseling in order to help staff members define for themselves a concept of continual professional development in which the needs of the individual and the organization can become compatible. And they will need to find creative ways to integrate planning and leadership functions so that they come to be seen as one integrated activity.

Bennis and Nanus (1985) confirm the fact that new forms of leadership will be essential to make our organizations as effective as possible in the future. They have identified four important strategies that leaders can use to become more effective: (1) creating focus and gaining attention through vision, (2) creating meaning through communication, (3) developing trust through positioning, and (4) developing self through positive self-regard. Their research on leadership in high-performance organizations emphasizes the sophisticated nature of the work force because of the increased education of its members. Such employees want to play important roles in planning the direction of their organizations. They want a say in defining missions and in developing goals and objectives to achieve these missions.

In the Bennis and Nanus study, effective leaders were those who consistently helped create a vision of where the organization should be going. Effective leaders never lose sight of this vision. In fact, they cling to it with a tenacity that is basically not negotiable, and they develop specific strategies and plans to achieve this vision. Such leaders are good communicators and use a wide variety of channels to help create meaning for work that is done in the organization. They develop trust by positioning their people in ways that enable them to be as successful as possible. And they always give attention to the development of themselves and others through emphasizing the worth of the individual and his or her accomplishments. Such leaders are future oriented, and yet they are also oriented toward producing results today. These leaders get results through the use of both intuitive and formal planning.

2. How can leaders come to understand and develop strategies for the effective management of organizational culture? Increasingly we are understanding the impact that corporate culture has on the effectiveness of the organization (Peters and Waterman, 1982; Deal and Kennedy, 1982; Grove, 1983; Schein, 1985). Schein (1985) offers the following valuable definition of organizational culture: It is "a pattern of basic assumptions— invented, discovered, or developed by a given group as it learns to cope with its problems of external adaptation and internal integration—that has worked well enough to be considered valid and, therefore, to be taught to new members as the correct way to perceive, think, and feel in relation to those problems" (p. 9).

Current research on organizational culture has revealed the importance of planning for the successful management of cultural change within the organization (Lippitt, 1982; Lippitt, Langseth, and Mossop, 1985; Schein, 1985). Thus effective leaders are students of organizational culture and change. They give time and attention to developing plans for changing culture in ways appropriate to the needs and the tasks of the organization.

3. What important aspects of group dynamics will impact on strategic planning and continuing education leadership? Organizations get things done through mobilizing groups of people. Therefore it is important for leaders to understand group dynamics. All organizational work groups deal with two basic issues simultaneously: (1) accomplishing the task at hand and (2) creating satisfactory social-emotional relationships among group members (Halpin, 1966; Bales, 1970; Kast and Rosenzweig, 1979; Zander, 1982; London, 1985). Thus people are always dealing with both the task and maintenance roles of the group. It is important that leaders understand this dual nature of group interactions because these task and maintenance dynamics act as powerful and influential forces within the group.

Schein (1985) has identified the following as major task and maintenance issues that all groups face as they conduct their daily work:

1. Developing a common language and set of conceptual categories. This enables group members to organize work and manage group issues in ways that increase the chances of promoting effective problem solving. Developing a common language and set of conceptual categories for organizing information enables all members of an organization to improve their daily problem solving.

2. Reaching consensus on group boundaries and the criteria for inclusion in the group. This enables individual group members to develop a psychological support base for their activities so that tasks can proceed with minimal interference. People usually have difficulty working effectively together until they understand and are confident of their place in the group.

3. Reaching consensus on criteria for the use of power and influence within the group. Power and influence issues are central to the effective functioning of any group. Groups give people the ability to use power and influence to achieve goals. However, they can also take away this power and influence and render individuals ineffective. Understanding how groups use power and influence is central to effective leadership because leaders spend so much of their time managing these dynamics in getting work done.

4. Reaching consensus on criteria for friendship and intimacy within the group. This deals with such important issues as helping individuals get a satisfactory answer to such questions as, "What does it take for people in the group to like me and want me for a friend and colleague upon whom they can rely?" Groups quickly establish norms for giving friendship, and such friendship is usually highly valued by individuals.

5. Reaching consensus on the criteria for giving out rewards and punishments. Since the reward and punishment structure is central to the effective functioning of any group, it is important that leaders understand these powerful dynamics that affect a group's productivity in achieving both the task and a satisfactory social-emotional relationship for group members.

Developing strategic plans to address these group issues makes it possible for individuals to function comfortably within the group and to concentrate on the tasks to be achieved. A collection of individuals does not become a high-performance group until it finds ways to manage the dynamics discussed above.

4. How can systems analysis and environmental scanning become an integral part of strategic planning and effective leadership? Systems analysis is a way to analyze complex issues by breaking them down into their component parts. Mitroff (1983) provides a useful way to engage in systems analysis through his concept of stakeholders. Stakeholders are those people and forces with a stake in the outcomes of the organization. Stakeholders affect organizational policy making and managerial leadership at all levels.

People who are stakeholders constantly engage in environmental scanning—surveying the environment for early warning signs that may be of importance to the organization. The assumptions of these stakeholders then become the basis for action. The stakeholder concept makes it possible to develop sophisticated approaches that can be used to analyze complex social systems.

Mitroff has developed four propositions that are useful for leaders to consider in relation to systems analysis, environmental scanning, and stakeholder analysis:

1. The world's growing complexity has made obsolete old notions of the world and the nature of individuals in relation to organizations. For example, we increasingly realize that there are not sharp distinctions between what goes on inside and outside people. Psychology has gradually moved from studying the surface characteristics of individuals to studying them from a holistic point of view. Integrating these two approaches has important implications. Just as psychologists now emphasize the importance of using holistic approaches to the study of human behavior, effective leaders must use similar holistic approaches when working with people.

2. Traditional approaches to organizations emphasized a relatively limited number of stakeholders. Such stakeholders were usually considered primarily in economic terms—such as

maximizing income for corporate shareholders. But we have increasingly come to realize the importance of interdependency as we engage in managing today's complex organizations. In an economy where estimates are that 90 percent of the work force will be employed in the service sector by the end of the century, traditional economic models do not tell the whole story. More complex, dynamic models of analysis must be created in order to help leaders and their organizations achieve higher levels of success.

3. A special set of stakeholders has emerged in recent studies of organizations—stakeholders whom Mitroff calls *archetypes.* Archetypes are abstract, inspirational images of what people and the organization can become. These images are most frequently concerned with an organization's basic values and mission. Effective leaders learn how to develop strategic plans for creating and maintaining these important archetypal images as a total part of their leadership effectiveness.

4. As our old pictures of the world and organizations become less effective, our methods of solving organizational problems are also becoming less effective. Traditional problem-solving concepts were founded primarily on a mechanistic view of the world. As a result, such problem solving usually attempted to achieve closure, certainty, and completeness before taking action. Newer methods of problem solving emphasize the fact that most organizational decisions will be made in an environment of incompleteness, uncertainty, and ambiguity.

Mitroff's concept of stakeholder analysis is of great importance to continuing education leadership. It offers a new set of images and conceptual schemes for achieving effectiveness in systems analysis and environmental scanning. Stakeholder analysis necessitates introspection to promote effective leadership. In addition, it deals with the internal and external organizational realities with which leaders must cope. The Club of Rome uses the term *problematique* to describe the ability to think about the entire complexity of a problem before acting on any aspect of it. The *problematique* concept emphasizes the ability to problem solve within an environment of ambiguity, diversity, uncertainty, and decentralization (Cleveland, 1985).

5. *How can leaders use strategic planning as a vehicle to help all organizational members create successful leadership strategies for themselves?* Kilmann (1984) has identified five tracks to organizational success. Leaders need to become expert at developing strategic plans for managing (1) the culture track, (2) the management skills track, (3) the team-building track, (4) the strategy-structure track, and (5) the reward system track.

Utilizing systems approaches, a leader constantly gives attention to developing strategic plans for analyzing and managing these five tracks. He or she engages in systems analysis and environmental scanning. Such a leader becomes a developer of people. He or she recognizes the role of group dynamics in creating high-performance organizations and gives constant attention to finding effective ways to monitor and shape these group dynamics for the good of the organization. Thus the leader's success is measured by the results achieved by the group under his or her supervision or influence. The major portion of such a leader's own work is developing strategic plans in order to achieve organizational results (Grove, 1983; Hickson, Butler, Cray, Mallory, and Wilson, 1986).

Toward New Directions for Strengthening Continuing Education Leadership

Success in an organization usually does not happen by accident. Instead it is a result of giving deliberate attention to managing cultural change, developing people and their management skills, developing teams of problem solvers, establishing effective organizational structures, and developing meaningful reward systems. Effective leaders ensure that the entire organization is aware of the efforts and successes of teams (Kaufman and Stone, 1983; Kennedy, 1984; Kilmann, Saxton, Serpa, and Associates, 1985; Kirkpatrick, 1985). Developing strategic plans for such a recognition system is a primary job of leadership in today's continuing education organizations. For many of us this is a new activity that demands a new set of assumptions, concepts, and language to be used in daily problem solving (Nash, 1983, 1985; Odiorne, 1984; Kotter, 1985; Apps, 1985). It involves creating independent relationships within the organization rather than relationships that are dependent on the leader (Powers and Powers, 1983; Pennings, 1985; Pinchot, 1985). Through decentralization and the giving away of power, the leader encourages the development of problem solving and strategic planning by individuals and teams.

Today's successful continuing education leader is a behavioral scientist who continually looks for new and effective ways to study the health and productivity of the organization. This, in turn, leads to appropriate action steps for achieving organizational goals. Thus strategic planning becomes an integral part of our never ending struggle to find newer and more effective ways to strengthen leadership.

2

The Strategic Planning Process

Seven Essential Steps

ROBERT G. SIMERLY

Strategic planning is a process that gives attention to (1) designing, (2) implementing, and (3) monitoring plans for improving decision making. Like many other processes in organizations, strategic planning often results in a product—in this case, a specific written document that enables all personnel to comprehend, analyze, and critique the goals, objectives, and strategies that are being used to achieve the organization's mission. It is this ongoing analysis, critique, and revision of plans that provides for the dynamic personal interaction characteristic of strategic planning (Allen, 1982; Bradford and Cohen, 1984; Cleveland, 1985). Strategic planning gives everyone in the organization a chance to participate in decision making and thus make a personal impact on the organization's future. Anomie, the loss of a feeling of personal power to influence decision making, is virtually eliminated.

These two ideas of strategic planning being both a process and a product, or actual written plan, are related to each other in such complex and overlapping ways that it is almost impossible to analyze one without considering the other (Michael, 1973; Steiner and Miner, 1982; Pfeiffer, Goodstein, and Nolan, 1985). Tichy (1983) conceptualizes this dynamic quality of strategic planning by using a rope as a metaphor. Ropes are composed of individual strands of fiber wound around each other to create a stronger product—the rope. He sees strategic planning (the rope) as composed of three important strands. There is the technical design strand that includes such activities as goal setting and strategy formation. The political allocation strand deals with how power and resources are used to bring about change. And the cultural strand deals with beliefs, values, and the interpretations people place on events. The role of leadership becomes one of keeping the strands of the rope bound together, through planning, in such a way that they contribute in positive ways to accomplishing the work of the organization.

Steiner (1979) has identified two classic approaches to planning: intuitive, anticipatory planning and formal, systematic planning. Each is equally important. However, in many organizations these two approaches are viewed as being in conflict with each other. Leaders who feel most comfortable with intuitive planning often tend to avoid formal, written plans and instead rely on the informal influence network to bring about change. Leaders who feel most comfortable with formal, systematic planning often tend to emphasize the development of long-range planning documents and discount the importance of intuitive planning approaches. But if they are to be as effective as possible, leaders need to accommodate both types of planning and learn to use each with equal ease and effectiveness.

Steiner has also been helpful in identifying and analyzing the following four points of view regarding planning. First, planning is concerned with the consequences of today's decisions. This means that planning is concerned with cause and effect relationships and alternative courses of action. Thus today's decisions are made in relation to how they probably will affect the organization in the future. Second, strategic planning can be thought of as a process. This process is concerned with creating consensus on organizational goals and objectives that are established as a means for achieving the overall mission. Third, strategic planning is a philosophy of how to lead an organization. That is, it is a comprehensive thought process that guides all daily actions. Fourth, strategic planning is a structural method designed to prepare for the future and hence one that emphasizes formal, written plans.

It is useful to think of strategic planning as composed of all four of these elements rather than only one or two. These elements are bound together like a rope to produce important organizational benefits. Strategic planning is a dynamic, ever changing process designed to improve the future of the organization. And if it is to be effective, it needs to become an integral part of the thought processes of everyone in the organization.

A Model for Step-by-Step Planning

This chapter integrates these four approaches through creation of a strategic planning model and suggests how continuing education leaders can use these ideas to strengthen their organizations. The model is flexible enough to be adapted to any continuing education organization. It should be emphasized that there are many approaches useful in thinking through planning issues. The idea of engaging in strategic planning as an important part of all daily leadership activity is more important than adopting any particular model. However, models are useful because they provide a structured way to think about an issue. The strategic planning model is illustrated in Figure 1, and an analysis of each step follows.

Step 1: Management Audit. Conducting a management audit is the first step in strategic planning. Chapter Four illustrates how to do this. The management audit serves to analyze the present situation of the organization. It should deal with such critical issues as: (1) What are the organization's strengths and weaknesses? (2) What are the windows of opportunity? (3) What should be changed and why? (4) How difficult will it be to change things? Basically this first step provides a snapshot of the organization. This snapshot, or analysis, lays the basis for designing strategies that will be effective in planning for the future. This initial step of strategic planning should develop a heightened awareness on the part of staff of the strengths and vulnerability of the organization.

Step 2: Values Clarification. The reason for identifying important organizational values is that such values directly influence how people behave. This step asks staff to identify the core issues, feelings, and attitudes that are important to them. These values determine the organizational culture, which is, perhaps, the most powerful internal force affecting any organization.

Figure 1. Strategic Planning Model.

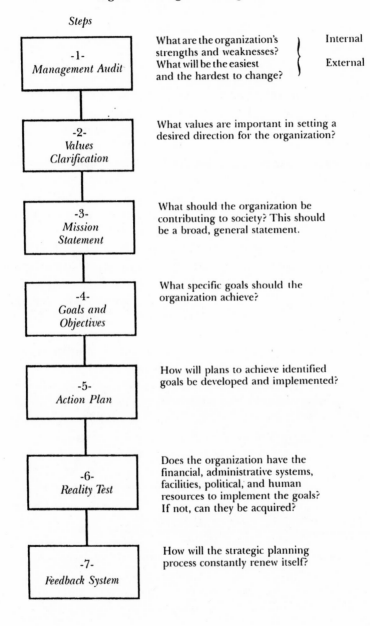

Steps

| -1- Management Audit | What are the organization's strengths and weaknesses? What will be the easiest and the hardest to change? | Internal / External |

-2- Values Clarification — What values are important in setting a desired direction for the organization?

-3- Mission Statement — What should the organization be contributing to society? This should be a broad, general statement.

-4- Goals and Objectives — What specific goals should the organization achieve?

-5- Action Plan — How will plans to achieve identified goals be developed and implemented?

-6- Reality Test — Does the organization have the financial, administrative systems, facilities, political, and human resources to implement the goals? If not, can they be acquired?

-7- Feedback System — How will the strategic planning process constantly renew itself?

Organizational culture defines expectations about behavior, how work is done, how decisions are made, how social interactions are structured, and how people communicate. In order to be effectively implemented, strategic plans must be created to enhance the organization's important values and thus its culture. Chapter Five provides a comprehensive discussion of this process of values clarification. A strategic plan that is inconsistent with the organization's culture stands little chance of success.

Increasingly we are becoming aware of the importance of understanding the dynamics of organizational culture, if we are to become more effective in our leadership roles. One of the chief characteristics of high-performance organizations is that they have strong organizational cultures that are driven by a central core of values shared by employees. Successful leaders in these high-performing organizations spend considerable time talking about and thus reinforcing their organizational culture. They also spend a great deal of time emphasizing the importance of creating an organization that is sensitive and responsive to its many publics. And they develop effective ways to monitor or scan the environment in order to demonstrate accountability and responsiveness to major constituencies.

Step 3: Mission Statement. A mission statement should reflect the basic purpose of the organization. The statement itself defines the organization by dealing with such issues as (1) what the organization should be contributing to society, (2) whom the organization should serve, (3) how it should serve people, and (4) the benefits to society as a result of its service and programs.

Good mission statements provide a yardstick against which daily decisions can be measured. Because they are so critical in the first phases of strategic planning, it is important that mission statements be clear and concise and that they be feasible. In addition, they should be challenging to staff. The mission statement of a continuing education organization should identify a purpose greater than accomplishing the routine of daily work. In other words, there should be a good answer for the question, "How is what I am doing enhancing the quality of people's lives?"

The following are useful guidelines for writing a mission statement:

1. A mission statement should never be stated only in financial terms.
2. A mission statement should set future directions for the organization.
3. A mission statement should be clear and concise in order to appeal to as wide a constituency as possible.
4. A mission statement should have an inspirational quality to it. We all want to work for organizations that make a difference in the quality of life for humanity. Good mission statements should reflect this need.

There are many good ways to state the mission of the continuing education organization. For example, an effective mission statement for the continuing education division of a state university might read as follows:

> The mission of the Division of Continuing Education is to provide the highest quality credit and noncredit continuing education opportunities to the state, region, and nation. Such programs will be designed to build on the strengths and expertise of our faculty and their departments and colleges for the purpose of assisting attendees to become more effective in their professional roles.

Step 4: Establish Goals and Objectives. Within the language of strategic planning, the terms *goal* and *objective* have very specialized meanings. A goal is a large, generalized statement that points directions for the future. Usually a goal statement should be general enough so that it cannot easily be measured in time and space. In addition, it should be short and easy to understand. One or two sentences should usually be adequate for stating a goal effectively.

An objective is a subset of a goal. The characteristics of an objective are that it can be (1) measured in time and space, (2) delegated to someone to implement, and (3) assigned a deadline for completion. An essential part of strategic planning is establishing goals and then developing specific objectives to achieve each goal.

Without these specific objectives, goals remain only idealized visions. Following are examples of effective statements of goals and objectives. These statements cover the major goal areas found in most continuing education organizations.

Professional Development of Staff

Goal: The continued professional development of all staff will be one of the highest priorities for this organization.

Objectives:

1.   A fund of $8,000 to be used for professional development will be established by September 1.

2.   The director will appoint a professional development committee to be chaired by Laura Matson. This committee will develop guidelines for the use of this fund and make recommendations on appropriate activities. Its report will be given to the director by January 15.

3.   The committee will consider two basic thrusts for professional development: (1) in-house professional development programs and (2) development programs people might design for themselves or attend outside the institution. The purpose of this is to allow for as much flexibility as possible in encouraging professional development.

Marketing

Goal: A total marketing plan for our organization will be developed—a plan that is consistent with the first-class standing of our institution.

Objectives:

1.   The associate director will be in charge of creating a committee to develop a marketing plan. This committee will deliver its final report by August 1.

2. The committee will be charged with developing input from all staff as well as from the major constituent groups that we serve.

Financial

Goal: We will end up with a positive net balance at the end of each fiscal year.

Objectives:

1. John Wilson, our business manager, will present the total budget to the staff for discussion, debate, and revision by February 1.

2. Each department head will have a chance to talk with his or her staff to suggest modifications in the budget.

3. The final version of the budget will be ready by July 1.

4. Each department head will be totally responsible for managing his or her department budget, realizing that no negative balance will be allowed at the end of the year.

5. The business manager will have monthly meetings with each department head to review the departmental budget records.

Management of Physical Facilities

Goal: Since physical facilities represent a major capital investment, we will maintain our physical facilities in good repair to the extent allowed in each year's budget.

Objectives:

1. Francis Thomas, our head of physical plant, will develop a long-range plan for facility needs by July 15.

2. This report will be discussed at a meeting of the director and department heads by October 1.

3.   The plan will be revised at least yearly to take into account the changing needs of physical plant and the amount of money required to maintain it.

The errors most frequently made when writing mission statements are (1) not developing specific, measurable objectives to achieve goals and (2) not developing feedback mechanisms to monitor on a regular basis how people are doing in achieving the objectives. The important thing is to engage in the setting of goals and objectives in a way that is appropriate and meaningful for a given organization. However, it is also important to keep in mind that specific objectives need to be established for reaching each goal. Otherwise goals have a tendency to become the unfilled dreams of their creators.

There are no hard-and-fast rules that govern which resource areas should be included when writing goals and objectives. However, to be comprehensive enough to be useful in strategic planning, goals and objectives should usually be developed for at least the following areas: human resources, financial resources, physical resources, political resources, administrative systems resources, and communications/public relations resources.

Because goals are the large, generalized statements that provide vision and direction for the organization, it is important that they be clear and concise. Also it is important not to create too many goals. This can lead to information overload. Most continuing education organizations find that five to ten major goals are an appropriate number to include in an effective strategic plan. However, any single goal may have a number of objectives.

Step 5: Action Plan. An integral part of strategic planning is to develop an action plan for implementing all objectives. This action plan should address two basic issues: (1) What are the possible problem areas in implementing the strategic plan? (2) How will new strategies be developed if the main plans begin to go astray? The purpose of Step 5 is to ensure that plans actually get implemented. Such an action plan should consider the following issues:

1. How, in specific terms, will the comprehensive plan be implemented?
2. Who will be in charge of implementing it?
3. What is a realistic timetable for implementation?
4. How will the success of achieving the plan be measured?

Step 6: Reality Test. Discussion of values, mission, goals, and objectives usually generates considerable excitement and enthusiasm. While this is important and desirable, it can also pose a danger. It is not hard to become so future oriented and visionary that one begins to lose touch with reality. Step 6 of the strategic planning model prevents this from happening. It is designed to provide an answer to the question, "Are our goals and objectives realistic and attainable, given the very real constraints of our situation?" Important questions to ask during the reality test are:

1. What resources do we need to accomplish our goals and objectives and thus fulfill our mission?
2. If the needed resources do not exist, can they be acquired or created?
3. Who can help us obtain these resources?
4. What are the important constraints that might keep us from achieving our goals and objectives?
5. Is it possible to decrease these constraints? How?

The reality test provides the last chance to modify mission, goals, and objectives before actually implementing the strategic plan. At this point there should be a reasonably clear answer to the question, "Can we do it successfully?"

Step 7: Feedback System. Feedback systems are an essential and critical part of strategic planning. Such systems should answer the following questions:

1. How will we know when our goals and objectives have been achieved?
2. How will we develop a series of checks and balances to provide an early warning that there is trouble in meeting a goal and/or objective so that corrective action can be taken?

3. How will failure be dealt with if it occurs?
4. How can we avoid punishing people if they try and fail?
5. How will we reward people for successfully achieving objectives and goals?
6. Who will be in charge of periodically checking on the implementation of the strategic plan?
7. What will be the process and structure for this?
8. How will progress in implementing the strategic plan be measured?
9. Is the feedback system comprehensive enough to successfully implement the strategic plan?

Characteristics of Strategic Planning

In order to further analyze strategic planning as both a process and a product, let us summarize the following major characteristics of strategic planning:

1. Specific action-oriented strategies to implement all plans that are developed
2. Constant monitoring so that plans can be modified to fit the changing realities of organizational life
3. Statements of overall general goals to achieve within the organization
4. Statements of specific objectives to achieve—objectives that are directly related to achieving identified goals
5. Effective systems of delegation so that it is always clear who is in charge of implementing any project or objective that is part of the strategic plan
6. Definite deadlines for completing all projects that are part of a strategic plan
7. Effective evaluation for all stated goals and objectives
8. Integrating strategic planning into the organization so that the planning process comes to be seen as an important and necessary component of daily work life
9. Active consideration of the human resources of the organization

10. Involving a wide variety of people within the organization in designing and implementing strategic planning
11. Considering the complex and often diverse motivations of people who will be charged with implementing plans and achieving results
12. Maintaining a balance between what people would like the organization to be and the realities of what is possible
13. Designing substantive ways to address the major issues in the organization—issues that are crucial to overall organizational success

Strategic planning is a very appealing process in most organizations. In fact, it is so appealing that it is difficult to develop a logical argument against it. However, the fact that there are so many positive benefits to be gained from it does not mean that strategic planning will automatically succeed. The following are ten important issues to consider when implementing strategic planning.

Issue 1—Having Support for Strategic Planning Come from the Highest Levels of Management. Strategic planning does not have much chance of succeeding unless support for it comes from the highest levels of management. Indeed, strategic planning must have the wholehearted support of top managers if it is to work (Hopkins and Massey, 1981; Behn and Vaupel, 1982; Bennis, Benne, and Chin, 1985; Hickson, Butler, Cray, Mallory, and Wilson, 1986). Top leadership constantly sends very important verbal and nonverbal messages to lower levels about what is and is not important. Thus, for strategic planning to succeed, management must make it clear through written communication, as well as through verbal and nonverbal communication, that such planning is one of the highest priorities in the organization.

Top managers must be willing to reinforce this on a daily basis through routine interactions with people as well as through special meetings devoted to strategic planning. If they are not willing to do this, it would be better not to try to implement strategic planning throughout the whole organization. However, it might still be possible to implement the process in a department if the head of the department is willing to support it fully through a total personal commitment (Craig, 1978; Jedamus, Peterson, and Associates, 1980; Gardner, 1981; Kaufman and Stone, 1983).

Issue 2—Creating Organizational Readiness for Strategic Planning. Any new organizational process with such far-reaching implications as strategic planning will probably meet with some resistance. This resistance will often center on getting satisfactory answers to questions such as the following:

- Is this a hidden plan to get me to double my productivity without any additional resources?
- Will I be able to succeed at this type of planning?
- Will I receive recognition if I put forth extra effort to implement strategic planning?
- How will strategic planning benefit the organization in ways that I can see and that are meaningful to me?
- Will it make my work life more enjoyable?
- Will I be able to do a better job as a result of this kind of planning?
- Will strategic planning increase or decrease the autonomy I value in my daily problem solving?

These are some of the questions that staff will have regarding any proposed change. Therefore it is important to prepare the organization for this activity and, specifically, to let staff members bring their concerns to the surface. Addressing this emotional or feeling level of behavior is important if strategic planning is to succeed. In the final analysis, most people's basic concern about strategic planning is, "Will it help me to become better at my job and will others recognize this?"

Issue 3—Creating a Planning Committee to Guide the Process. Designing and implementing strategic planning are time-consuming processes. In anything other than very small organizations it probably is not realistic to expect that all staff can become involved in such steps as writing a mission statement, identifying important values, establishing a comprehensive set of goals and objectives, and developing a feedback system to monitor the implementation of the plan. Therefore it is important to establish a committee to take charge of designing and implementing the strategic planning process. It is also important to communicate throughout the organization that this planning committee will be seeking advice and suggestions from a wide variety of staff and possibly from groups outside the organization that represent important constituencies.

This planning group should be small enough so that data gathering and decision making can proceed smoothly. Probably the minimum number of members required for such a committee is five, with the maximum being eight to ten members.

Issue 4—Carving Out Adequate Time to Make Strategic Planning a Success. To successfully design and implement a comprehensive and effective strategic plan is a labor-intensive and time-consuming business. Therefore it is important to give the planning committee adequate time to gather data, organize it, seek advice from staff, and make recommendations.

As with other aspects of the planning process, it is difficult to give accurate time lines for such deliberations because of the unique requirements and demands of individual organizations. However, as a general guideline, many leaders find that it takes approximately six to nine months for such a planning committee to find the time to meet regularly, condition the organization to accept new ideas, work out specific plans, and develop effective strategies to implement such plans.

Issue 5—Monitoring the Implementation of the Strategic Plan. How does one begin to monitor the implementation of a comprehensive strategic plan? First, it is important to note the reasons for monitoring such plans. Organizations are complex systems. Given this complexity, it is easy for any plan to begin to go astray if there is no one in a position to take corrective action as required. Therefore the purpose of a monitoring process for strategic planning is to provide an early warning system so that corrective action can be taken if it becomes apparent that there will be difficulty in reaching particular goals or objectives. In order to be effective, such a monitoring system should have the following characteristics:

1. It should provide for a regular review of the progress in meeting all goals and objectives.

2. It should be designed to act in a supportive rather than a
    punitive manner.
3. It should deal with measurable events.
4. It should clearly establish who is ultimately in charge of
    implementing each objective.
5. It should be easy to use.

One way to achieve success with this monitoring process is
to have monthly meetings with the major people involved in
implementation of the strategic plans. Such meetings will be most
effective if they are devoted solely to reviewing and discussing the
progress to date on the strategic planning process. At such a
meeting everyone who has been delegated important goals and
objectives reports on the progress in meeting them. The advantage
to this method is that it puts the evaluation in a public forum.
Thus a certain amount of peer pressure to achieve comes into play.
Another advantage to this public forum is that it enables the key
players to discuss among themselves the problems that will
inevitably be encountered in implementing strategic planning.
Discussing these problems openly as a team is the first step toward
developing effective solutions to them.

Whatever method is chosen for a monitoring system, it is
important that meetings take place approximately once a month.
If a longer time elapses, those involved may come to think that
strategic planning is not really that important to the organization
or more time would be devoted to it. Moreover, if too much time
elapses between monitoring sessions, interest in the whole process
tends to decline. All staff pick up a wide variety of organizational
signals sent from top management. And one of the first and most
important signals they pick up is that the amount of time spent on
any organizational issue is usually in direct proportion to the
importance top management places on it.

*Issue 6—Building Flexibility for Change into the Strategic
Planning Process.* Any planning process should remain flexible.
For example, it often happens that when organizations decide to
implement strategic planning, individuals agree to take on more
responsibility for achieving goals and objectives than they can
realistically accomplish in relation to their existing work.

Therefore strategic plans must be kept flexible, so that they can be changed in ways that will not dampen enthusiasm and decrease energy and interest in the process.

Developing such flexibility is a two-edged sword, however. You want to be sure that you do not legitimate poor performance. Therefore the following guideline can be helpful: If a person has agreed to try to achieve a particular goal or objective and if it has also been agreed in advance how success in doing this will be measured, he or she will be held to this contract unless the contract is renegotiated. And if the contract has to be renegotiated, it can probably be done most effectively with the planning committee in one of its regularly scheduled monthly meetings. In this way, the entire planning committee becomes responsible for the success of the monitoring system.

Issue 7—Actively Managing the Higher Levels of Conflict That Often Occur When Strategic Planning Is Implemented. One of the things that often happens when organizations are effective in implementing strategic planning is that they experience higher levels of overt conflict. Often a leader reacts to this by asking, "What am I doing wrong?" Often the answer is, "Nothing." In fact, he or she is probably doing everything right.

Conflict in all organizations is natural and inevitable. The leadership issue is how to manage conflict for productive results. When an organization implements strategic planning, individual staff productivity often takes on a new meaning. Suddenly people are asked to commit themselves in a public way to defining and reaching specific goals and objectives. In addition, it is agreed on ahead of time how success in reaching these new goals and objectives will be measured.

Such changes can be very threatening to people who have been used to operating without measurable accountability. Until people begin to feel comfortable with the new procedures, there may be frequent and severe arguments over such issues as the fairness of resource allocations, the advisability of introducing measurements of productivity, and what measures of productivity are fair and equitable.

Issue 8—Behaving on the Job in Ways Perceived by Others to Support the Total Concept of Strategic Planning. Leaders need to pay particular attention to the signals they give off in all their actions. This is particularly important in relation to strategic planning. Some of the important signals are related to the tone in which problem-solving meetings are conducted and the language that is used. Consider, for example, the leader who begins a meeting by saying, "Okay, it's time to get started. The sooner we get started, the sooner we'll be out of here." Such a tone really conveys this message: "I do not consider this topic, the time spent on it, or the people involved to be important enough to warrant my attention."

Therefore it is critical that leaders decide in advance what kind of general tone they want to create for all the planning activities. This tone will be most effective if it is upbeat and positive. Anything less than this will decrease the effectiveness of strategic planning as a self-renewing system for the organization.

Issue 9—Rewarding People for Participating in Strategic Planning. We all like to be rewarded for making an extra effort to accomplish something. That reward does not have to be a monetary one. But there should be some appropriate reward for helping to make strategic planning a success. It is also important that the reward be consistent with the value system of the organization. For example, a framed plaque of appreciation would be considered an excellent reward in some organizations, while in others it would be laughed at as being beneath the dignity of professionals. Therefore it is difficult to suggest specific rewards for participating in strategic planning. However, the planning committee is in a good position to consider this and to come up with suggestions for rewarding participation.

Issue 10—Conditioning Staff to Accept the Fact That Strategic Planning Should Be a Continuing Process Throughout One's Professional Career, Not Just Something That Happens Periodically. It is important to present the concept of strategic planning as something that will become a part of the daily process of conducting organizational work. Care should be taken not to leave the impression that at some point such planning will be over. Instead it is important to emphasize that as initial goals and objectives are achieved, new ones will take their place. Thus strategic planning is a never ending circular process. And as such it is designed to be one of the chief ways to accomplish organizational renewal. An important characteristic of high-performance organizations is that they give extensive attention to developing such self-renewal systems.

Moreover, it is through constant attention to this self-renewal process that the organizational environment becomes an exciting place in which to work. In such an environment new goals and objectives are constantly being created. The pros and cons of major organizational issues are debated. Conflict is managed for productive results. And people come to feel that their work is important in enhancing the quality of life for all.

Most leaders who decide to make strategic planning an integral part of their organizational culture have a very real and practical question: "How long will it take?" While there are no easy answers to this, the following are some guidelines to consider:

1. It often takes a number of months in order to build enough support so that staff will be receptive to engaging in a strategic planning process—particularly one that results in a written long-range planning document.
2. It is often possible to see positive results from strategic planning within a year after staff becomes involved in designing and implementing such a plan.
3. It often takes up to three or four years before strategic planning becomes an accepted routine of organizational life.
4. Allowances must be made for possible failures in implementing some aspects of the strategic plan—especially at the beginning stages of the process.
5. It is important not to punish people for failure at strategic planning. Instead leaders can provide a supportive environment that encourages people to analyze reasons for failure and can help them design new plans that have a better chance of success.
6. Reward people for participating in strategic planning in ways that are meaningful to them.

Summary

Strategic planning, like other aspects of successful leadership, is never finished. However, successfully implementing strategic planning is a rewarding process. It is an effective means by which to build a continuous process of self-renewal into an organization. We all want to be a part of organizations that have a larger purpose and somehow make a difference to humankind. Once you have been a part of creating this kind of environment, you will never want to work in any other type of organization.

3

The Leader's Role in
Strategic Planning

JOHN W. SCHMIDT

"Building bridges not walls" is a symbolic phrase. It envisions a particular kind of relationship between an institution, its continuing education leader, and the external environment. It is both an idea and a commitment to how institutions ought to deal with change. And both ideas and commitment are necessary before we can proceed with decisions about structure and resources.

"Bridges" and "walls" represent two schools of thought about the purposes and responsibilities of higher education with respect to society. One group argues in favor of building bridges because it sees a need to respond to shifting demographic, educational, and societal forces. In this view, failure by institutions of higher education to acknowledge the external environment and reexamine their roles and responsibilities in relationship to it may well create a significant gap between the campus and the world outside. Further, this group notes that the service function is not linked strongly to teaching and research and is often discharged by individual faculty as paid consultants. Thus service is often not perceived by either the public or faculty members as being integral to the mission of the institution. As this gap widens, institutions of higher education will come to be viewed by society as increasingly irrelevant and ineffective. Ultimately, many institutions will simply be ignored (Boyer, 1979; Niebuhr, 1982; Lynton, 1984; Schuh, 1984).

Those who advocate having a wall between the institution and the environment do so out of a profound concern for what they see as the institution's central purpose. That purpose is threefold: (1) the discovery of new knowledge, (2) the creative resynthesis of knowledge, and (3) the critical evaluation of knowledge (Shoben, 1971). In combination, these constitute the traditional goals of scholarship and learning. The primary activities associated with this tripartite purpose are cultivating the brain power of students and carrying out basic research.

The purpose of the university, from this viewpoint, is accomplished best by turning inward and pursuing these goals as ends in themselves. To do otherwise is to lose a sense of purpose for the university; its mission and goals will become diffused as it tries to be all things to all people. The negative consequences of departing from the singleness of knowledge as the goal are a loss of cohesion and the risk of exposing the institution to forces that are incompatible with, and may even threaten, academic values (Bok, 1982).

Continuing education leaders must prepare a response to the position that walls are to be maintained between the external environment and the institution—its colleges, departments, and faculties. Ideally, the approach used should establish a ground-work for a planning strategy that will facilitate the building of both internal and external bridges. We can find a basis for such an approach by examining the historical relationship between American colleges and universities, on the one hand, and external trends and needs, on the other. For example, consider the significance of the following examples and events:

- American universities since inception have been responsive to and shaped by society. The desire for literate, college-trained clergy was probably the most important single influence leading to the founding of the colonial colleges (Brubacher and Rudy, 1968). Shortly after the Civil War, institutions of higher education began to embrace the concept of utility, particularly in the form of professional schools (Veysey, 1965). Since that time a consistent trend has been for universities to offer programs that respond to society's need for technically trained people (Shoben, 1971). Currently, of the more than 1,100 different undergraduate programs and majors, more than 50 percent represent occupational fields (Rhodes, 1985).

- The academic curriculum is the result of a process of give-and-take. It responds to what society wants, and in turn it helps to shape society (Rudolph, 1977). Contemporary examples of this symbiotic relationship are women's studies, programs in urban and regional planning and in criminal justice, and various ethnic studies (The Carnegie Foundation for the Advancement of Teaching, 1977). Continuing education units have often played important roles in the development of such new programs.

- Public policy is a vehicle to achieve national and state goals. Examples abound. Among them are the GI Bill as a means to help veterans readjust to the postwar world; the response to Sputnik by development of curricula geared to strengthen science education; and assisting minorities to enter the mainstream of American life (The Carnegie Foundation for the Advancement of Teaching, 1977; Edgerton, 1983).

- Major economic and cultural transformations taking place in society have led to the formation of new models of higher education. One example here is passage of the Morrill Act in 1862, which established the land-grant colleges. In 1873, the University of Cincinnati was founded and became the forerunner of our urban, commuter universities (Brubacher and Rudy, 1968; Diebold, 1984).

- The Wisconsin Idea was developed early in this century. Ashby (1967) characterizes the Wisconsin Idea as the great American contribution to higher education and one of the rare innovations in the evolution of the university. It dismantled the "walls" around the campus by expanding the borders of the campus to the boundaries of the state. A major reason for its success was economic. The shift of Wisconsin agriculture from a wheat-growing to a dairying basis required both efficient business management and specialized technical knowledge. The university helped provide these essential skills to the state's dairy farmers, thus laying the foundation for popular support for public higher education (Brubacher and Rudy, 1968).

When the purposes of higher education are placed in historical perspective, it becomes clear that we have always had to seek a balance between the views of traditionalists and the views of those who seek change. Most parties in this debate agree that universities ought to serve society. However, they differ in their view of how institutions can make their most important contributions (Bok, 1982). Which viewpoint dominates at any given time depends on the shifting consensus in society about its most urgent needs (Shoben, 1971).

The Importance of Strategic Planning

To plan is to anticipate the future—its problems and opportunities—and to attempt to shape that future by intelligent and informed action. Planning gives purpose and direction to an organization by allowing it to determine in advance what it wishes to accomplish and the means it will use to achieve its ends.

Systematic and ongoing planning will be a critical imperative for colleges and universities in the remainder of this century. An organization dependent on faculty members who are highly individualistic and who cannot be managed by issuing orders must still find a way to give focus and unity to their activity (Keller, 1983). Strategic planning can help provide that focus and unity. Moreover, strategic planning is the best means to handle pressures for accountability and to determine how external forces of change will manifest themselves in our institutions of higher education. In fact, the ideas generated through a planning process often have a more direct bearing on the future of the organization and its activities than do changes in either its structure or personnel (Bean and Kuh, 1984).

What Hinders Planning in Continuing Education?

It is difficult for continuing education leaders to engage in anything other than short-term planning. One reason often cited is that most adult education agencies have no separate policy board to establish long-range goals, plans, and policies. In addition, the usual approach to program development mitigates against long-range planning because the focus is on immediate client needs and on offering individual courses and workshops as the response to those needs. These responses lack academic coherence in the sense of being part of an overall curriculum. Finally, the method of financing adult and continuing education often makes long-range planning difficult (White and Reed, 1980).

Nevertheless, continuing education leaders can no longer ignore the need to engage in long-range planning. They should not sidestep the splendid opportunities to come to terms with the dynamics of change brought about by society's pressures. Now is the time for such leaders to get ready to meet the future.

The steps that must be taken to meet the future are similar to those found in the strategic planning approach. In their adaptation and application to higher education, there is a commonality to the approaches outlined in the literature (Cope, 1978; Hollowood, 1979; Mayhew, 1979; Peterson, 1980; Cope, 1981; Keller, 1983; Uhl, 1983; Morrison, Renfro, and Boucher, 1984). The steps are based on these concepts:

1. Scan the environment to identify trends or potential changes and their implications for the institution. These changes may open up opportunities as well as pose threats.
2. Assess institutional strengths, weaknesses, problems, and capabilities.
3. Review the mission, tradition, values, and roles of the institution.
4. Match the staff's strengths to the mission of the institution so that change can be planned effectively.
5. Devise strategic alternatives to achieve goals.
6. Choose from the alternatives identified.

Subsequent sections of this chapter will illustrate ways to adapt these steps to the continuing education setting. But first I want to emphasize the value of strategic planning to today's continuing education leader.

Continuing education leaders have knowledge of the external environment and are already familiar with the trends, needs, and expectations of those external to the university. They are familiar with the questions that need to be raised about the adult education mission and how appropriate distribution of adult education activities might be brought about (Smith, 1985).

Continuing education leaders know adult learners. This expertise can be invaluable in helping institutions develop goals that address the needs of adults.

Finally, strategic planning is a tool through which leaders can address the view that continuing education is peripheral to the institution (Knox, 1979). Such planning should help to clarify the interrelationship between the continuing education function and the other functions of the organization. Thus it will help to "build bridges" between those functions and move continuing education more into the mainstream of the institution.

Environmental Scanning

Environmental scanning is an activity familiar to continuing education leaders. Client needs are the backbone of program planning and marketing, and both require an understanding of the forces at work outside the institution. Consequently, continuing education leaders are already favorably predisposed toward the concept.

Environmental scanning both expands the concept of needs assessment and routinizes the process. A broader base results from focusing on an identification of trends or potential changes in the environment. This kind of scanning concentrates on trends that cut across various relevant groups and the institution. Therefore, its perspective is more macro than micro, more institution wide than client, department, or discipline specific. The purpose is to discover and describe opportunities that an institution may choose to exploit. The process will also reveal environmental constraints that the institution may have to circumvent.

Setting Up Categories

In order to deal with the complexity of the environment, an institution needs to segment it. Various approaches to this task have been suggested. Cope (1981) recommends using four categories—economic, social, technological, and political trends. Keller's (1983) scheme uses five categories—technological, economic, demographic, political-legal, and social-cultural. The futures paradigm of the American Association of State Colleges and Universities (Alm, Buhler-Miko, and Smith, 1978) employs two categories—societal trend areas and societal value shifts. Included in the first category are population, government, global affairs, environment, energy, economy, science and technology, human settlements, work, life-style, women, and participation. Included in the category of value shifts are such issues as change, freedom, equality, leisure, foresight, pluralism, localism, responsibility, knowledge, quality, goals, and interdependence.

The taxonomies offered are suggestions. The best course of action is for each institution to identify the trends in the external environment that it believes will influence its planning. For example, the Wisconsin Cooperative Extension Service has focused its environmental scanning efforts on population, education, economics, environment and natural resources, interdependence, support for and expectations of public agencies, and support for research. A similar effort has been undertaken in Missouri, where the focus has been on educational, demographic, economic, work force, governmental, and social trends.

The preceding examples attempt to focus on the smaller rather than the larger picture. A problem with focus on global or abstract trends, such as the information revolution, is how to translate the global trend into individual institutional reality. A balance needs to be struck between stretching the vision in order to capture the possibilities and limiting vision to the smaller realities, since the latter may be more acceptable to the institution's leaders and more amenable to coherent interpretation and decisions (Hearn and Heydinger, 1985).

Methods and Sources

Adaptation of strategic planning to higher education is in its infancy. Consequently, there is no generally accepted procedure for scanning the environment. Without an established methodology, acceptance by faculty will likely be marginal. Academics are trained in the use of rigorous methodologies, and their inclination is to do little until the intradisciplinary methodological cornerstones of research are in place (Keller, 1983; Morrison, Renfro, and Boucher, 1984).

In spite of this reservation, continuing education leaders must encourage their institutions to proceed without the certainty typically desired by an academic discipline. The external environment simply does not recognize the methodological desires of a discipline. Further, in an age of convulsive change, the future quickly becomes the present and soon recedes into the past. In reality the only choice is to do the best we can in scanning the environment.

Support by institutional governance representatives for environmental scanning is important. One approach that should help gain their support is to involve them in a pilot screening process. The project could survey their perception of the external environment by covering these items:

1. Identification of external trends that may have the greatest impact on institutional governance over the next ten years
2. Identification of external trends that may have the greatest impact on the institution over the next ten years
3. Identification of the two or three issues listed under number two that will be most critical to the institution and why
4. Sharing with institutional governance representatives a list of sources particularly useful in understanding identified trends

The results of the pilot project will provide information on the perceptions of the environment by key campus leaders. In addition, their responses will suggest either directly or indirectly what additional data and background material might be helpful to them in understanding the linkage between the institution's external environment and their own departments.

Other sources of information about external trends are internal studies done by departments. These include feasibility studies for a new degree or program, career path profiles of graduates, professional development activities of the faculty, and reports on public service and consulting activity. For example, a state university undertook a study of regional industries to measure demand for a graduate program for industrial scientists. The departments developed a profile of the technical assistance provided to many of these industries. The results of the study showed that it was questionable whether there were enough potential students to support a graduate degree program. However, the analysis of the data also indicated an emerging trend toward more continuing professional education. Both of these outcomes proved useful to decision makers involved in developing strategies for educational programming.

One of the most widely used approaches for implementation of the scanning function is establishment of an in-house interdisciplinary committee. Such committees are usually composed of various institutional leaders, including leaders from several of the disciplines. This facilitates the analysis of trends that cut across disciplines. Interdisciplinary teams are also less susceptible to methodological fads that rise and fall within single disciplines (Asher and Overholt, 1983). Morrison, Renfro, and Boucher (1984) recommend that selections be made by the institution's chief executive officer.

Whatever appointment process is followed, it should be perceived as legitimate in light of institutional traditions. It is usually best to limit the committee size to no more than twelve members and to have the chairperson named by the appointing officer. The objectives and responsibilities of the committee should also be specified.

The University of Minnesota's experimental team for environmental assessment directed its effort toward (1) providing background information for institutional planning themes and various planning efforts, (2) expanding the perspective of university planners and thus reducing their chances of overlooking crucial issues, and (3) producing environmental scenarios to aid planning (Hearn and Heydinger, 1985).

The charge given to a committee composed of faculty and administrators from institutions at the University of Wisconsin was to advise the author on major theme areas, based on their assessment of the environment, which would serve as the basis for setting statewide priorities and goals. Both of these approaches identify clearly the purpose of environmental scanning, thereby minimizing the ambiguity of its goals. Reducing the ambiguity of goals at every state of a planning process will maximize use of resources (Bean and Kuh, 1984).

Sole reliance on internal resources, even if a committee uses external materials, runs the risk of limiting the environmental scanning perspective. Use of a panel of experts from outside the institution is a technique frequently employed to promote a broadened viewpoint. Criteria for selection and organization of the panels can be based on the categories to be scanned.

Evaluation of Trends

Each environmental category will produce more issues than the institution has the capacity to address. The issues should be structured in ways that will help the institution do three things: (1) describe problems and/or opportunities identified in the scanning stage; (2) evaluate their relative importance; and (3) establish priorities.

Questions can be used to determine the relative importance of the trends and issues identified. One series of questions could deal with the turbulence, placidity, and rate of the trends and issues (Smart and Vertinsky, 1984). Questions about turbulence measure the changes in the factors or components of the institution's environment—the greater the uncertainty facing an organization, the higher the turbulence. Placidity is the opposite of turbulence. Questions about rate assess the dimension of time for each of the changes in the institution's environmental factors or components.

A second series of questions examines the relative and expected importance of the trend and its issues. Importance has two dimensions, probability and impact, and three questions will evaluate both.

The first question asks how probable it is that the issue will actually occur. A second question projects how widespread the trend will be. Assuming that the trend actually emerges, the third question asks for an assessment of its impact on the future of the institution. A variation of the preceding approach was used in the strategic planning effort of Wisconsin's Cooperative Extension Service. Task forces were formed for agriculture/agribusiness, 4-H youth development, community and natural resources and economic development, and family living education. These task forces used five questions to structure the analysis and interpretation of external trends. These five questions involved (1) identifying the number and complexity of the future needs or problems brought by each of the trends, (2) assessing the acuteness of the emerging need or problem, (3) determining the impact of the trend on basic and/or individual needs, (4) estimating client readiness to seek or to receive assistance, and (5) estimating whether the trend data suggest that the demand will likely continue and/or increase.

One technique for displaying the information gathered is a probability-diffusion matrix, as illustrated in Figure 1 (Cope, 1981). This technique assesses the relative probability that a trend will occur as one dimension of the matrix. The other dimension is its scope. By placing an issue in the appropriate box along a continuum, it is possible to assign a relative rate to the issue. Placement of the issues in the matrix can serve as a vehicle for soliciting faculty assessment and comment.

Institutional Strengths and Weaknesses

The focus of the planning effort thus far has been on the external environment. Opportunities and constraints constitute what the institution *could* do with respect to the external environment. What an institution *can* do is determined by knowing its strengths and weaknesses.

Institutions of higher education have unique strengths. An extensive knowledge and research base undergirds their curricula and professorial staffs. For example, colleges and universities account for nearly one-half of the basic research done in the United States (Johnson, 1984). These resources are supported by a spirit of academic freedom and inquiry that permits uncompromised pursuit of knowledge. The knowledge and research base, freedom of academic inquiry, and concern for quality education are in contrast to the resources many other providers bring to their programs. Nowhere is this distinction more sharply drawn than in the area of freedom to teach. The economic, political, or social

Figure 1. Probability-Diffusion Matrix.

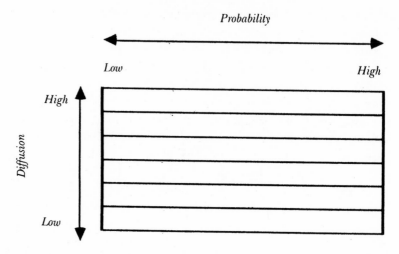

viewpoint of owners and/or stakeholders may limit what is taught by many other providers of continuing education.

In order to capitalize on these inherent strengths, both credit and noncredit continuing education programs must be an extension of academic programs. The following outline can serve as a basis for an analysis and interpretation of the relative strengths and weaknesses of the knowledge and research base of these programs.

Analysis and Interpretation of Institutional Resources

I. Research and knowledge base
    A. List the institution's majors and degrees.
    B. Identify and describe existing research and knowledge applicable to opportunities for new programming.
    C. Determine what unique forms of research and knowledge the institution can contribute.
    D. Project whether new research results are imminent.
    E. Estimate the institution's capability to identify, create, and stimulate relevant knowledge.

II. Faculty and staff

    A. Identify faculty and staff with disciplinary competencies required to deal with opportunities.

    B. Estimate the number of faculty members and how much of their time will be required in relation to the scope and intensity of the problems associated with strategic long-range planning.

    C. Evaluate whether faculty have the skills to provide innovative leadership for developing new programs.

    D. Assess additional training needed or faculty willingness to participate in professional development if needed.

    E. Project which departments and other knowledge bases are ready to participate in continuing education.

III. Institution

    A. Review personnel policies and procedures to see whether they recognize faculty participation in continuing education activities. If not, determine the likelihood that such changes could be accomplished.

    B. Evaluate the extent to which the institution can respond to opportunities efficiently and competitively.

    C. Determine the degree to which the institution will accept financial responsibility for continuing education activities.

    D. Assess the abilities and priorities of the institution's leaders.

    E. Determine the institution's ability to overcome its limitations, shortcomings, barriers, or obstacles.

Each institution will need to tailor these questions to meet its specific situation. Whatever method an institution chooses to assess its strengths and weaknesses, its potential in the marketplace must not be overlooked.

Determining Position in the Market. One way to determine an institution's position in the market is to (1) categorize the market according to discrete blocks of clients or potential clients; (2) develop a list of significant stakeholders—business leaders, influential persons in the community, and key legislators; (3) ask individuals in the two groupings about their perception of the nature of the institution and its strengths and weaknesses. This information makes it possible to position an institution on the basis of its image with a variety of its publics as well as its relationship to other competing institutions (Cope, 1978; Keller, 1983).

Values Assessment. The final phase in analyzing an institution's strengths and weaknesses is a values assessment. Values are imbedded in the fabric of the institution in the form of its traditions, aspirations, and culture. I have previously discussed the position taken by those who wish to preserve these internal values by building walls. Whether seen by a continuing education leader as strengths or weaknesses, these qualitative forces must be uncovered and examined openly. Responding to the opportunities in the external environment may alter the institution's aspirations and even bend its traditions and the faculty culture. As Keller (1983) wisely observes, these powerful intangibles cannot be ignored. It is best if the new opportunities in continuing education can be linked with an institution's traditions and ambitions.

Strategic Decisions. A strategic decision emerges from matching the institution's strengths and weaknesses to external environmental opportunities and constraints and then to its traditions, values, and aspirations (Shirley and Volkwein, 1978). A strategic decision is a conscious effort to plan for the future by using intelligence and foresight to set the direction for the institution.

The material on external opportunities and threats and institutional strengths and weaknesses constitutes a profile of present and prospective realities and potentials. A strengths/weaknesses/opportunities/threats (SWOT) profile, illustrated in Figure 2, provides a summary analysis useful in making strategic decisions.

Continuing education leaders can also help their institutions reach strategic decisions by using a nine-cell matrix such as that in Figure 3. The matrix matches internal capabilities with external probability-diffusion.

The process builds on the probability-diffusion matrix in Figures 1 and 3 and evaluates trends by adding an assessment of the institution's strengths and weaknesses. The matrix provides a

Figure 2. SWOT Profile.

Internal   *External*

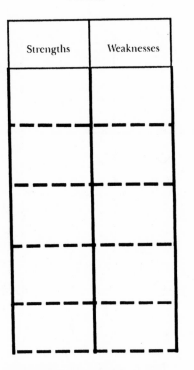
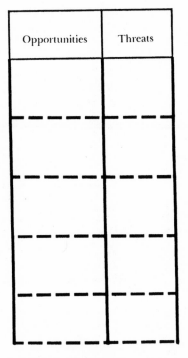

| Strengths | Weaknesses | | Opportunities | Threats |

This column summarizes
strengths/capabilities
and weaknesses/
limitations
in the internal
educational market.

This column summarizes the
important opportunities and
threats in the external
educational market.

visual comparison of these two dimensions and thus serves as one
indicator of the most promising prospects for building bridges.

Strategic decisions based on use of a SWOT analysis and the
nine-cell matrix also help to establish priorities. Continuing
education leaders should embrace this outcome. Such leaders
frequently try to be too many things to too many people and in so
doing engage in some activities peripheral to the institution's

Figure 3. External Probability-Diffusion Matrix.

	High	Medium	Low
High			
Medium			
Low			

mission and goals. Setting priorities communicates a clearer focus and better understanding, both internally and externally, as to what continuing education and the institution's service function are and are not. Priorities help to build a bridge between the external environment and the academic resources of the institution through the extension function.

Strategic decisions that build these bridges between the external environment and the institution, through the continuing education function, are implicit statements about the developments to which the college or university intends to dedicate its resources. These statements should be explicitly spelled out in the institution's mission statement. Since the purpose of a mission statement is to integrate the variety of roles that an institution plays, either revision or clarification of an existing mission statement may be required in order to accurately reflect the strategic decisions reached.

When a mission statement needs revision or clarification, the worth and validity of the changes will depend on how accurately the institution understands its external environment and how well it relates this understanding to its mission. An orientation based on the discharge of a service responsibility to society by individual faculty members is not sufficient. Instead, the orientation needed is institutional. It should reflect the decision to mobilize the institution's resources to address external issues and needs (Schuh, 1984). These qualities provide the institution with a mission statement that will have the overriding purpose and cohesion needed to facilitate internal planning in an integrated way (Ackoff, 1984).

Goals. Goals provide a sense of direction and serve as a statement of broad ends with regard to specific issues or needs contained in a strategic decision. A statement of direction offers a frame of reference for planning continuing education activities. It also provides a means by which to evaluate these activities. The following example illustrates the sequence of theme (environmental category), issue/need/opportunity, and goal. The format is one used by the author as part of a strategic plan for the University of Wisconsin—Extension.

Theme: Economic Development
Issue: Entrepreneurship
Goal: To assist entrepreneurs with "business idea" evaluation, project feasibility, market analysis, site selection, and staffing.

Linking Strategic Decision to Program Planning

Thus far this chapter has outlined a process for making strategic decisions from an institutional perspective. This serves as the framework for planning at the program level. The process for sharing that framework will differ from institution to institution based on a variety of factors. Among these are the institution's system of governance, style of organizational communication, and experience with planning efforts. However, the framework should contain the elements of (1) theme, (2) opportunities/needs/issues,

(3) justification, (4) goals, (5) type of activities, (6) resources, (7) target clientele, and (8) objectives. The first four elements set the institution-wide strategic direction. The last four make up the tactical plan developed at the programming level in support of a strategic direction. The following outline incorporates additional details for each of these eight elements:

1. Theme—one of the environmental trends.
2. Statement that identifies a need, issue, opportunity followed by no more than two paragraphs of detail and analysis.
3. Justification—brief analysis of institutional strengths applicable to need, issue, and opportunity.
4. Goal statements for this particular need, issue, opportunity.
5. Description of types of activities that the program planning unit proposes in support of the goal statements.
6. Resources—projected number of faculty and staff from planning unit, other faculty and staff, ad hoc consultants to offer proposed activities.
7. Identify potential clientele.
8. Incorporate 5, 6, and 7 into objectives that are supportive of the goal statements specified in 4.

This approach focuses on the external environment and asks each planning unit to relate its specific internal strengths to that environment. Its dominant view is "outside-in," which is the opposite of the typical approach to planning. A further advantage is that continuing education leaders will have material organized by theme and issue, need, and opportunity. This provides a composite of the institution's capabilities. In addition, it supplies information helpful to the coordination of the institution's efforts. Finally, the planning unit's proposals to implement its contributions to the institution's strategic direction can serve as a basis for development of budgets and the allocation of resources.

Summary

The agenda for continuing education leaders is to build bridges between the environment and their institutions. Favorable economic, societal, and educational trends offer the opportunity to build these bridges. To carry out this agenda, continuing education leaders must have a commitment to do longer-term planning. An adaptation of strategic planning concepts can provide continuing education leaders with the needed tools. Key tools are included as part of the following summary, which highlights the basic steps in the strategic planning process:

Step 1. Scan the environment.
    A. Set up categories to segment the environment.
    B. Involve faculty. This will provide internal expertise about external trends and help to legitimize the activity.
    C. Consider using an in-house interdisciplinary committee. Be sure that appointment to the committee is in keeping with the institution's traditions and that its role and responsibility is clearly stated.
    D. Evaluate trends by specifying issues, needs, opportunities, and their relative importance.

Step 2. Examine the institution's strengths and weaknesses.
    A. Assess the institution's research and knowledge base. This is the strength of higher education and must serve as the foundation of its continuing education programs.
    B. Determine whether research and knowledge base apply to opportunities in continuing education.
    C. Become familiar with the faculty and disciplinary competencies required to take advantage of opportunities.
    D. Assess the institution's readiness to undertake strategic planning.

Step 3. Make strategic decisions.
    A. Match the institution's strengths and weaknesses to the external opportunities.
    B. Evaluate whether strategic decisions require revision of the existing mission statement.
    C. Set goals for each strategic decision.

Step 4.   Link strategic decisions to program planning.
  A.   Provide planning units with the strategic decision framework composed of theme, opportunities/ needs/issues, justification, and goals.
  B.   Use planning at unit level to specify objectives in support of goals.

It is through use of these four steps that a continuing education organization can create and maintain a position central to the overall mission of its parent organization. Environmental scanning, a key aspect of strategic planning, becomes the basis for building bridges. Such scanning, when used routinely, becomes an important part of the organization's method of daily operation and decision making. No important decisions are made without engaging in such an environmental scanning process.

Goals for each strategic decision are established. Thus a direct link is established between decision making and program planning. This builds the important bridges necessary to encourage support and dialogue between the continuing education unit and its parent organization.

4

How to Conduct an Internal Diagnosis of a Continuing Education Organization

ROBERT G. SIMERLY

Leaders in all types of organizations have experienced the frustrations of trying to implement effective planning systems. They often mistakenly assume that planning is a rational process that consists of establishing goals, identifying objectives to achieve these goals, assigning a person to achieve each objective, and establishing a deadline for checking to see whether or not the objective has been met. Yet everyone who has ever engaged in any type of planning has found that it often does not proceed smoothly in a rational, step-by-step way.

Strategic planning is a way to systematically introduce change into an organization. However, because traditional long-range planning has been based almost entirely on rational models, many handsomely bound planning documents have ended up gathering dust in the bottom drawer of filing cabinets. Often such documents have not helped leaders improve their daily decision making. And if a planning process does not help leaders in their daily decision making, it becomes very difficult to implement the plans (Lippitt, 1973; Mason and Mitroff, 1981; Kanter, 1983). Strategic planning, however, differs from traditional planning. It produces better results for organizations. In addition, it allows for meaningful input from staff (Craig, 1978; Steiner, 1979; Hopkins and Massey, 1981; Steiner and Miner, 1982; Tichy, 1983).

A basic assumption of planning is that strategies will be worked out to make the implementation of the plans successful. Strategic long-range planning is a structured process for (1) designing, (2) implementing, (3) monitoring, and (4) revising plans for improving decision making.

Creating a Balance Between Maintenance and Change

When we consider strategic planning, the relationships between organizational maintenance and change activities become important (Kast and Rosenzweig, 1979). Thus to function effectively, all organizations have to plan for maintaining those activities and programs that are already working well and contributing to the goals of the organization. In addition, organizations have to plan specific ways to introduce change that will help improve daily operations and lead to continued long-term strength and productivity.

Good strategic planning should assist in developing change strategies. However, developing effective maintenance strategies is equally important. In most organizations a dynamic tension exists as leaders wrestle with two basic questions: (1) what kind of time and resources should be devoted to maintaining the status quo in order to get the work of the organization done and (2) what portion of time and resources should be devoted to introducing change? These internal forces, along with various external ones, create powerful dynamics that push the organization this way and that as it seeks to develop an effective way to function within this maintenance/change tension (Bennis, Benne, and Chin, 1985; Bennis, 1976; Schein, 1978).

Continuing education organizations, like all organizations, need a stable base of activity in order to develop effective programs (Flanagan and Smith, 1982). Therefore an important part of any planning process is to design active strategies for maintaining those activities and programs that have proved effective. In fact, leaders usually have to spend the majority of their time on this important maintenance activity. In addition, it is important to find enough time to devote to change and innovation (Astin and Scherrei, 1980; Boyatzis, 1982; Deal and Kennedy, 1982; Bolman and Deal, 1984).

Negotiating a satisfactory balance between maintenance and change often determines the success or failure of strategic planning

(Kaplan, 1983; Kaufman and Stone, 1983). Finding creative ways to accomplish this is therefore a primary job of leadership. By conducting a management audit of the overall health of the organization, leaders can successfully address the issue of achieving an effective balance between maintenance and change. In addition, such an audit should also provide for ways to plan for the development of human resources (London, 1985).

Leaders sometimes introduce changes without adequately determining whether or not they will help the organization meet its goals more effectively. When this happens, the rationale for change is only the change itself. The end result of a given change should always be a stronger and more productive organization— one that meets its major goals more effectively and efficiently (Argyris and Schön, 1974, 1978; Argyris, 1982).

Conducting an Organizational Diagnosis

A basic guideline is to conduct a comprehensive diagnosis of an organization's overall health before attempting to introduce change (Lippitt, Langseth, and Mossop, 1985). For a treatment model to use in assessing organizational health, we might in fact turn to the medical profession. Physicians do not prescribe treatment without first diagnosing what is wrong with a patient. Then, after the diagnosis, appropriate treatment is begun. Moreover, the treatment often has to be modified along the way because of the wide variety of variables that can affect human health.

Similarly, organizational leaders are most effective when they become skilled diagnosticians. Such leaders are social scientists who constantly diagnose the health of the organization on both a formal and informal basis (Golembiewski, 1972; Grove, 1983). And like the physician, leaders should not try to prescribe treatment for organizational problems or develop strategic plans until they have first diagnosed what should be changed, what should be maintained, and why. This helps to avoid establishing an organizational agenda of change just for the sake of change. In addition, it allows leaders to develop specific strategies to deal effectively with those who resist change (Adizes, 1979; Odiorne, 1981; Mitroff, 1983).

The issue then becomes one of finding an effective method for conducting a reliable and easy-to-use diagnosis or management audit. The Maintenance/Change Diagnostic Model depicted in Figure 1 is a very useful diagnostic tool. It provides a way to

1. identify what programs and activities actually contribute to reaching organizational goals.
2. identify what programs and activities are ineffective and thus need to be changed or modified. In addition, identify new programs and activities that should be created to help reach organizational goals.
3. identify programs and activities that are amenable to change as well as those that are not amenable to change.
4. prioritize the implementation of any change activities.

The major idea behind the Maintenance/Change Diagnostic Model is that successful strategic long-range planning requires active management of both maintenance and change after a comprehensive diagnosis of the health of the organization's activities and programs has been undertaken. Getting agreement on major problem areas that need to be addressed or changed is often a difficult and time-consuming process (Michael, 1973; Powers and Powers, 1983; Blake and Mouton, 1984). The Maintenance/Change Diagnostic Model shows a four-quadrant view of organizational conditions. The least resistance to change will probably be experienced with those issues listed in quadrant 1. These are activities that are healthy and amenable to change.

The following explanations illustrate how to use the Maintenance/Change Diagnostic Model as a comprehensive organizational diagnostic tool. If the ease with which change can be brought about is a major criterion for deciding to change, success should be easier to achieve by changing conditions that can be classified in quadrants 1, 2, 3, and 4—in that order. It is important to note, however, that ease of implementing change will not always be the major criterion for making a change. Therefore an important aspect of the model is that it needs to be used in

Figure 1. Maintenance/Change Diagnostic Model.

	Healthy	*Unhealthy*
Easy to change	Quadrant 1	Quadrant 2
Difficult to change	Quadrant 3	Quadrant 4

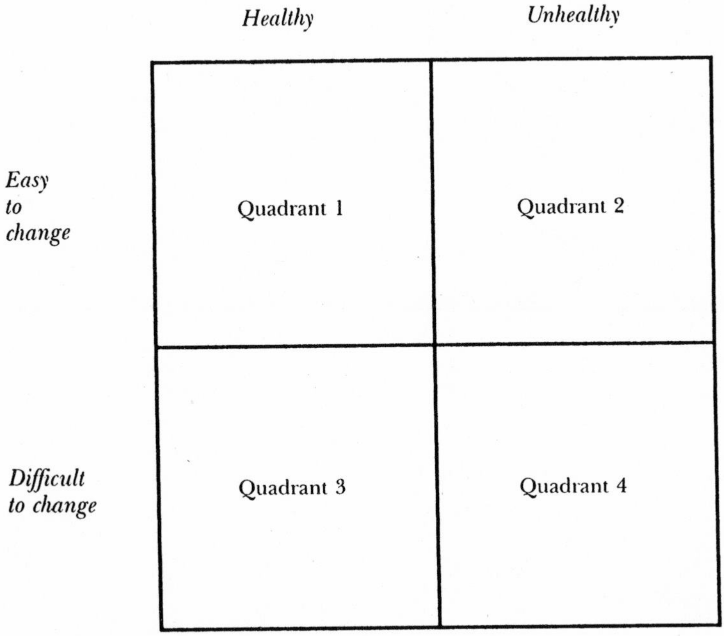

Source: I am grateful to Steve Ruma, organizational development consultant, for conceptualizing the Maintenance/Change Diagnostic Model during several weeks I spent at the National Training Labs in 1974-1975. I have used it with great success in a wide variety of organizational settings and have found it to be an invaluable conceptual tool. I developed the decision rules to be used with the model after many experiences in using the model as a diagnostic tool in continuing education settings. Therefore the theoretical model has been tested successfully in continuing education. Leaders often mention that the model helps them improve their daily problem solving as well as their long-range planning.

conjunction with three important decision rules to be discussed later in the chapter.

Quadrant 1: Healthy Conditions—Easy to Change. This quadrant identifies programs and activities that are basically healthy and are contributing to meeting the organization's goals but are also easy to change. Programs and activities in this area contribute to the following:

1.   Functional organizational problem solving
2.   The meeting of organizational goals and objectives
3.   Overall positive staff morale

Changes related to items classified in quadrant 1 usually consist of a revision or slight altering of existing healthy conditions. In such cases there is often little resistance. Indeed, such change often serves to sharpen the focus of activities and make them even more effective. Case 1 provides an example of organizational conditions that can be classified in quadrant 1.

Case 1

Jonathan Hull is director of noncredit programs in a continuing education office at a small community college in the Northeast. He, an assistant, and a secretary comprise the staff for the entire noncredit programming operation. Together they plan and coordinate the eighty-five noncredit programs that are offered each semester. The total number of participants in these programs during the year comes to 3,200. John's portion of the continuing education enterprise is small, but it has been growing steadily. And the evaluations consistently demonstrate that the programs are fulfilling real needs in the community.

John, however, has been trying to create some strategic plans. Specifically he is trying to develop some concrete strategies to make his noncredit operation more productive. Using the Maintenance/Change Diagnostic Model, he identifies an important activity in the noncredit operation that is basically healthy but at the same time would be relatively easy to change.

"I don't think Janice, my assistant, will mind changing our approaches to brochure design," John thinks to himself. "After all, the brochures are good now, and they produce results. However, we should be experimenting with ways to make them even better and thus increase our registrations. If we do this, we both will become more skilled at direct mail marketing. This will provide the organization with major benefits as we become more competent in this area."

Analysis of Case 1

The brochures to advertise courses are well written, and they produce the required number of registrants in order to break even in almost all courses. But John feels that improved brochures might increase registrations. Since he and his assistant do all the copywriting and both are willing to change, he decides that this activity can be classified in quadrant 1 of the Maintenance/Change Diagnostic Model. He has diagnosed the brochure-writing activity as healthy but easy to change. John's problem now will be to

1. identify specific results that would be accomplished by changing the brochure format.
2. analyze the cost of the proposed change.
3. develop appropriate implementation strategies.
4. decide how to evaluate the results of the change.

By taking this structured approach to diagnosing organizational conditions, John will not fall into the trap of introducing change simply for the sake of change. Rather he will be forced to think through a comprehensive rationale for the change as it relates to other important activities in his total organization. A significant benefit gained from using the Maintenance/Change Diagnostic Model is that it encourages leaders to take a logical, structured approach to problem solving. This structured approach is based on diagnosing organizational conditions in a comprehensive way before instituting any major change.

Quadrant 2: Unhealthy Conditions—Easy to Change. Issues classified in quadrant 2 are those that are basically unhealthy but at the same time are relatively easy to change. For example:

1. Areas in which people are willing to change dysfunctional problem solving when it is pointed out to them
2. Areas in which there has been a breakdown in meeting

organizational goals but where people would be willing to change if appropriate conditions were created

Case 2 illustrates an organizational issue that can be classified in quadrant 2—a condition that is unhealthy and does not help the organization achieve its goals. At the same time, however, the condition is amenable to change.

Case 2

Martha Travers had just taken a new job as director of training and development for a large, national, nonprofit association that conducts workshops for its membership. Each year over seventy-five workshops are offered. These programs attract an average attendance of 50 people each for a total of 3,750 participants per year. The workshop tuition per participant averages $575, resulting in a total annual income to the organization of $2,156,250.

Shortly after Martha assumed her new position, she noticed that many of the brochures to advertise programs were being mailed first class rather than at the special bulk rate available to nonprofit organizations. Martha became concerned about this because she realized that her organization could save a significant amount of money by mailing brochures at the cheaper rate. When she raised this issue at the next staff meeting, she learned some interesting facts about the problem.

"Yes, it's a problem that we've had for some time now," said Wendell Foxworth. "We all have tried to change this, but our problem comes from the faculty we use to teach the workshops."

"Yes," agreed Susan Menton. "They just won't get their brochure copy in so that we can meet all the printing deadlines. As a result we can't get the brochures printed in time to take advantage of the bulk rate. For example, if you're mailing at bulk rate across the United States, you need to allow thirty days from the time you give the mail to the post office until it arrives in people's mailboxes."

Martha listened carefully. Then she said, "If the problem is with the faculty not meeting copy deadlines, it seems to me that there should be some reasonable ways to correct the problem. One solution would be to work more closely with faculty and help them understand the reasons why they must meet copy deadlines. Another solution would be to change the date of the workshop if copy deadlines can't be met in order to provide enough time to enable us to use bulk mailing rates. There are probably other solutions that we could think of too. Solving this problem would save our organization a great deal of money."

"I need some time to think about this," said Wendell Foxworth. "I'd be willing to do some investigating and estimate how much money we'd save each year by mailing all our brochures at the bulk rate. I think I could get the data together within a week and report the results at the next staff meeting."

Analysis of Case 2

Martha judged the condition described in case 2 to be unhealthy for the organization because it encouraged people to spend more money than necessary for mailing expenses. However, Martha also judged that the staff was interested in learning to be more effective in their budget planning. Therefore, using the Maintenance/Change Diagnostic Model, she classified this problem in quadrant 2—unhealthy but easy to change.

Quadrant 3: Healthy Conditions—Not Easy to Change. Quadrant 3 represents those conditions that are basically healthy but are not easy to change, such as the following:

1. Activities that effectively meet organizational goals
2. Areas in which there is a high degree of resistance to change for reasons other than rational ones
3. Areas in which staff have developed an unusually strong psychological bonding to programs or activities

The next case illustrates a situation that can be classified in quadrant 3 of the Maintenance/Change Diagnostic Model.

Case 3

Sam Jameson was director of continuing education for a large hospital. Each year he and his staff planned forty programs that served 4,500 participants. Sam had come to realize that all registration information on participants was being processed by hand. He thought that such data could be more effectively handled by computer. However, when he suggested the idea to his staff, the person in charge of processing all registrations, Tim Donald, made a good point.

"I don't think it's the best use of our money," he stated bluntly. "It will cost about $6,000 to purchase a personal computer by the time we buy all the hardware and software. And according to our best forecasts, the number of participants enrolling in our programs is not projected to increase substantially during the next three to five years."

"I agree," stated Sue Fisher, another staff member. "We don't have any problems with the current system. Things are going smoothly. Why should we change?"

Sam listened carefully and mentally assessed the situation, using the Maintenance/Change Diagnostic Model.

"The registration process does not cause any problems. Therefore we have to acknowledge that this area of the organization is healthy. People appear to be resisting the idea of computerization, and I find it difficult to push this issue—particularly in light of the fact that according to our best data we do not project substantial increases in enrollments. We think attendance at programs will remain fairly stable for the next several years. Therefore this may not be the highest priority for organizational change at this time."

Sam decided to take the advice of his staff, and he dropped the idea for the present. "There are other pressing management issues in the organization, and they should have a higher priority for attention at this time," he concluded.

Analysis of Case 3

Case 3 illustrates some important points about deciding what to change and what not to change in organizations. The existing registration process is effective. And from the conversation at the staff meeting, it is clear that it is not going to be easy to change the thinking of staff on this particular issue. But why are they not amenable to change? Some possible reasons might be:

- They are afraid of the whole concept of computerization with its stereotyped emphasis on mechanization versus concern for people.
- They might fear that introduction of a computer would eliminate jobs.
- They might not want to spend the time and energy it takes to acquire computer skills.
- They might genuinely think that the $6,000 can be used more effectively in other ways. And they might also have a suggestion for using this money in a different way.
- There is a sound organizational rationale for maintaining the current system—namely, staff members can see no major increases in future registrations, and current procedures are effective and efficient.

In analyzing this case, it is important to emphasize that the central issue has to do with Sam and how he and his staff decide what in the organization needs to be changed and in what order. As the Maintenance/Change Diagnostic Model illustrates, the programs and activities classified in quadrants 1 and 2 will probably be easier to change than those classified in quadrants 3 or 4. This does not mean that programs and activities in quadrants 3 or 4 should not be changed. Rather the model illustrates that changes in the other areas will probably meet with less resistance than those classified in quadrants 3 and 4.

Quadrant 4: Unhealthy Conditions—Difficult to Change. Organizational conditions that can be classified in quadrant 4 are almost always difficult to address. They are conditions that are basically unhealthy. Often such conditions prevent the organization from reaching its goals effectively. At the same time, issues that can be classified in this area are very difficult to change. Such problems are often characterized by

- dysfunctional problem solving.
- major breakdowns in meeting organizational goals.
- major difficulty in introducing change because the unhealthy conditions have been institutionalized to the point where significant numbers of people have come to live with them over an extended period of time. Thus there will be high resistance to change because people have learned to adapt and thus feel a certain degree of comfort with even unhealthy conditions.

The next case illustrates a problem that can be classified in quadrant 4.

Case 4

Jean Stimpson had just been hired as the new director of training and development for a large international manufacturing association. One of the ways the association earned money was by coordinating a large number of national and international workshops and conferences each year. The previous director had not given much attention to the departmental budget. As a result, the department had a deficit of $55,000 that had to be repaid.

During her first week on the job, Jean met individually with all ten staff members in her department. She learned that no budget had been prepared for five training workshops that had already been advertised, even though registration fees had been listed in the brochures. When she expressed concern about this, her staff quickly pointed out that they had never been actively involved in the budgetary process.

"We've always just done the programming," said one staff member. "In fact, I've never been involved in actually building a budget from the beginning for any of our conferences."

"Wouldn't it be helpful if you were involved with the budget building?" Jean inquired.

There was a lively discussion in which the staff generally agreed that they were happy with their current responsibilities. "We're so busy with administering the programs that we really don't have time to do the budgeting too," said Warren Westin.

Jean left the meeting remembering the charge she had received from Edith Wilcox, her boss, when she was hired. "We're hiring you to shape up the training department," Edith had stated firmly. "You cannot run a deficit as has been done in the past. We expect you to establish a good budget-planning system and follow it."

Remembering the Maintenance/Change Diagnostic Model, Jean analyzed the situation. She decided that the budgeting system represented a condition that could be classified in quadrant 4. It was definitely unhealthy, and changing conditions in this area would probably be very difficult because in the past the staff had not experienced negative consequences as a result of the budget deficit. Therefore she concluded that making changes in this area would probably meet with major resistance. But she also remembered that classifying an activity in quadrant 4 does not mean that you can or should step away from it.

"In fact," she thought to herself, "the staff has been allowed to ignore the budgetary aspect of training activities for so long that if I start to change this immediately, I'll probably run into active resistance. And if I don't begin to change the budgeting system immediately, I'll be out of a job in six months. The charge I have from Edith, my boss, is very clear. I was hired to improve all aspects of the departmental operations. And bringing about a successful budgeting system is the area that needs immediate attention."

Analysis of Case 4

Case 4 illustrates conditions that can be classified in quadrant 4 of the Maintenance/Change Diagnostic Model. These conditions are unhealthy. They do not contribute in positive ways to helping the organization meet its goals of sound financial management. At the same time, it will be difficult to change these conditions. Yet the survival of the training department is dependent on making such changes quickly.

The central management questions here are:

1. What guidelines can be used to make the Maintenance/ Change Diagnostic Model useful for improving daily decision making?
2. How can the Maintenance/Change Diagnostic Model help show where to begin changing programs and activities?

For example, in case 4, guaranteeing survival of the training department is one of the most important things for Jean as a leader to consider. Delaying initiation of a major change in the budgeting process, even though it will probably be one of the hardest activities to change, is not a good alternative.

Even thinking about changing conditions that can be classified in quadrant 4 often seems like an impossible task. Therefore in using the Maintenance/Change Diagnostic Model, it is important to analyze carefully the programs and activities that can be classified in all quadrants of the model so that conscious choices can be made about comprehensive change strategies. Even if leaders decide not to change a particular item in one of the quadrants, they are making a conscious choice to do this, and it represents a decision based on logical analysis. As many decisions as possible regarding planned change and maintenance need to be made as a result of conscious choice after a careful analysis of the major variables affecting the issues. The Maintenance/Change Diagnostic Model provides the analytical tool for accomplishing this. However, it is important to use the model in conjunction with certain decision rules.

Three Decision Rules for Using the Maintenance/Change Diagnostic Model

Vroom and Yetton (1973) have contributed much to our understanding of the importance of helping people develop decision rules when faced with alternatives during complex problem solving. When issues are complex and there are many alternative courses of action from which to choose, guidelines become a necessity. The following three decision rules should be considered when using the Maintenance/Change Diagnostic Model.

Decision Rule 1

If ease of achievement is the major criterion for deciding to institute change, develop strategies for changing activities classified in quadrant 1 and proceed through the model to quadrant 4. Thus a leader begins with the areas that are most amenable to change and proceeds in a logical sequence to the areas that are diagnosed to be the least amenable to change.

Analysis of Decision Rule 1. In case 4, Jean would be making a big mistake if she did not address the budgetary issue immediately, even though the Maintenance/Change Diagnostic Model identifies this as an area that would be hardest to change. Decision rule 1 provides Jean with a way to prioritize what she will begin to change in the organization. Ease of bringing about this change is not the main criterion for changing the budgeting system. Planning for financial stability of the department is the main criterion for instituting the change.

Thus decision rule 1 demonstrates that if an activity has been judged to be of major importance in helping the organization remain effective, dealing with that issue supersedes the guideline of beginning with the easiest things to change. Jean should change the budgeting system immediately even though change will probably meet with great resistance.

Major Advantage of Decision Rule 1. The advantage of using decision rule 1 is that it enables leaders to begin changing things for which there is the least resistance. Therefore these changes stand a greater chance of succeeding. A major way to implement planned change is to build on small successes before tackling larger, more difficult issues that may be highly resistant to change.

Major Disadvantage of Decision Rule 1. Ease of bringing about change is not always the best criterion to use when deciding what to change. For example, in case 4, Jean Stimpson was hired and given the charge to put the training department on a sound financial footing. "You cannot run a deficit as has been done in the past," Edith Wilcox, her boss, had emphasized. "You must establish a good budget-planning system and follow it."

If ease of bringing about change were the best criterion for Jean to use, she would not be encouraged to address the dysfunctional budget-planning system in her office. As a result, she would do a great disservice to her organization. She would not help the organization meet its goals of establishing good financial planning systems. In addition, since her charge to bring about better financial management was very clear, she would probably be out of a job soon if she diagnosed the health of the organization using the Maintenance/Change Diagnostic Model and decided not to begin immediately changing the budget-planning system.

Decision Rule 2

An effective way to begin a change process is to collect reliable data to present to people. These data should demonstrate how their present behavior is not effective in helping the organization meet its goals.

Analysis of Decision Rule 2. In case 4, Jean was aware that she had a specific charge from her boss, Edith, to bring good financial management practices to the department. Therefore, according to decision rule 2, a logical way for Jean to proceed was to immediately gather reliable data about the current, unhealthy financial planning conditions and then present these data to her staff for analysis and discussion. Some of the things she decided to do were:

1. Analyze the office budget for the last three years in order to show clearly how a $55,000 deficit had occurred.
2. Present these data to the staff for discussion and analysis.
3. Share with her staff Edith's mandatory charge to improve the budgeting process immediately.
4. Clearly state that she is not negotiating with her staff over whether or not to bring improved financial management to the department. Whether or not she should do this is not a topic for debate.
5. State clearly that she will be working to introduce an effective budgetary process since this is the charge she has from her superiors.

6. Establish clearly that what is open for negotiation is how everyone on the staff can work together with her to help improve the budgeting process.

7. Work with staff to establish a series of written procedures for improved budget management—procedures that everyone will have a part in designing and that everyone will agree to follow.

8. Establish the necessary checks, balances, and review procedures to ensure that the new written procedures will be followed.

9. Review successes and failures with the new procedures at weekly staff meetings so that everyone will be able to learn better daily problem-solving techniques regarding financial management. In addition, this will provide the entire staff with an opportunity to monitor the change process as it proceeds.

10. Establish clearly that all staff have a responsibility for improving daily budget management.

11. Establish specific deadlines by which people will begin using the newly developed budget procedures.

Advantages of Decision Rule 2. Collecting reliable data on organizational issues helps get agreement on what the problems are. Most people are willing to change if they are presented with the "facts." However, one of the major issues that blocks change is that people often do not reach agreement on (1) what activities need to be changed and (2) in what order such changes need to be made.

Disadvantages of Decision Rule 2. Collecting reliable data on organizational problem areas often generates defensive reactions. Such behavior can be manifested in a wide variety of ways, including direct attacks on the leader, withdrawal, flight, denial, avoidance, and so on. Therefore a leader must be able to skillfully manage the inevitable conflicts that will result during the change process. It should be emphasized that conflict is a normal part of the planned change process and should not be viewed negatively.

Decision Rule 3

 The most successful change in organizations usually occurs when people can see an important reward for instituting change.

Analysis of Decision Rule 3. Reward systems in organizations are always complex. Basically, however, they can be classified as follows:

- *Extrinsic Rewards.* These are concrete rewards that are provided by the organization—rewards that are usually clear and easy to quantify. Money is an example of an extrinsic reward. The chief characteristic of an extrinsic reward is that the recipient is dependent on someone else to give it to him or her.
- *Intrinsic Rewards.* These are the internal rewards that people give to themselves for a job well done. The major characteristic of an intrinsic reward is that no one has to give it to a person. Rather people learn to reward themselves inwardly. Often such a reward takes the form of feeling very satisfied with a job well done or of feeling more competent because of succeeding at something.

In case 4, Jean decided to try to change the management of the budgetary process even though she knew she would encounter considerable resistance from the staff. Hence she turned to the Maintenance/Change Diagnostic Model and the three decision rules. In considering decision rule 3, she immediately realized that it would be impossible for the organization to give her staff extrinsic rewards for instituting this change. In particular, the organization would not give the staff additional money for improving an unhealthy budgeting situation. If management did this, it would send a signal that the way to get a raise is to perpetuate a dysfunctional activity until the organization bribes you into changing.

Therefore Jean decided that she would have to engage staff members in designing an intrinsic reward system for themselves. Since becoming more skilled at daily problem solving and having the organization recognize this as an important intrinsic reward for most people, she conceptualized her role during the entire change process as being that of a:

- *Data gatherer*—to help present concrete data to the staff demonstrating that the budgeting process they were using was ineffective.
- *Clarifier of consequences*—to help the staff clarify the consequences of not bringing good management practices to financial planning.
- *Continuing educator*—to help educate the staff in ways to become better at daily problem solving, particularly in areas involving financial management.
- *Intrinsic reward designer*—to help the staff develop a series of intrinsic rewards that they could give themselves for becoming more effective problem solvers.

An important point to remember is that the most effective staff members are usually people who see themselves as actively helping the organization solve its daily problems more effectively. Because they see themselves as effective problem solvers and not simply as staff members who carry out the orders of others, they tend to develop very strong psychological commitments to the organization and its success. These are the people who become the best creative problem solvers on a daily basis. And solving problems more effectively on a daily basis is a critical step in instituting a comprehensive strategic planning system.

Summary of the Maintenance/Change Diagnostic Model and Decision Rules

The Maintenance/Change Diagnostic Model presented in Figure 1 provides a way to analyze an organization through a management audit before deciding what programs and activities should be changed. If it is to be an effective diagnostic tool, the model must be used in conjunction with the three decision rules that accompany it.

The model is a valuable conceptual tool for analyzing healthy and unhealthy organizational conditions. In addition, it helps determine what will be easy to change and what will be difficult to change. The three decision rules provide useful guidelines for establishing the priority in which changes should take place. In the fast-paced world of busy leaders, conceptual models must be simple enough to learn quickly if they are to be readily adopted by staff (Behn and Vaupel, 1982). This enables leaders to spend their time concentrating on opportunities rather than always seeing the world as a set of problems (Knox, 1982).

The case studies have emphasized the role of the leader in analyzing conditions and classifying them in the four quadrants of the model. However, the model can be used with equal effectiveness during staff meetings or strategic planning discussions as a way of encouraging staff participation in problem solving. Temporary work groups or "adhocracies" (Toffler, 1980) can be set up to develop and implement both change and maintenance strategies.

Through use of the model in such situations, everyone can begin to contribute to a management audit. For example, during a retreat on long-range planning, all staff members could be asked to classify issues in the four quadrants of the model. Then through general discussion and debate, consensus will begin to develop around a central core of issues. Involving staff members in the total strategic planning process is critical to successful implementation of plans (Stodgill, 1974; Sayles, 1979; Zander, 1982; Peters and Waterman, 1982).

The Maintenance/Change Diagnostic Model and its accompanying three decision rules can become the conceptual framework for involving people in a dynamic, internal management audit that assesses in a comprehensive way the total health of the organization. A major advantage of the model is that it is just as effective when used by individual managers as it is when used with groups of people.

❖ 5 ❖

Matching Programmatic Emphases to the Parent Organization's Values

MICHAEL J. OFFERMAN

Programming is *the* essential function of the continuing education organization. It is through programming that a financial and political support base is built. Programs constitute the organization's product and identity. Decisions about which programs to maintain, develop, or terminate ultimately determine the organization's long-term health and vigor. Thus a leader's influence on programming is an important aspect of strategic planning.

Every organization develops a certain character based on its history, product, self-perception, and dynamic generation of new striving and needs (Selznick, 1957). That character results either from the distinctive competency or from the inadequacy of the organization. The leader plays a key role in developing that character. Selznick outlined the essential tasks that the leader must carry out to create key values and the social structures that embody them. These are (1) defining mission and role, (2) setting institutional purpose, (3) defending institutional integrity, and (4) ordering internal conflict.

Defining integrity as "the persistence of an organization's distinctive values, competence, and role," Selznick (p. 119) emphasized that goals should not be established without a clear enunciation of principles. Some twenty-five years after his conceptualization of the importance of values as a means to infuse day-to-day behavior with long-range meaning and purpose, Selznick's ideas formed one of the synthesizing theories for Peters

71

and Waterman's *In Search of Excellence* (1982), one of the most popular books on leadership in the 1980s.

A more recent work (Vicere, 1985) argues that the pursuit of integrity is essential to the enhancement of continuing education's relative position in the university. For Vicere, integrity consists of four components: holism, continuity, participation, and distinctive excellence. The term *holism* refers to the unity of effort and interdependence of all institutional subgroups necessary to ensure mutual efforts toward the same goals. By continuity, Vicere means the logical progression toward those goals and toward development of an institutional saga that claims a sense of uniqueness. *Participation* of all staff in policy and decision making helps to bring about coordination, integration, continuity, and consistency. Finally, emphasis on areas of *distinctive excellence* assures that programming focuses both on quality and the existing mission of the parent institution. The pursuit of integrity and its component parts results in a greater understanding of and respect for continuing education within the parent institution. This, in turn, contributes to a stronger power base for continuing education. The same basic argument has been made regarding the human resource development effort in business, industry, and government (Janov, 1985).

The Leader's Role in Values Clarification

The premise of this chapter is that the continuing education leader can best influence programming efforts by infusing them with basic guiding values. These values become the parameters within which the multitude of day-to-day programming decisions are made. If they are consistent with the values of the parent institution and the ethics of the field of practice, the continuing education organization will then develop a character notable for its excellence and integrity.

The pursuit of excellence and integrity makes sense from both a business and a political point of view. First, the continuing education organization that grounds its practice in the values, mission, and strengths of the parent institution not only will develop congruence of purpose with the institution but will move toward a position of greater centrality within it. This is a result of definable contributions to the vitality of the parent institution. Second, the focus upon institutional strengths will result in high-quality programming, readily distinguishable from that of the competition. It will result in a committed clientele and a definable niche in the marketplace. Third, the sense of vision that develops from a clear definition of purpose adds meaning to the continuing education effort and serves as an inspiration to staff. An inspired staff will develop programming that is not only consistent with the institution's strengths but congruent with its purpose.

Certainly the challenges facing the continuing education leader require clarity of vision and purpose. Continuing education has always had to live with certain contradictions. On the one hand, it must identify its role and fit within the parent institution. On the other hand, it must develop an external orientation that seeks ways to extend service to new groups and to utilize new delivery modes. An aspect of this paradoxical situation is the need to balance innovation with tradition (Sparks, 1985).

Attempts to embrace core values and at the same time engage in risk taking will produce conflicts (Project on Continuing Higher Education Leadership, 1985). In addressing this challenge, the members of the National University Continuing Education Association's consultation group recommended that continuing education be made more central to the mission of higher education. In addition, they recommended that its programming coincide with institutional role and mission and that emphasis be placed on what distinguishes institutions of higher education from other providers of continuing education. In making these recommendations, which parallel those already outlined here, the group focused on such value-laden issues as the identification of the true mission of higher education and decisions about whom higher education is to serve.

Relationship of Values to Innovation

Where innovation has ignored the need for clear mission congruence with the traditions and roles of the parent institution, the result is often viewed as dysfunctional. It has been argued that in order to avoid that pitfall, university-based continuing education organizations should offer only traditional academic programs and deal only with knowledge obtained through rigorous study and practice. This assures congruence with the parent institution's mission and best serves the learner (Campbell, 1982).

The challenge is complex. Innovation is essential, but it must be carried out within the domain defined by the parent institution's mission, role, and saga. Innovation undertaken outside that domain may remove continuing education even further from a role of institutional influence. The leader's role is to provide a sense of vision about how continuing education may strategically enhance the institution's mission. The leader can actively bring legitimacy to the organization by providing vision and a guiding cluster of values even while promoting change (Gros Louis, 1985).

Recognizing that educational leadership is based on something other than authority and power, the leader may seek influence through pursuit of organizational integrity (Cyert, 1985). The identification of institutional goals, deeply shared values, and priorities is a vital part of strategic planning (Keane, 1985). Internalization of those beliefs is an important step toward value-informed programming. Understanding those values, goals, and priorities helps members consider what their organization is now like and what they want it to be. In essence, this helps to provide a sense of meaning, purpose, and vision that in turn allows them to find opportunities in seemingly paradoxical situations. Thus they will be in a better position to develop unique, innovative responses to continuing learners' needs and the saga of their institutions (Comfort, 1981).

Role of Values in Programming

The role of values in programming is significant. Knox (1981) describes programming as a series of connected decisions that are personal, situational, and value based. He sees values as the basis for all decision making and believes that leaders need to develop breadth of vision in order to define desirable directions for continuing education (Knox, 1985). Others have reached similar conclusions about the importance of values and what is here termed integrity. Comfort (1981) calls for service to adult learners within the confines of the parent institution's values and expectations. Votruba (1981) believes continuing education will become strategically important to the institution only if it attends to the traditions, distinctive faculty, and curricular strengths of that institution.

Peters and Waterman (1982) describe how we often become glassy eyed when values are discussed because we believe that such discussions necessarily involve soft and esoteric considerations. But they argue that the best leaders operate on a faith grounded in a clear set of values. This faith is the basis for what Peters and Waterman call a "loose-tight" operation, that is, one that allows considerable staff autonomy within the parameters defined by shared values. These values are the basis for a stern, tight discipline. However, they focus on building business and on not constraining it. In addition, there is a strong emphasis on the customer and quality. Peters and Waterman outline the four elements of leadership as people's need for (1) meaning, (2) a certain degree of self-control, (3) positive reinforcement, and (4) beliefs shaped by actions. Each element is profoundly affected by a commitment to a clearly defined set of shared values. This is not soft, esoteric "stuff." Rather it is the key differential between effective leaders and ineffective ones.

The fact is that every action, every decision, every program is value based but that the underlying values in continuing education are seldom examined (Merriam, 1982). Whether consciously or not, programming reflects values. Leaders are those who clarify their own values, integrate them with their institution's values, and work to instill a synthesized value set into the day-to-day programming effort. A philosophy has been described as a form of long-range planning (Strother and Klus, 1982) and values clarification as a means to maximize our strategic planning by development of a sense of purpose. Such attention to values has the potential to be motivating, inspiring, energizing, and meaningful (Merriam, 1982). Elias (1982) sees practice guided by a philosophy as invigorating, rewarding, explanatory, and imaginative. Selznick (1957) argues that meaning and purpose can be added to an organization through myths presented in uplifting, idealistic language that focus on what is distinctive in the aims and methods of the organization.

Defining a clear value base, which is the key component in a commitment to integrity, is not merely an academic exercise. It is very practical since it takes into account real-world financial and political concerns. In fact, it is astute behavior that can lead to consistency, coherence, and congruence for programming and to a better fit between continuing education and the parent institution. Such definition of values is guided by commitment to institutional strengths, quality, learner's rights, and support for colleagues. It can lead to a better understanding of continuing education, mutuality of purpose, and greater internal and external support.

Opposing Tendencies

There are, however, potential pitfalls that must be considered. A commitment to integrity involves a dual orientation to innovation and institutional tradition. These orientations are based on assumptions that are not easily bridged. They can be bridged only through informed, persistent effort. Grounding programming in existing institutional patterns can become an easy means to avoid innovation. There must be an offsetting value placed on expansion of service and customer orientation if continuing education is to remain dynamic and viable. Leaders must not become prisoners of their own doctrine but rather increase organizational vitality by constantly seeking better ways to pursue goals (Ryan, 1985). Moreover, overcompensation for their perceived marginality can make continuing educators even more inflexible and wedded to tradition than mainstream academic colleagues (Cunningham, 1982). The problem is to manage paradox, a key to leadership in the modern world (Peters and Waterman, 1982).

Another potential pitfall is an institutional history that relegates continuing education to a marginal position. Institutional history can serve as a limitation, a constraint to the potential of the continuing education organization. Blake and

Mouton (1983) suggest that "ideal modeling" is the means to overcome this pitfall. Ideal modeling is a process that focuses on developing a clear view of what is possible if historical limitations are recognized and consciously addressed. It allows the identification of historical barriers to excellence and presents ways to overcome those barriers. At its simplest, it is an argument that demonstrates how continuing education efforts have been constrained historically and how removal of those constraints could strategically serve the institution. It is a means to assess and demonstrate how continuing education would be capable of innovating within the domain of the institution's mission and saga if it were allowed to overcome historical limitations.

Ideal modeling involves development of a strategic vision that consciously incorporates an awareness of potential problems and a valuing of innovation and flexibility. This suggested approach certainly does not eliminate pitfalls. Rather it focuses awareness on them and approaches them through a dynamic, value-based process. The process neither overcompensates nor becomes doctrinaire.

The pursuit of integrity can most easily be constrained by doctrine when the question of ethics arises. As part of an effort to professionalize the field of continuing education and in reaction to concerns about the potential dangers of rapid growth and competition, increasing attention has been directed to ethical behavior. As qualitative principles that guide program operations, ethics are a vital part of the value system that contributes to the integrity of the continuing education organization (Mason, 1979; Dill, 1982). However, the determination of what is right or wrong behavior is easily misinterpreted as something static and universal rather than dynamic and multidimensional. Ethics, in fact, arise out of the values held by individuals, organizations, and communities. They arise out of the beliefs established through the social process and therefore are informed by the context, goals, means, and implications of that social process (Singarella and Sork, 1983). The commitment to ethical behavior and the process of ongoing values clarification are more important than the potential product—a code of ethics.

Attempts to Develop a Code of Behavior for Continuing Education

Despite warnings that development of a code of behavior for continuing education would be difficult and even undesirable given the diversity of the field (Wooten and White, 1983), attempts have been made to codify ethics. One comprehensive attempt to develop a code of ethics emphasized programming and dealt with learning needs, outcomes, experiences, evaluation, and administration (Council on the Continuing Education Unit, 1984). This attempt has been criticized as doctrinaire in its reductionism and its emphasis on only one program development model (Collins, 1985). Other attempts have had to struggle with the same problem: how to be definitive while capturing the tremendous diversity of the field. None of these attempts has been successful, and each, in fact, has ended in the adoption of one or another philosophical approach to the question of ethics. Because such a large number of philosophies are available, the futility of attempting to develop a universally acceptable code is obvious.

What is important, however, is the commitment to good faith and good practice—in effect, to integrity. The process of assessing values and beliefs is important and is, in fact, desirable in itself rather than being only a means to develop a universal code. What these attempts at codification have helped to do is demonstrate that there are widely shared basic concerns that underlie our practice.

There have been several agendas for consideration offered by national groups concerned with the future of continuing education. One group of consultants called for continuing education to define how it may affect both economic development and social progress, to determine what groups should be the focus of educational efforts, and to set forth the implications for the field (Project on Continuing Higher Education Leadership, 1985). Another commission cited the need to address the problems of employability, adult illiteracy, equal access to education, maintenance of skills during technological change, and assuring a knowledgeable citizenry (Commission on Higher Education and the Adult Learner, 1984). In effect, these agendas represent current national concerns that require value-based decisions about how the field and individual organizations should respond.

In addressing these agendas, the leader must consider the overriding questions that require values clarification. This, in turn, offers the opportunity to see how a commitment to integrity can enhance and inform programming. Those overriding concerns include the following questions: (1) What is the purpose of continuing education? (2) Who should be served by continuing education? (3) How should those persons be served? (4) What responsibility does continuing education have for the consequences of its programs? (5) How shall honesty, fairness, equity, and human and civil rights be accrued? The leader must consider these questions in developing his or her own set of guiding values.

How Leaders Can Communicate a Commitment to Integrity

Some issues do represent near-universal principles of justice (for example, concerns about honesty or civil and human rights). Other issues are universal concerns, but the responses to them may vary. The common elements in a commitment to operate with integrity are a concern for people, especially learners, for the institution, and for society. Selznick (1957) suggests that in creating an organizational myth that encompasses both meaning and purpose, it is not the communication of the myth that matters but having the insight to see the necessity for myth in the first place.

So it is with the need for integrity. Actions, not the commitment itself, are the telling points of integrity. What is offered now is a list of commitments that a continuing education organization might make to ensure its integrity. The list is not meant to be prescriptive, universal, or exhaustive. But I hope that it has captured the issues related to integrity listed above.

Important Programming Values

The nine interrelated programming values that would contribute to organizational integrity for continuing education are:

1. Congruence with overall institutional mission and goals
2. Maintenance and innovation in areas of institutional strength
3. Delineation of whom to serve with a commitment to equity
4. Emphasis on quality
5. Nonduplication of effort
6. Acceptance of responsibility for all programming consequences
7. Respect for learners' rights
8. Commitment to fair and honest practice
9. Commitment to the improvement of society

Congruence with institutional mission assures mutuality of effort and continuing education's contribution to institutional vitality. Emphasis on areas of strength, existing and potential, helps to define better the market to be served and ensures that the institution will deliver its best services. An outgrowth of this commitment is a decision about whom to serve. As long as a commitment to equity exists, there will be efforts to extend services to previously unserved or underserved groups. A related issue is service to society. The need to address problems of illiteracy, unemployment, and maintaining an informed citizenry must be included in the decision about whom to serve. Much of the continuing education effort is directed at groups already educationally advantaged (Cross, 1981). Leaders should seek ways to prevent development of an educational underclass and to address societal needs.

Quality is a nearly universally agreed on goal that is, unfortunately, not universally attained. The emphasis on an institution's strength and distinctive excellence works in tandem with a commitment to quality. Excellence requires that the leader not merely duplicate what is already available. Mere duplication is a waste of resources and does not necessarily improve or extend opportunities.

Accepting responsibility for all programming consequences requires that all means employed are appropriate to desired ends. Does programming emphasize a belief in the dignity of the learner and the integrity of the organization? Efforts should be made to develop independent, self-directed learners. Unfortunately, continuing education has been accused of creating permanently deficient learners dependent on lifelong schooling. The leader who is pursuing organizational integrity must attend to and overcome this criticism.

Respect for human and civil rights demands more than mere compliance with laws. It demands a deep and sincere belief in the integrity of all persons. A philosophy grounded in that belief will also lead to honest and fair practice. Leaders should ensure that the learner as consumer is provided with all the information that he or she needs to make decisions about participation. All promotional materials must be clear and honest. In addition, programming based on integrity will ensure consideration of how such a program can contribute to the improvement of society through the improvement of the individual program participants.

These ideas sound fine to most of us, but the crucial point is the extent to which they actually guide our practice. How will programming be affected by these values? Will the organization be viewed as operating with integrity if it follows these values as guidelines? The following two cases illustrate these principles.

Case 1

The Continuing Education Division at Regional University has worked with a department in the College of Education to offer several credit workshops (one semester hour each) at an off-campus site for the past four years. These workshops have been very popular with teachers who are able to acquire credit for pay scale and continuing certification needs by attending them. Both division and departmental budgets have been favorably affected. However, problems have begun this summer. First, some students have complained that they have accumulated six, eight, even ten hours of workshop credit only to find that this credit will not be accepted in a degree program. Second, there have been complaints from other students and departments that courses critical for certification and degree completion purposes have been canceled because of a loss of students to the two-day workshops. The students and departments look to Continuing Education for resolution of the problem. How should the leader respond?

Obviously there are many ways to respond. One approach to this dilemma would be to consider the situation in terms of the values discussed earlier. The mission of the university is to offer courses, degrees, and noncredit programs for professional career preparation and advancement. Emphasis is placed on academic and vocational programming. The strength of the university, which distinguishes it from other providers of education, lies in its credit- and degree-granting ability. The teachers attend for credit purposes. However, the leader might question whether it is strategically the most appropriate decision to award credit for a program with no student requirements or evaluation. Is this an educational need that is being served or a certification need? Does it enhance the integrity of the organization and institution to remove traditional academic requirements in this situation? Or would this open the workshops to the charge of hucksterism?

The leader who answers these somewhat loaded questions—loaded in terms of the values outlined earlier—will most likely decide that there are some real problems with this popular program. The values will help the leader to decide in what ways the programs need to be changed. Obviously, the values will not solve all problems. But they do lend a sense of purpose to what the leader is pursuing—a vision of what kind of programming is appropriate. The leader now realizes that he or she must address this problem, perhaps by pushing for adoption of an institution-wide policy to set guidelines for credit-bearing workshops. Issues for consideration might include minimum numbers of contact hours, disclosure regarding credit for degrees, evaluation, and so on.

Unfortunately, there are popular topics and programs that may need to be rejected given the values appropriate for organizational integrity. Equally unfortunate is the fact that often these programs are not rejected, and continuing education does not receive the respect of colleagues or clientele. For example, we can easily imagine the reaction of the science faculty to programs sponsored by continuing education that support the existence of unidentified flying objects or of the psychology faculty to programs on astrology. Clientele can also be turned off, for example, if in the mad scramble to serve business and industry, a small liberal arts college develops continuing engineering education programming with neither the faculty nor resources to support such efforts.

However, the above examples demonstrate only how the pursuit of integrity can limit programming. The more difficult task is to find ways to innovate and expand services within the limits of that pursuit. The following case is an example of program extension.

Case 2

A government agency has a continuing problem involving work processing and routing. The training branch has traditionally provided management and supervisory training. It has offered specific training to overcome these problems with the assumption that there would be follow-up in-office training for nonsupervisory employees. In fact, the problems have not been resolved. The vast majority of problems occur at the clerical and paraprofessional levels. The training branch is asked whether it believes training can help solve these problems and what it would recommend.

Research into the question results in three conclusions: (1) the problems are skill based, (2) the supervisors know processing well but are not skilled at training the staff, and (3) there is a morale problem among staff members who fail to see how they fit in the overall work processing. There are two options offered: (1) train the supervisors to become trainers or (2) extend the training branch's role to include work-processing training for support staff. What shall the leader do?

Applying the values outlined earlier, the leader might conclude that the branch's extension of service is congruent with the agency's mission (effective work processing) and emphasizes a branch strength (training). It also emphasizes the right of all employees to have adequate job training. The training of support staff by the branch helps the agency focus on its real mission and creates more equality of opportunity. This may lead to greater respect for the training branch by its clientele and parent organization. Just as importantly, providing opportunities to a previously unserved group may stimulate that group, and the potential payoff will enhance morale and commitment. Ideally all groups involved will benefit from program expansion.

There are numerous opportunities for innovation within the areas of institutional strengths. However, it is easy for continuing education organizations to forget the need to address social problems. One such problem is illiteracy. Kozol (1985) states that colleges, universities, businesses, and industries all have a role to play in resolving the functional illiteracy of some sixty million adult Americans. The political, economic, psychological, and sociological implications of this problem cry out for creative, cooperative, institution-stretching responses. There is also a need to consciously and persistently pursue ways that continuing education can reach unserved or underserved populations. One means is to develop community-based, self-directed projects supported by university resources, including faculty, staff, and researchers, with the intent of resolving community problems. Such an effort would allow a university to develop independent learners and address problems in its community while serving new populations often ignored by continuing higher education. Development of the Lindeman Center in Chicago by the Community Services Office of Northern Illinois University is an excellent, although uncommon, example of this type of approach (Northern Illinois University, 1984).

Gaining Organizational Commitment to Values of Integrity

The leader must not only be committed to values that bespeak integrity. The leader must also ensure that the continuing education organization shares and reflects that commitment. There are no easy answers to the how-to-do-it question. But some suggestions can be made. First, the leader must critically assess and clarify his or her own values. Knox (1985) suggests that there must be time specifically set aside to deal explicitly with values—both one's own values and those of the institution. Next, the leader must integrate these personal and institutional values and synthesize them into a meaningful set. The leader encourages staff members to do the same and provides opportunities for them to do so.

The leader serves as coach, model, and evangelist in clarifying values (Peters and Waterman, 1982). However, the key lies in his or her actions. While the leader may present a soaring vision to staff members, it is, according to Peters and Waterman, deeds, not words, that instill values. Good role modeling is essential. The leader must believe in values that promote integrity, must live them, and must demonstrate them over and over again in daily and mundane tasks. The leader can help to ensure that this happens by reflecting a concern for these values in staff discussions, meetings, evaluations, goal setting, and recruitment and promotion. Over time, the leader and staff will begin to enact these values unconsciously and with confidence.

Bennis (1984) has captured the essential ingredients of what is required of leadership to assure value-based behavior in his study of the competencies of leadership. He found that ninety of the most effective leaders in the United States shared exceptional capabilities in four areas: (1) the management of attention, (2) the management of meaning, (3) the management of trust, and (4) the management of self. Effective leaders know what they want and provide an extraordinary focus of attention that attracts people to them and their agendas. They also communicate their vision in a way that provides meaning through the integration of facts and concepts. Leaders are reliable and constant in their focus, with the result that people can trust them and predict their responses to issues.

Finally, leaders know themselves, their skills, and their beliefs. Working with a leader who manages these four key elements is an empowering experience that offers significance to a staff's efforts, makes work exciting, and develops a sense of community. Bennis concludes that feelings of quality are connected ultimately to our experience of meaning, beauty, and value in our lives. Closely linked to these feelings are dedication and love of our work.

A better sense of our values and a commitment to incorporate those values in our leadership can provide self-inspiration, focus staff attention, provide meaning to our actions, and develop a sense of trust for the leader and the continuing education operation. In the final analysis, what separates a leader from a manager is the ability to understand himself or herself through values clarification and thus give focus, meaning, and integrity to his or her actions. Rather than an abstract exercise, the clarification of values emphasis on integrity is a practical, essential aspect of leadership. A focus on integrity is the hallmark of the successful, resilient, and supported continuing education program.

Building an Effective
Organizational Culture:

How to Be Community-Oriented in a Traditional Institution

TERRENCE E. DEAL

Institutions of higher education have become highly complex. New majors, cross-disciplinary programs, campuses abroad, and internship programs give higher education a look far different from what many alumni can remember. Professional schools have grown in size and scope, and their combined enrollment often exceeds that of undergraduate programs. In addition, most colleges and universities have both traditional and nontraditional programs on the same campus. Differences between the two can be characterized as follows:

Traditional programs cater to younger, full-time students and follow age-old academic canons. The professor is the unquestioned authority imparting knowledge and wisdom to novices—mainly through lectures and classroom discussions. Periodic examinations provide students an opportunity to show how well they have mastered the subject. Term papers and essays allow students to inquire into highly specialized topics. Grades, assigned by instructors, array students into performance levels that label present and potential academic ability. The conventional scenario is highly predictable, unchanged over centuries, and widely recognized by anyone who has experienced higher education directly—as a student, professor, or administrator.

Nontraditional programs are given many names: adult education, lifelong learning, or continuing education. Whatever they are called, nontraditional programs are far more varied and less familiar than their traditional counterparts. Although it is difficult to specify general patterns, programs in continuing education often have certain characteristics in common. Students tend to be part time and older, with work experience outside the university. Professors' success is directly dependent on their performance in the classroom and their ability to link theory with the practical world. Instruction often relies heavily on experiential activities such as simulations, role playing and case discussions, and on media such as videotapes, television, and interactive computer programs. There is an emphasis on the world outside the classroom, and external visits sometimes form part of classroom instruction. There is more emphasis on how well students can apply and act on theories or ideas rather than on what they can recall. And finally, there is a stratification of students based on their projected career paths, not on their academic grades. To a person whose experience in universities has been confined to traditional programs, the objectives and activities of nontraditional programs can seem strange—even alarming.

The differences between traditional and nontraditional programs carry even more deeply into their respective organizational fabrics. Traditional programs in higher education have typically been thought of as existing in "domesticated" organizations (Carlson, 1975). Historically, such programs have been assured an admission pool. Once admitted, their clientele tends to stay—and to accept what it is given. To be traditional means to take a conservative stance and change very slowly, if at all. Bennis (1975) has noted that universities are harder to change than cemeteries.

Nontraditional programs can be characterized as "wild" organizations (Carlson, 1975). They must attract a client pool and compete with other programs—on and off campus—to hold students. Students are less prone to accept what they do not like and quicker to leave if the program does not suit their immediate needs. "Wild" organizations must always walk a fine line between their conception of what students need and what students will actually accept. In the case of California's community colleges, Clark (1975) noted that the institutions were captives of the clients rather than the other way around. Balancing quality and palatability is necessary to hold clients yet still maintain a topflight program. Continuing educators take risks, market their programs, and change rapidly in response to opportunities and shifts in the external environment—or in their clientele.

Tension between traditional and nontraditional programs in colleges and universities has always existed. However, recent demographic shifts may intensify these tensions into deeper conflicts. The pool of students who apply to traditional programs is shrinking while the potential pool for continuing education is expanding. In most universities, programs in continuing education are growing while many traditional ones are holding at a steady state or declining. Resources generated by continuing education are frequently used to subsidize traditional programs even though regular faculty typically look with disdain upon their nontraditional colleagues. As squabbles erupt on campus between traditional and nontraditional proponents, an increase in nonuniversity-based education threatens to capture a slice of the market. Education is big business. And if universities do not deliver, they will create a profitable opportunity for someone else.

Whatever the outcome of these shifts and conflicts, it seems clear that those who administer continuing education will need to think and act differently in the decade ahead. Three issues are worthy of special attention:

1. How can leaders shape both the identity and image of continuing education?
2. How can conflict be managed between the cultures of traditional and continuing education within the same institution?
3. What are some specific leadership strategies that can be considered in building culture and tradition under nontraditional conditions?

Interwoven among these three issues are two important concepts: culture and leadership. Both have become almost a preoccupation of business people across the country and abroad. The main purpose of this chapter is to apply these emerging concepts to continuing education. The overriding question is how can continuing educators become leaders who build nontraditional cultures in response to community needs without undermining traditional programs?

Building Culture Through Leadership

Leadership is often confused with management (Bennis and Nanus, 1985). One primary difference between the two is where one's time and attention are focused. Management is concerned with goals, the organization chart, roles, policies, evaluation, planning, and decision making. Leadership emphasizes values, symbols, rituals, ceremonies, and "meaning making." Managers worry about short-term accomplishments (what gets done today), control (keeping the lid on), and their power (the ability of one person to get another to do what he or she might not otherwise do). Leaders focus on long-term vision (what might be someday), process (encouraging people to be comfortably out of control), and influence. In some universities, managers have created predictable, well-controlled, accountable organizations. In other cases, leaders have created "beloved institutions to which participants may be passionately devoted. . . . The participants have added affect, an emotional loading, which places their conception between the coolness of rational purpose and the warmth of sentiment found in religion and magic" (Bennis, 1975, p. 99).

True leaders create institutions—traditional or otherwise—that inspire people, that command their loyalty and commitment. To exercise their leadership, continuing educators need to develop strategic plans that attend to the two axes of organizational effectiveness: identity and image. Identity is what an organization thinks it is; image is what others think it is. Identity and image can be seen as two separate dimensions. Assigning dichotomous values for each, one can construct a matrix, such as that found in Figure 1, that shows the differences among organizations.

Institutions with a solid identity and an exemplary image would include IBM and Harvard University, among others. A shaky fraud is an organization with a past exemplary image but a shaky current identity based on a reputation bound in the past. A

Figure 1. Types of Differences Among Organizations.

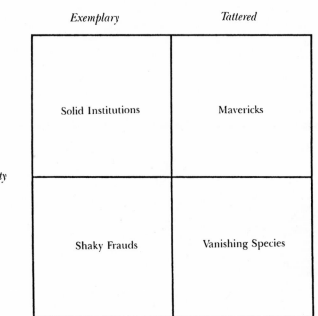

Image

Exemplary   *Tattered*

Identity

Solid Institutions   Mavericks

Shaky Frauds   Vanishing Species

vanishing species is an organization with neither a positive image nor a positive identity—Chrysler before Lee Iacocca, Antioch College before Arthur Morgan. A maverick is an organization with a solid identity and a tattered image that needs revitalizing. Mary Kay Cosmetics, or Apple Computer (in its earlier days) are examples of cohesive organizations that, at one time, had not yet caught the positive glance of the public eye.

It is interesting to apply the matrix to continuing education. The key to organizational success centers on a positive identity. Many continuing education programs have built a strong collective sense of themselves. The identity then becomes the basis for marketing and image building rather than the other way around. Building the foundation before erecting the walls makes sense in most enterprises. Iacocca took Chrysler Corporation from vanishing species to maverick by working on the internal issues first. Once the new identity began to solidify, marketing campaigns challenged the consumers: "If you can find a better car, buy it." The message also reaffirmed the internal dictum: "Unless we build a quality car, we are out of business." Chrysler seems well on its way to institutional status if the company continues as it has.

Leaders shape the identity of an organization by working on the culture—the informal, unconscious consensus that determines "how we do things around here," that is, how hard people work, whether or not they stay, how satisfied they are, as well as their loyalty and commitment to the organization (Deal and Kennedy, 1982; Kilmann, Saxton, Serpa, and Associates, 1985; Schein, 1985). Culture gives meaning to work and to collective actions. Culture interweaves individual strands into a unified pattern or mosaic, provides the glue that bonds individuals to each other and to the organization, or, in short, "keeps the herd moving roughly west" (Deal and Kennedy, 1982).

Leaders, such as Marvin Runyon of Nissan of America or Gerald Mitchell of Dana Corporation, spend a significant amount of their time working on the culture of the workplace. They do so by articulating and reinforcing core values, by anointing and celebrating heroes and heroines—those individuals who personify core values—by convening and participating in key rituals and ceremonies, by telling and serving as subjects for vivid stories, and by working the informal network of priests/priestesses, storytellers, gossips, and spies who watch over, protect, and make the culture accessible and real to other employees (Deal and Kennedy, 1982; Bolman and Deal, 1984; Bennis and Nanus, 1985).

In this view continuing education programs need a strong cultural heritage based on values they stand for rather than on a reaction to traditional academic values. They need heroes and heroines, ceremonies, symbols, and stories. At a recent Harvard commencement, a graduate of the university's continuing education program likened himself and his fellow classmates to "ghosts who make footprints in the snow"—a metaphor for invisible people on the campus who nonetheless leave their mark on the institution. His commencement address was a challenge to

Harvard's relationship to its nontraditional programs and a reaffirmation of the values of continuing education.

Traditional professors, students, and alumni are linked in a common cause. They have symbols, ceremonies, and rituals. For example, as an activity to promote learning, the lecture has no real value. However, as a ritual it usually has meaning to both professor and students. As the professor enters to open a window and erase the chalkboard, the ritual begins. It ends as the professor closes his or her notes. Because most students believe that they are learning, the lecture remains the model teaching strategy—and it probably works. Lecture notes become symbols of newfound knowledge to students. They will faithfully transport them from place to place thereafter.

In a similar way, continuing education needs to spin a symbolic web of meaning around its unique values, rites, ceremonies, and practices. Because continuing education departs from tradition, it is crucial that it build a mythological saga around its unique differences. Unless that happens, both the identity and image of programs will suffer. The next decade's challenge to leaders of continuing education will be to develop strategic plans for building the cultural foundation for nontraditional programs. Management approaches are seldom equal to the task. The influence of leaders can be.

The Clash of Cultures: Traditional Versus Continuing Education

Let us suppose that the culture of continuing education becomes stronger and traditional programs become more threatened in the face of declining enrollments and shrinking resources. What can university campuses expect? The obvious answer is more conflict. But the conflict will be over more than questions of power and resources. It will be primarily a clash of values and beliefs—a contest between two very different cultural patterns. If the conflict can be understood and approached as a cultural issue, it may be possible to keep battles from becoming all-out wars that may unduly damage a college or university.

In *Corporate Cultures*, (1982), Allan Kennedy and I developed a simple typology of corporate cultures. Our intent was to construct metaphors that would help people think about the relationship between culture and the business environment and to help them understand the obvious consequences of bringing members of one cultural type together with others.

Our first step was to conceptualize the environment. We imagined it to have the following two dimensions: (1) the amount of risk involved in a typical action or decision and (2) the length of time required to know whether an action or decision was successful or not. These are depicted in Figure 2. By splitting risk into values (high and low) and feedback time into fast and slow, we devised a matrix that yielded the four basic types of corporate personalities depicted in Figure 2.

"Macho" or tough-guy cultures arise in an environment of high risk and quick feedback. These are corporations in areas such as advertising, marketing, broadcasting, and oil. Values reward risk takers and winners. Heroes and heroines are gamblers for whom risks paid off; the losers will invariably try again. Rituals and ceremonies reinforce competition, risk taking, and celebrate the triumphant. Stories extol the exploits of those who won—or those who failed, tried again, and eventually succeeded. The greater the risk, the sweeter the victory.

"Bet-your-company" cultures are especially attuned to an environment of high risk and slow feedback. Boeing builds an airplane and puts all the resources of the company behind it. The company waits for years to see whether or not it has produced a commercial success—or a flop that will severely affect both the company and the entire Seattle area. The military continually prepares for catastrophic war. We all hope it will be decades—or an eternity—before it will be necessary to test the worth of its weapons, tactics, and equipment. In such endeavors, the main values are thoroughness and deliberateness. Heroes are granitelike figures who have enough experience to be wise and enough patience to withstand long periods of uncertainty. Rituals focus attention on subtle details, trying to find the fatal flaw ahead of time. Ceremonies recognize carefulness and patience. Stories extol those who found a minute fissure in an airframe or noted design problems in a vital assembly before a plane went into production. Nothing can be left unturned or unexamined.

Figure 2. Feedback Patterns.

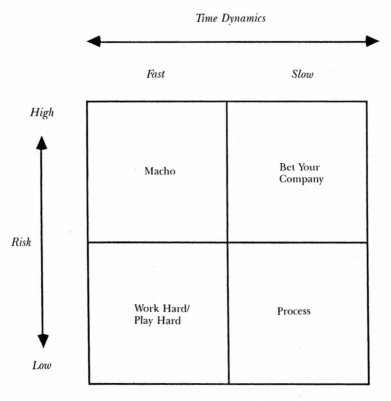

Time Dynamics

	Fast	*Slow*
High	Macho	Bet Your Company
Low	Work Hard/ Play Hard	Process

Risk

"Work hard/play hard" cultures thrive in the world of low risk and quick feedback. These are the sales organizations of the world: Mary Kay, IBM, and Xerox. The driving value is action. The prevailing heroes are the top salespeople, but always in the context of the sales team. The rituals that surround the sales call are taught to all beginning salespeople. Year-end parties are lavish displays of extravagance and hoopla designed to keep the action level high and the morale up since people hear "no" as often as "yes" from potential customers. Stories abound about the last big bash. No one can wait for the next one to roll around.

Process cultures such as banks and insurance companies, along with government agencies such as the Internal Revenue Service, do best in an environment of low risk/slow feedback. The main value is to manage details without making mistakes. The heroes and heroines are the detail workers. Holding meetings and sending memos become key rituals. People jockey for office space and location as symbols of their status and power. Ceremonies celebrate longevity and seniority. Stories describe the exploits of someone who keeps two sets of books to maintain accuracy or shifts the responsibility for an error to someone else through the memo process.

These types of feedback patterns help to categorize companies in the world of business. They may also be useful in pinpointing some of the key cultural differences between continuing and traditional education.

Although anyone could dispute the precise differences, it seems obvious that traditional education and continuing education operate in different environments. For traditional education, the environment is relatively benign—risks are relatively low. Adding a new instructional program is not that much of a gamble. Any risks that exist are minimized by tenure or the endowment. In addition, whether or not the new program works will be difficult to determine. The presumed acid test is whether students learn more and graduates do better. Short-term results are difficult to determine; knowing long-term results is almost impossible.

The multiple influences on career success or failure complicate the relationship between instruction and eventual performance or success. And even if it were possible to link instruction to longer-term outcomes, it is not clear that program advocates would interpret negative relationships as an indictment of classroom activities. There is a well-documented inverse correlation between academic performance in medical schools and clinical performance following graduation. But do medical schools change instructional patterns? Most have not. Ambiguities of measurement, outcomes, and cause-effect relationships make traditional education's feedback loop mushy, almost nonexistent.

The snapshot of the environment can be laid on a composite caricature of traditional academic cultures. They have multiple values. Heroes and heroines are typically those with the longest tenure. Meetings of committees occupy a large amount of time. Invocations and graduations reaffirm tradition and the status quo.

Memos are an important communication medium. Old-timers usually dominate the informal network. In research universities, a somewhat different pattern is found; that is, they tend to conform more closely to the bet-your-company profile. But most people who have spent a significant portion of their lives in colleges and universities would probably agree that they follow the patterns found in banks and insurance companies. (Note the similarities between the power of the registrar in a college when grades are due and that of the chief auditor in a bank when a balance does not add up. It is very important that banks and universities manage details well.)

The environment of continuing education provides a striking contrast to the low risk/slow feedback world of traditional education. Launching a new program or series typically requires significant planning and marketing costs. The level of risk involved can vary from low to moderate. In most colleges and universities, the investment in a particular continuing education program would not equal the costs of a national advertising campaign in business. In most instances, the feedback loop for determining the success of continuing education is quite rapid. If no students enroll, the program simply fails. If students leave midway, the program's success is questionable. Costs are expected to yield profits. Evaluation results at the end are carefully scrutinized for quality control purposes. The return on investment is calculated in terms of both quality and profit.

While I am sure that it varies from place to place, my experience with continuing education confirms a cultural pattern that is an amalgam of the work hard/play hard and macho types. There is a premium placed on action and competition. Heroes and heroines are risk takers and team players. Rituals and ceremonies seem more flamboyant than in most educational organizations. Stories are told about innovative programs that have gone big and entrepreneurs who have struck it rich for the university.

Thus most universities currently house two very different subcultures. And if the subcultures are not contained by superordinate values of the college or university, the expected scenario will probably play itself out. Neither group will understand the language or behavior of the other. Mutual conversations will be dialogues of the deaf. Different ritualistic rules and tempos will keep everyone off balance. Each group will try to undermine the efforts of the other. In the meantime, educational programs outside the university will make inroads into the market share much as the private adult education entrepreneur has done in large cities such as New York.

Recognizing and dealing with the obvious differences between traditional and nontraditional programs represent a significant challenge to colleges and universities. Continuing educators need to exercise their leadership in reaching a pact of coexistence. This involves finding a suitable university-wide umbrella to reconcile the differences and to view the conflict as an opportunity to transform higher education. In a sense, continuing education may be signaling new directions for the culture of higher education.

Building the Culture of Continuing Education

How can leaders begin to develop strategic plans that will strengthen the existential fiber of programs that serve mainly part-time adult students? While many feel that culture cannot be produced by fiat, it certainly can be encouraged. Culture arises from the interaction of people; thereafter it shapes them. Anyone's actions, especially those of leaders, can alter the chemistry and affect the blend. How can continuing education leaders plan to enhance their culture? The following nine ideas should prove helpful.

1. *Survey the environment, map its movement, and determine what it will take to succeed.* Leaders in continuing education cannot afford to focus all their attention inwardly. They need to anticipate and respond to emerging opportunities. Will the local community (or wider sector) respond favorably to a variety of inexpensive, short-term seminars? Or might they make their mark by investing a substantial amount of money and time to develop an integrated series of courses around a timely topic? Leaders need to know what the community wants or needs. They must also be aware of—and even anticipate—trends that might create a new education market. Mapping the environment can be done in a

number of different ways. Formal surveys can be used to pinpoint existing needs. But the antennae of continuing educators must be constantly attuned to informal signals and their gaze riveted on divining rods that point to new opportunities.

2. *Try new approaches.* Successful businesses take calculated risks. They launch pilot efforts to test the market and their assumptions. In the process, they separate things that work from those that do not work. Experience is the wellspring of cultural values and economic success alike. Very few people would have predicted the instant success of the Hula-Hoop or the long-term staying power of Ivory soap or Monopoly. Each was launched as a trial product, and for different reasons each was a success. From successes, companies learn values. Procter & Gamble learned to pay attention to the consumer as a result of its experience with Ivory soap. However, organizations also learn from failures. In the aftermath of the Vietnamese War, the United States Air Force returned to one of its traditional values: "Cohesion is a principle of war." Leadership in continuing education requires an entrepreneurial attitude: Leaders must be willing to try things to separate the wheat from the chaff. Inaction will not permit the sorting to take place. Continuing education requires continual experimentation.

3. *Articulate core values.* No company or institution of higher education can do everything. Successful organizations stand for something. Through symbols and slogans, effective companies make core values accessible across and up and down levels of the organization. Traditional programs do not have to put the same effort into defining core values. The value of a traditional diploma is assumed. But continuing education must stand for more than a loosely defined alternative to regular education. Its values of relevance, excitement, and articulation between ideas and action must be expressed in memorable statements and meaningful symbols. Just as the motto *Veritas* anchors the meaning of a Harvard education, continuing education organizations need to articulate their special character.

4. *Anoint and celebrate cultural heroes.* In any organization, there are people who embody and represent its essential character. These people serve as role models for others. In their

anointing and celebration, people come to know their values and bond together in a common quest. Consider the dropout who finishes a degree in mechanical engineering, the housewife who finishes first among her peers in a liberal arts program, the business person who receives a promotion on the basis of newly acquired knowledge and skills in an experimental marketing program. Such individuals embody and represent the central values of continuing education. Their recognition provides role models for other continuing education students and helps to attract new applicants to programs. Continuing education exists to serve the adult learner who would otherwise not have the opportunity to take full advantage of an academic program.

5. *Amplify and underscore cultural rituals.* The lecture method works in traditional education because of a long history that makes students believe they learn when they take notes and makes teachers believe they teach when they talk. Alternative forms in continuing education need a similar kind of symbolic support. The philosophic base of new practices needs to be shared and reaffirmed.

If continuing education encourages the case method, internships, or simulations, such practices need to be imbued with meanings. Unless leaders in continuing education take a stand and articulate the rationale behind its practices, students will not see the connection between activities and learning—nor will employers. Continuing educators can follow the example of the Harvard Business School, an institution that has given its case method special status in the eyes of students, faculty, alumni, and the business community.

6. *Convene and give special attention to cultural ceremonies.* One leader in continuing education told the president of her university that she wanted to sponsor an alumni reunion for students who had taken part in the program. The president raised questions about the event because poor attendance might damage the university's reputation in the field. The event was held, and the president was embarrassed—not because of a poor turnout, however, but for two other reasons. First, the event was better attended than the reunion for the traditional program. And second, the alumni were obviously more successful—at least as

measured by the quality of cars they drove to the event. Ceremonies express and reinforce the values of a culture. Continuing education needs to pay special attention to key ceremonies. These provide splendid occasions to communicate unique values and assumptions.

7. *Tell vivid stories.* Stories carry values. In most continuing education programs, late bloomers blossom and dramatic changes take place in people's lives and careers quite regularly. These need to be shared and retold—both for identity and image purposes. One continuing educator recently captivated an audience with a vivid description of a graduation ceremony in which a group of handicapped students received their diplomas. The program was designed to prepare severely handicapped students for the social, economic, and other realities of making it on their own. In the story, outsiders were able to experience the values of one facet of continuing education. The graduation ceremony also brought together administrators, faculty members, and students involved with the program.

8. *Work the cultural network.* The cultures of continuing education, like those everywhere, need constant attention and nourishment. Priests and priestesses, gossips, storytellers, and spies play pivotal roles behind the scenes. Every continuing education program has a variety of secretaries, custodians, clerks, food-service workers, and faculty who play important, informal roles. Such people need to be worked with so that they become an integral part of the success of continuing education.

9. *Spend time working on symbolic issues.* Gerald Mitchell, Chairman of Dana Corporation, noted recently that he spends nearly half his time working to reinforce and communicate the culture of Dana. In continuing education, an even greater emphasis may be required. Continuing educators need to set aside even more time to work on the culture than do their counterparts in traditional programs. Both the image and identity of continuing education must be carefully cultivated by its leaders.

Summary

In the next decade, continuing education will undoubtedly play a more important role in the life of individuals and institutions than it does now. This will require a legion of leaders at the helm of continuing education programs who realize their key roles in shaping the identity and image of their organization. Such leaders will understand and work to bridge the cultural differences between continuing education programs and those of the parent organization. And they will work continuously to reinforce the system of values and beliefs that give meaning to life and work in organizations. Developing strategic plans to achieve this is one of the highest priorities for today's continuing education leadership.

✤ 7 ✤

Managing the Tensions That
Go With the Planning Process

FRANCIS M. TRUSTY

The role of conflict in human affairs has been documented by numerous authors (Coser, 1956; Boulding, 1970; Deutsch, 1973; Likert and Likert, 1976; Duke, 1976; Trusty, 1971; Brown, 1983; Blake and Mouton, 1984). In fact, in most organizations the absence of conflict is a rarer phenomenon than its presence. (Duke, 1976; Blake and Mouton, 1984). Managing organizational conflict is thus an important process in strategic planning. It first of all involves accepting conflict as a natural phenomenon. But it also involves analyzing one's own approach to conflict management and making plans to enlarge one's repertoire of conflict management skills as an integral part of the strategic planning process.

Conflict Defined

The type of conflict discussed in this chapter is that which naturally occurs among people as they pursue different goals and objectives. It is those differences that lead to conflicts.

Filley (1975) sees the source of conflict existing between incompatible goals and values. However, he emphasizes that such differences are often only perceived differences rather than real ones. Brown (1983) emphasizes that conflict is simply incompatible behavior among people who have different interests and values.

Various forms of conflict have been identified. Among these are personal, interpersonal, group, intergroup, organizational, and interorganizational conflicts (Smith, 1971; Blake and Mouton, 1984; Bercovitch, 1984). Most of the conflict to be addressed in this chapter will be interpersonal and organizational. However, because conflict is a dynamic phenomenon, there is no definition that can separate the various forms of conflict into mutually exclusive categories.

Our expectations for individual success are shaped by early exposure to conflict through competitive activity in sports, education, business, and social relations. This exposure produces winners and losers, and success is measured by the evidence of winning (Robert, 1981). This evidence is reflected in the acquisition of goods, the achievement of difficult objectives, the control exercised by supervisory personnel over employees and resources, and the authority to make decisions that affect other people.

At the heart of this kind of competition is an assumption of scarcity. In some cases the scarcity is real; in others it is contrived. In either case, however, individuals are motivated to compete and achieve success. Conflict increases as individuals strive to maximize their acquisition and consumption of goods, gain control of people, or determine goals and objectives for organizations (Duke, 1976). In other cases, a lack of trust or a failure in communication will create conflict (Blake and Mouton, 1984).

Conflict can be both functional and dysfunctional in organizations. Some of the major dysfunctional aspects of conflict include:

1. Conflict can be stress producing for individuals.
2. Conflict can disrupt the harmony of work groups.
3. Conflict can hinder decision-making processes.
4. Conflict can challenge the status quo.
5. Conflict can be a cost to the organization.

Conflict also serves functional purposes (Coser, 1956; Pondy, 1967; Trusty, 1971; Jandt and Gillette, 1985). The following are some of the functional ways in which conflict can assist organizations:

1. Conflict with other groups establishes the group's separate identity and strengthens its boundaries.

2. Conflict preserves relationships by allowing the venting of hostilities.
3. Conflict with other groups leads to greater internal cohesion, centralization, and mobilization of resources.
4. Conflict leads to greater social participation in group life by members of the group.
5. Conflict leads to the establishment of new norms and a reaffirmation of old ones.
6. Conflict leads to the clarification of issues.

Conflict accompanies every change of any significance. In fact, it helps to motivate individuals and organizations to make needed changes. While efforts to eliminate conflict from human affairs and organizational settings are constant, its total elimination would be dysfunctional. Conflict can and should be managed in productive ways as an integral part of strategic planning and effective leadership.

Causes of Conflict

Establishing the cause of a conflict is important when developing a posture or stance from which to engage in win-lose conflicts. It is less important to do so when engaged in problem solving or win-win activities. There the goal is not to locate blame but to improve the individual's performance or the organization's effectiveness. Knowing the causes of conflict can, however, provide the continuing education leader with a set of conceptual tools that will improve the leader's ability to manage conflict.

Typical causes of interpersonal conflict include differences in the values people have (Turner, 1974; Duke, 1976), challenges to their sense of self-worth or importance (Blake and Mouton, 1984), and threats to their identity (Parsons, 1959; Erikson, 1963; West, 1967; Glasser, 1972). Organizational conflicts often arise from changes in goals or procedures (Robbins, 1974; Blake and Mouton, 1984), efforts to exert control over others (Turner, 1974), the existence of overlapping responsibilities (Heilizer, 1964; Brown, 1983; Blake and Mouton, 1984), the scarcity of resources (Duke, 1976), and attempts of organizational units to suboptimize

(Robbins, 1974; Brown, 1983). These causes are reflected in the problems and crises continuing education leaders face on a daily basis—problems associated with personnel assignments, organizational structure, the allocation of resources, program development, and relationships with the environment.

A Win-Win Approach

It is the thesis of this chapter that management of conflicts in continuing education should focus on win-win problem solving. Such an approach is both rational and productive. As Schellenberg (1982) notes, people in conflict who search for a solution that is acceptable to all parties are seeking to develop a rational approach to resolving their conflict. This position is similar to the thinking of Rawls (1971) on the question of justice. According to Schellenberg, justice is usually not the only variable involved in attaining a mutually satisfying resolution to a conflict. True, win-lose strategies based on adversarial strategies are common, but there are also many other ways to manage conflict. For example, in most continuing education endeavors there are a sufficient number of rewards available for the persons involved; hence, a distributive or win-lose approach is unnecessary and even dysfunctional in most cases.

What is needed is an ability to conceptualize problems in such a way that win-win (integrative) rather than win-lose (distributive) solutions and strategies are appropriate (Walton and McKersie, 1965; Folberg and Taylor, 1984; Jandt and Gillette, 1985). The use of creativity in generating alternatives, selecting strategies, and involving people is needed if win-win outcomes are to be achieved. However, moving from traditional win-lose models of conflict resolution to win-win models also requires a high degree of sensitivity to the needs of the parties involved. Both organizational expectations and individual needs must be satisfied.

The ability to redefine conflict situations and to see the potential for use of win-win strategies is critical. This ability helps to differentiate between genuine win-lose conflicts and those that can be transformed into win-win problem solving. Filley (1975) notes that if conflicting parties can view their resources as being abundant rather than scarce, then it is often possible to deescalate the conflict so that it becomes a simple issue of engaging in mutual problem solving. Further support for the win-win approach is offered by McCarthy (1980), who emphasizes the use of nonadversarial procedures in the decision-making process. If this is to happen, however, it is often necessary to change fundamental organizational processes. For example, management structures will have to be altered to accommodate more collaborative and consensual approaches.

Several problems face the continuing education leader in working toward use of win-win strategies, including:

1. Outmoded organizational structures that govern the relationship of the continuing education unit to the parent organization.
2. Inadequate funding formulas and procedures that limit the resources available to the continuing education unit.
3. Inflexible values that govern the kinds of programs and services available.
4. Established ways of reviewing daily problems that inhibit the development of creative or alternative solutions.
5. Restrictive organizational procedures that govern the internal allocation of resources and the assignment of personnel.
6. Limited expectations that screen out programs for clients not previously served.

Strategy Selection

When these kinds of problems are confronted, the selection and use of a strategy should be a function of the situation. Whether an individual uses power, negotiates, or collaborates with others will depend on the similarity of their goals, the procedures they use, and the nature of their power relationships (Derr, 1972). Although collaboration is the most desirable of the three strategies, the conditions for genuine collaboration are the most exacting.

The goals and procedures of the parties involved must be similar, and any power differences need to be neutralized.

In addition to focusing on mutual goals, a win-win or collaborative approach also focuses on fact finding, expressing needs, accepting constructive disagreements as helpful, and solving problems (Filley, 1975; Jandt and Gillette, 1985). Critical to the win-win approach is the need to find solutions to people's problems rather than locating blame. This is a first step in becoming win-win oriented. A second step is selecting strategies that will create a climate conducive to the use of win-win strategies. Important strategies for building this climate include developing trust among members of the work group. This can be done by promoting effective communication and involving colleagues in decision making. Such activities encourage the development of mutual respect and build a sense of commitment and accountability. Win-win strategies are most acceptable in such a cooperative climate.

A third step is the selection of strategies to ensure the development of human resources. The implicit assumption here is that continuing education leaders, by helping their staff learn from their involvement in conflict, will make those staff more capable of handling routine disputes in the future. The modeling behavior of the continuing education leader in the use of human, conceptual, and technical skills is a critical element in this process. Such modeling provides evidence of the leader's awareness of the issues involved and his or her skill in addressing these issues. Successful management will encourage employees to work toward solutions acceptable to the major parties in conflict. As staff members demonstrate their problem-solving ability, this can, in turn, offset the need or desire to use win-lose strategies.

A fourth step involves the selection of strategies that will facilitate needed changes. Since conflict represents dissatisfaction with existing conditions or relationships, effective win-win strategies must address dissatisfactions and suggest acceptable and workable solutions to them. Such solutions will take into account the needs of individuals, their competencies, and the resources available. The solutions also will consider the future needs of the organization and its environment. This approach should increase the probability of success in implementing alternative changes.

More specifically, a collaborative or win-win approach to managing the conflicts often encountered in strategic planning might include the following:

For the Problem of the Outmoded Interorganizational Governance Structure

1. Establish a joint task force representing all interests to develop a set of goals and objectives consistent with the continuing education unit's mission.
2. Schedule a two- or three-day retreat for leaders from the parent institution and leaders from the continuing education unit to discuss the problems associated with the present organizational structure.
3. Use techniques, such as Delphi or nominal group process, to identify and prioritize the structural needs of the continuing education unit.
4. Create an advisory board for the continuing education unit that will recommend structural changes consistent with the needs of the continuing education unit and the parent organization.

For the Problem of an Inadequate Funding Formula

1. Conduct a financial assessment of the expenses of the continuing education unit and the income it earns in relation to support available to similar units on other campuses.
2. Develop a profile of the contribution of continuing education as a means of justifying requests for greater support.
3. Analyze the present funding formula to show inequities and how they adversely affect the continuing education unit's ability to deliver expected services.
4. Conduct a campaign to make the appropriate policy makers aware of the continuing education unit's programs and financial needs.

For the Problem of Inflexible Values

1. Meet with people with inflexible values to determine their interests and the level of support they are willing to provide to programs attuned to their values.
2. Provide programs that do not challenge or threaten the values in question until such time as a positive relationship has been established and support for more innovative programs has been gained.
3. Recognize that inflexible values may be a result of great insecurity. When this is the case, careful consideration should be given to the use of power strategies in the negotiation process. Power strategies are often based on win-lose strategies, and these do not contribute toward providing an environment that encourages the examination of inflexible values.

For the Problem of Overcoming Established Ways of Handling Daily Problems

1. Modify the membership of those groups that are charged with developing solutions to crises or daily problems.
2. Identify the inadequacies of established ways of solving problems and request that a task force develop better ways of proceeding.
3. Hold a retreat session to discuss current ways of handling problems and to generate alternative ways to proceed with exploration and study.
4. Use techniques such as Delphi to generate better procedures for handling problems.

For the Problem of Restrictive Procedures for Allocating Internal Resources

1. Review the goals and objectives of the continuing education unit to determine the relationship between such goals and the allocation of resources.
2. Review the existing policies, rules, and procedures that govern the allocation of resources in relation to the continuing education unit's goals.

3. Assess the continuing education unit's personnel to determine which of their priorities and objectives serve to maintain existing practices.
4. Form a task force to reallocate the available resources consistent with identified needs.

For the Problem of Limited Expectations

1. Arrange for staff development programs to acquaint personnel with emerging trends and practices in continuing education units at other institutions.
2. Conduct an assessment of potential clientele for new or revised program needs and share the results with continuing education personnel.
3. Provide funds for establishing innovative programs that address needs not now filled by current programs.
4. Hold regular brainstorming sessions to discuss the functioning of the continuing education unit.

Role of Negotiation in Conflict Management

In the absence of similar goals and an equal distribution of power, negotiation is a realistic conflict management strategy. One form of negotiation is that provided for in the Wagner Labor Relations Act, as well as by the policies and procedures of the United States Mediation Service. This kind of negotiation represents a formal approach to the settlement of disputes. However, it is usually employed to address economic concerns and systemwide working conditions as specified in labor-management contracts.

The type of negotiation referred to here, however, relates to the process of negotiation between individuals and between individuals and the organization. These conflicts often involve the continuing education leader either as a participant, as a leader in the organization, or as a third party. As a participant, the leader's role is straightforward. She will act in the same way as any other person who is experiencing a conflict; that is, she will place her self-interest first. The strategies that she selects, whether they be win-win or win-lose, will serve to promote that self-interest.

However, when acting as a representative of the organization, the leader's behavior may be circumscribed. She will probably be limited by a set of expectations as to how she "ought" to function. Violation of these expectations can have consequences for the organization and, subsequently, for the leader herself.

The leader may also be constrained by the nature of the conflict. If the conflict is over organizational issues, then the leader may be placed in the role of a mediator or arbitrator between the organization and its adversary. In such cases the leader is expected to be impartial or neutral and help resolve the conflict. If, however, the complaint is against the leader herself, it becomes difficult for her to remain neutral, wear the hat of mediator/ arbitrator, and also represent her own self-interest.

When the leader functions as a third party, she will be called upon to adjudicate conflicts between employees holding peer positions or superior-subordinate positions and between employees and the organization. Determining whether the leader is a mediator, arbitrator, administrator, or participant may some-times be a problem. In such cases astuteness and perceptivity are required. Rubin (1981) points out that one of the critical things a third party can do is to help conflicting parties communicate effectively with each other. The third party can act as a go-between who clarifies issues, positions, and choices using language that is acceptable to all the conflicting parties. Upholding the norms, rules, and regulations of the organization, while simultaneously playing the role of problem solver, requires considerable skill and practice.

As a third party, the continuing education leader should take on the mantle of an impartial person and weigh the various points of view. Especially in handling disputes among staff members, it is desirable for the continuing education leader to remain impartial and thus increase the chances of producing a win-win solution. Where the issue is one of adherence to the norms or rules and regulations of the organization, the role of the leader can more easily be that of an arbitrator.

Where agreement has been reached about the procedures to be followed in resolving disputes, this agreement becomes the basis for making decisions that will govern future relationships. In such situations parties are encouraged to state their expectations and priorities. As these emerge and come to be understood, procedural agreements can move the conflict toward accommodation and cooperation (Bercovitch, 1984), if not harmonious agreement. While absence of agreement provides the basis for continued conflict (Pondy, 1967), conflict management has as one of its goals the full utilization of available resources (Bercovitch, 1984). As such, accommodation and cooperation within the workplace are acceptable intermediate goals. Such situations do require, however, that leaders possess the skills needed to manage the periodic conflicts that will emerge.

In most situations, we should avoid using power to solve conflicts. By power we mean the ability to control behavior or to determine the actions of another person through the authority of position or status accorded by relevant others (Dahl, 1957). Further, a power differential exists when the ability of one party to coerce or influence is superior to that of the other party. In the absence of a clear power differential, the use of power may not succeed. Even if it does succeed, it often brings about resentment and a lack of cooperation (Jandt and Gillette, 1985). Power, especially in the form of force, tends to lose its effectiveness (Derr, 1972; Schellenberg, 1982). However, the use of authority and the power associated with it can be justified in cases of crises, extreme emergencies, or the inability of participating decision makers to make up their minds. The failure of a leader to plan or consider needed changes at earlier opportunities, however, should not be used to justify the use of power to achieve win-lose decisions. Such action may, in reality, represent incompetent leadership.

At the heart of the use of power are the question of legitimacy, the urgency of the situation, and the choice of solution. Thus the perception that power has been used legitimately in situations requiring immediate action and for the purpose of implementing a solution acceptable to the parties involved can lead to a win-win outcome. But the absence of one or more of these favorable conditions can lead to a win-lose outcome.

Examples of unwarranted use of power include the following:

1. Withholding information needed by a decision-making group and then rejecting its proposed solutions to the conflict by claiming that all critical variables were not considered.
2. Failure to consult with others in making decisions that affect them and over which they have jurisdiction.
3. Delaying the discussion of critical problems or issues until time does not allow for participation by or input from others.
4. Involving others in making decisions and then choosing a unilateral course of action contrary to the group's recommendations.
5. Transferring personnel or making personnel assignments without regard to employees' personal or professional abilities or interests.

Skills for Managing Conflicts

Managing conflict is not always easy or pleasant. However, it can become more satisfying if done in such a way that it contributes to the continuing education leader's effectiveness. One way of assuring this result is to acquire or improve the skills related to managing conflict.

Listening is one of those skills. Listening to both what is said and what is not said reveals the full message of the speaker. Observing verbal and nonverbal communications helps the listener interpret the message (Folberg and Taylor, 1984). Similarly, attending to the feeling as well as to the content that has been communicated is important. It is often the feeling that conveys the seriousness of the message and suggests the appropriate interpretation of that which is being communicated. Understanding and accepting the communication will make possible the development of an acceptable win-win solution. While listening and understanding do not guarantee a win-win solution, the absence of understanding almost certainly precludes it.

Listening is among the most helpful skills for managing interpersonal conflicts. It is also one of the least expensive skills to acquire and utilize. It does, however, require patience and energy on the part of the listener to become informed about the issues being discussed and the feelings being expressed. Careful listening communicates to the other person in the conflict that his or her ideas and feelings are being heard.

How well we listen is reflected in the questions we ask. Questions that encourage the speaker to explain further, to clarify points, or to clear up misunderstandings held by the listener are generally perceived as helpful (Folberg and Taylor, 1984). Questions that make the speaker defensive, attempt to demonstrate the listener's superior knowledge, or confront the speaker prematurely will more frequently hinder a mutual exploration of the problem. Statements such as, "I did not understand your last statement," will be more acceptable than, "You did not state your last point clearly," or, "Your last statement made no sense." Questions that request further information are more conducive to problem solving than statements that are judgmental or express strong opinions.

Another aspect of effective listening as a tool for managing conflict is the ability to paraphrase the previous speaker's comments to ensure understanding. This allows for immediate clarification of misunderstandings and establishes a basis for future effective communication. Finally, listening is the cornerstone of most effective conflict management strategies.

A second important skill for managing conflict is that of providing feedback. Positive feedback can strengthen relationships and generate trust between conflicting parties. It can reinforce cooperative behavior and establish the basis for continuing interaction. While positive feedback is desired by most people, it is frequently difficult to give and sometimes even more difficult to receive, especially if the party giving the positive feedback lacks credibility with the listener. Positive feedback tends to reinforce the self-concept people have of themselves. Perhaps because of this, giving positive feedback often provides a basis for a reciprocal relationship. This in turn makes it easier to achieve win-win conflict management outcomes.

Positive feedback is most effective when it is specific, timely, and given with a genuine feeling of respect. For example, to be told, "Your presentation was most interesting," is less effective than, "Your ideas on poverty really addressed the economic plight of older Americans living on limited incomes in the United States.

Your comments showed insight and concern. I wish you success in your work."

Giving and receiving negative feedback are also important in managing conflict. If done well, negative feedback helps to correct behaviors that may lead to conflict. If no change results, however, the feedback has served no useful purpose. Thus, questions about who is in charge of the desired change, the legitimacy of the change request, the process to be followed, and whether the behavioral change is possible all become critical.

Attempting to change another person's behavior within a win-win context also requires an understanding of the person, especially of his or her ability to change. It is generally conceded that there needs to be a trust relationship between the person providing the negative feedback and the recipient. Further, the proposed change must address something that can be changed. Also, the change should be seen by the recipient of the feedback as beneficial. This helps the person to feel in control of the change process.

It is difficult to give negative feedback because it has the potential for disrupting relationships. It also suggests superior insight and the assumption of responsibility for correcting the other person's behavior. Receiving negative feedback requires the recipient to make a decision. Accepting such feedback means that a change in behavior is in order. This, for most people, is not easy. If the feedback is rejected, however, it may interfere with the relationship of the parties.

As continuing education leaders strive to bring about program improvements and use their personnel most effectively, changes need to be made in the status quo as an integral part of strategic planning. This will inevitably lead to requesting changes in roles and assignments and, with those changes, modifications in patterns of behavior. It is here that the continuing education leader will find the ability to give positive and negative feedback helpful. While much feedback is provided on a one-to-one basis, giving such feedback in group settings can also be helpful. Where the purposes are clear and support for the employees undergoing change is evident, employees can be encouraged to discuss their needs to adjust and change patterns of work and behavior.

Knowing that everyone has to make some adjustments can alleviate some of the tension and pain associated with change.

Another important skill for managing conflict is the ability to conceptualize conflict. This involves putting the conflict in perspective. Such a perspective can include recognizing human needs, organizational expectations, emotional overtones, common areas of agreement, and areas in which compromise is likely or unlikely. Understanding the conflict helps determine the resources needed to manage it, select the strategies that are most likely to produce a win-win outcome, and determine the time required to deal with the conflict. Although no conflict is totally predictable, the intelligent use of conflict management skills over a period of time will usually result in a satisfactory outcome.

The ability to confront another person is also an effective conflict management skill. Effective confrontation does not have to be aggressive, abrasive, or sarcastic or consist of other inflexible behaviors. It does require the ability to understand the issues and a desire to determine the factual base for the conflict. It proceeds from an assumption that clarification of the issues through focused inquiry is a desirable approach for resolving conflict. Discrepancies become known, positions are clarified, and a new basis for maintaining relationships is usually established.

Confronting another person is not easy, especially if one is unsure of his or her own ability or needs. It is also difficult if the power distribution between the parties in conflict is unequal. Confronting someone to determine facts, as opposed to expressing opinions or making judgments, can be very helpful. Confronting provides a basis for exploring differences and or establishing mutually satisfactory procedures. The ability to make clarifying statements, to ask concise and clear questions, and to share observations of behavior is critical to effective confrontation. Further, the ability to differentiate between relevant pieces of information and inconsequential details helps in the confrontation process.

Whether the confronting is done privately or in a group setting, care must be exercised to see that the desired goal—understanding—is preeminent in the thinking of the parties involved. Confrontations that result in anger, hostility, or seriously bruised self-concepts should be avoided if at all possible. Preparations for confronting should include helping the participants understand the purpose of the meeting and the time constraints involved. If the conflict has existed for some time and has a moderate to high degree of intensity, several meetings should be planned. This will provide opportunity for the participants to review and digest the emerging information.

The participants may want an opportunity to share their doubts and insecurities with a third party prior to confronting these issues openly in a larger meeting. This can have the effect of making the participants more comfortable in expressing their feelings and needs. It is important for the participants to have an opportunity to clear away the doubts and misperceptions they have about the other party. When this is done, a climate is created that encourages appropriate strategies for future relations.

Continuing education leaders have, by virtue of their position, many opportunities to serve as third-party managers of meetings in which confrontations occur. While such experiences may be distasteful in the first instance, they can become opportunities to help staff develop their ability to manage conflict. Such experiences can help the organization improve its effectiveness.

The ability to remain flexible and resourceful in all situations is a mark of an effective conflict manager. Flexibility helps parties in conflict explore alternative behaviors and solutions to issues. This, in turn, makes possible joint problem solving and avoids premature win-lose posturing. It also enhances the negotiation process and helps the parties develop confidence that they can solve their differences.

Resourcefulness is another skill that is helpful in generating alternative strategies and solutions. Rarely is there just one way of resolving a conflict. As a result, the task for continuing education leaders is to work toward solving problems rather than locating blame or using other win-lose strategies. Leaders will be most effective if they accept the arguments of other people with whom they are in conflict and try to see the issue from the other person's point of view. This ability will help transform conflicts into productive win-win situations. Accepting the argument of the other party does not mean agreeing with him or her. It does mean being able to understand the conflict from the other person's point of view and to maintain working relationships with him or her in spite of the conflict. The following conflict management skill form will assist the continuing education leader in assessing his or her skills for managing conflict.

Exhibit 1. Conflict Management Skill Evaluation Form.

Respond to the following statements as candidly and accurately as you can. In each instance indicate (a) the extent to which you possess this skill and (b) the extent to which you use this skill when you are involved in a conflict. (Use "a" for possession; "b" for use)

1. Ability to listen to points of view other than your own.

   1   2   3   4   5   6   7   8   9   10   11   12   13   14

   High Ability   Low Ability

2. Ability to accept the ideas and feelings of others who have different views.

   1   2   3   4   5   6   7   8   9   10   11   12   13   14

   High Ability   Low Ability

3. Ability to confront and disagree with other people and their ideas.

   1   2   3   4   5   6   7   8   9   10   11   12   13   14

   High Ability   Low Ability

4. Ability to work with ideas and people with whom you disagree.

   1   2   3   4   5   6   7   8   9   10   11   12   13   14

   High Ability   Low Ability

5. Ability to see the broader context in which most conflict takes place.

   1   2   3   4   5   6   7   8   9   10   11   12   13   14

   High Ability   Low Ability

6. Ability to analyze issues and situations as to their potential for creating conflict.

   1   2   3   4   5   6   7   8   9   10   11   12   13   14

   High Ability   Low Ability

Exhibit 1. Conflict Management Skill Evaluation Form, Cont'd.

7. Ability to express emotion and to accept the expression of emotion by others in conflict situations.

1	2	3	4	5	6	7	8	9	10	11	12	13	14

    High Ability   Low Ability

8. Ability to respond creatively to conflict—such as developing new ways of thinking, behaving, reacting, and so on.

1	2	3	4	5	6	7	8	9	10	11	12	13	14

    High Ability   Low Ability

9. Ability to implement effective conflict management strategies.

1	2	3	4	5	6	7	8	9	10	11	12	13	14

    High Ability   Low Ability

10. Ability to develop a trusting relationship with a person with whom you are in conflict.

1	2	3	4	5	6	7	8	9	10	11	12	13	14

    High Ability   Low Ability

11. Ability to retain a sense of objectivity when you are involved in a conflict.

1	2	3	4	5	6	7	8	9	10	11	12	13	14

    High Ability   Low Ability

12. Ability to take a risk when involved in conflict.

1	2	3	4	5	6	7	8	9	10	11	12	13	14

    High Ability   Low Ability

13. Ability to be or remain authentic during your involvement in conflict.

1	2	3	4	5	6	7	8	9	10	11	12	13	14

    High Ability   Low Ability

14. Ability to disclose your own weaknesses when involved in a conflict.

1	2	3	4	5	6	7	8	9	10	11	12	13	14

    High Ability   Low Ability

Exhibit 1. Conflict Management Skill Evaluation Form, Cont'd.

---

15. Ability to acknowledge the strengths of those with whom you are in conflict.

1	2	3	4	5	6	7	8	9	10	11	12	13	14

High Ability   Low Ability

16. Ability to express negative feelings directly to those with whom you are in conflict.

1	2	3	4	5	6	7	8	9	10	11	12	13	14

High Ability   Low Ability

17. Ability to express positive feelings directly to those with whom you are in conflict.

1	2	3	4	5	6	7	8	9	10	11	12	13	14

High Ability   Low Ability

18. Ability to function effectively as a third-party mediator when you are not involved in the conflict.

1	2	3	4	5	6	7	8	9	10	11	12	13	14

High Ability   Low Ability

19. Ability to negotiate a conflict when you have the responsibility for seeing that a satisfactory agreement emerges.

1	2	3	4	5	6	7	8	9	10	11	12	13	14

High Ability   Low Ability

20. Ability to empathize with a person involved in a conflict.

1	2	3	4	5	6	7	8	9	10	11	12	13	14

High Ability   Low Ability

21. Ability to make a decision when involved in a conflict and to stand by that decision.

1	2	3	4	5	6	7	8	9	10	11	12	13	14

High Ability   Low Ability

22. Ability to cope successfully with personal conflicts for which there is no easy solution.

1	2	3	4	5	6	7	8	9	10	11	12	13	14

High Ability   Low Ability

Exhibit 1. Conflict Management Skill Evaluation Form, Cont'd.

23. Ability to maintain a sense of perspective concerning who is involved in the conflict.

1	2	3	4	5	6	7	8	9	10	11	12	13	14

    High Ability   Low Ability

24. Ability to accept being confronted as a way of dealing with conflict.

1	2	3	4	5	6	7	8	9	10	11	12	13	14

    High Ability   Low Ability

25. Ability to accept conflict and change as natural phenomena in the lives of people.

1	2	3	4	5	6	7	8	9	10	11	12	13	14

    High Ability   Low Ability

26. Ability to improve your conflict management skills as a result of participating in conflict.

1	2	3	4	5	6	7	8	9	10	11	12	13	14

    High Ability   Low Ability

27. Ability to objectively discuss your conflicts with other people.

1	2	3	4	5	6	7	8	9	10	11	12	13	14

    High Ability   Low Ability

28. Ability to function effectively in win-lose types of controversy.

1	2	3	4	5	6	7	8	9	10	11	12	13	14

    High Ability   Low Ability

29. Ability to function effectively in win-win types of controversy.

1	2	3	4	5	6	7	8	9	10	11	12	13	14

    High Ability   Low Ability

30. Ability to function effectively in lose-lose types of conflict.

1	2	3	4	5	6	7	8	9	10	11	12	13	14

    High Ability   Low Ability

Managing Organizational Conflicts

In addition to using effective conflict management skills, the continuing education leader needs, as an integral part of strategic planning, to establish procedures for managing organizational conflicts. Some types of conflicts can seriously hinder the effectiveness of an organization. The following procedures may help in managing these conflicts:

1. Establish grievance procedures for handling staff complaints.
2. Establish joint task forces to study issues and problems that involve more than one division of the continuing education unit.
3. Use data-gathering procedures and instruments such as Delphi, nominal group process, and survey questionnaires to identify problems and concerns.
4. Use third parties such as ombudsmen, mediators, and arbitrators to investigate complaints and to recommend solutions.
5. Use staff retreat sessions to discuss continuing education problems and issues as a means of reducing unnecessary conflict.
6. Use staff development sessions to upgrade and improve staff capability for managing new programs and coping with organizational requirements.
7. Create a coordinating council broadly representative of the continuing education unit's divisions that meets on a regular basis to discuss the implementation of programs and facilitate planning.
8. Maintain open lines of communication between the continuing education leader and staff through frequent contact, with the focus on job-related issues.
9. Reduce the ambiguity of work tasks by establishing clear lines of communication and areas of responsibility.

Summary

There is no panacea for managing interpersonal or organizational conflicts. However, attending to the needs of staff, to organizational requirements, and to environmental pressures through win-win approaches will go a long way toward alleviating unnecessary conflict. The refinement of one's conflict management skills and the establishment of organizational procedures for managing more complex problems and conflicts will prove to be very beneficial to the continuing education leader. Such an approach should be an integral part of strategic planning for effective leadership.

Linking Continuing Education to Community and Economic Development

GORDON H. MUELLER

The city is at risk. Its future is imperiled, not by competition or technological change, not by outside forces or dangers, but by the steady weakening and disintegration of its learning system at virtually every point—in the home, in the neighborhood, in the school and college, in church and temple, in the marketplace, and in government.

The problem manifests itself in many ways: in the city's persistent poverty; its staggering illiteracy; its high dropout rate; its low rate of academic achievement; the alarming number of teen-age pregnancies; the low level of entrepreneurship and business expansion; the high rate of crime and juvenile delinquency; its low per-capita spending on education, libraries, and museums; the poor management policies and practices of government; the city's disunity and increased racial tensions; and the decline of those old virtues—civility, respect for elders, self-reliance, and community pride.

The problem we face is so great and so grave that it cannot be met by schools alone, or by a mayor alone, or, for that matter, by all of government alone. The problem has been created by all of us; it can only be solved by all of us. The challenge must be met by a united city, mobilized at every level by a common concern and inspired by a common vision.

The common concern, which we all must address, is the crisis in learning that permeates and affects every aspect of our city's life. The common vision is that recommended to the nation by the National Commission on Excellence in Education. The challenge is to create a learning society. In a learning society, the value of learning imbues and informs all aspects of life—learning becomes ingrained in the culture. In a learning society, each institution contributes to this value by providing learning incentives and opportunities as well as by supporting the learning agendas of other institutions.

These ringing words were written for the mayoral platform of Sidney Barthelemy, a recent candidate for mayor of New Orleans. The author, Anthony Gagliano, is not a professional continuing educator but the project director of economic development for the Regional Planning Commission and former executive assistant to New Orleans Mayor Moon Landrieu.

The platform as adopted by Barthelemy's education committee is important as an illustration of the many opportunities for leadership and learning that can come to continuing educators from arenas external to the university. The platform is important as a reminder of the all-too-familiar litany of social, economic, and learning ills that currently threaten the fabric of our society and the way of life we have come to enjoy. The platform is also important in that it suggests we look for solutions "beyond the quick fix." Such solutions require linkages between all our institutions—solutions that can only emerge through adoption of a systems approach—a learning system. Finally, the platform is an example of how external partnerships placed a continuing education dean in a position to help shape the ideas and vision that framed Gagliano's powerful rhetoric for the aspiring mayor.

Leadership in the External Arena

From this starting point, it is my intention to address the challenge of continuing education leadership in the external arena. I will argue that the marginality of continuing education can only be overcome if, as academic leaders, we make it our highest priority to develop strategic plans that will allow continuing education to participate creatively and purposefully in the great transformation now underway in our universities and our society.

In developing the case for this type of strategic planning and leadership, I have been guided by several assumptions. First, I am convinced that a guiding vision must be present. I do not mean a charismatic vision but rather a vision that springs from knowledge and understanding. Second, I assume that this knowledge is acquired through efforts to gain a historical and theoretical appreciation of the changes that are presently transforming our society, our economy, and the learning enterprise. Emerging from this transformation is an improved way of thinking about the new interactions among society's institutions. Third, I assume that continuing education leaders require a conceptual framework to link academia with external institutions, especially with business and industry.

My own operational framework assumes that continuing educators can engage in three broad areas of external linkage: (1) joint research, (2) technology transfer and entrepreneurial assistance, and (3) human resource development (education and training). Within this framework of partnerships a wide variety of interactions occurs, from the most basic, short-term agreements to the highest level of partnerships that are long term in their benefits and are likely to imply significant adjustments in organizational structure, in policy, and in the very thinking of the partners (Johnson, 1984). My focus in this chapter will be on this higher level of partnership and on the theoretical and conceptual framework of a learning system that gives meaning to the vision of the continuing education leader.

Emphasis on Learning. It is important that those of us engaged in forging these new alliances speak of learning rather than of education. The latter word conjures up the image of separate institutions, each with the responsibility to deliver formal education in a traditional manner to a single group of students over a prescribed period in a fixed location. As we enter the new information age and become each day more of a learning society, it will be increasingly difficult to know "where the university ends and the corporate world begins and where they both fit with the large education and training system," which includes all our institutions (Gold, 1981, p. 9).

In addition, there are both psychological and symbolic reasons to make clear the distinction between learning and education. Learning is everybody's business. It is not something that occurs only in schools. Learning is a lifetime endeavor. Every individual is responsible for his or her learning agenda as well as for the learning needs of our society. The learning concept helps to dissolve institutional boundaries and leads logically to a systems consciousness—to the ultimate notion of a learning system. It is in this context that we can begin to appreciate the full meaning of the mayoral platform of Sidney Barthelemy cited at the beginning of this chapter. Without the framework of a learning system, without a broader focus on learning rather than on education, no mayor can find political benefit in or even have access to this issue. Barthelemy's call to action offers a unifying solution to social and economic crises in New Orleans—crises that far exceed the capacity of a single institution to solve. Finally, it was only through my research and investigations into the revolutionary changes transforming our economy, and the role of higher education in that process, that I was eventually able to bring this new vision to Anthony Gagliano and three years later to the platform of the aspiring mayor.

Hence, we see in this outcome a concrete example of how a continuing educator can exercise leadership in the direct application of knowledge to the solution of real-world problems in one of our nation's major cities. Put another way, the unifying vision of a learning system provides the framework for moving knowledge from the mind to the marketplace. It is around this vision that continuing education leaders can build the highest level of partnerships with institutions outside the academy. What more exciting or energizing development could happen than to see our communities make lifelong learning a matter of public policy? What better result could a continuing educator have than to succeed in making the development of a learning system the highest priority of politicians, business leaders, educators, and all institutions in a given city or region? What more practical or purposeful application of knowledge can we imagine for the new information age?

The Meaning of Vision. For the remainder of this century and into the next, continuing educators will have unlimited opportunities to become the architects of significant partnerships with a wide variety of people, businesses, government agencies, political leaders, health organizations, and civic, religious, and other nonprofit organizations. Indeed, many of these partnerships are already forming throughout the country. But without a strong conceptual framework, without a clear vision to cement the partnerships within a broader social purpose, without reminding all the partners of the differences between growth and development, without anchoring partnerships in the emerging paradigm of a learning system, the foundation of the partnerships will be weak, and the continuing educator will not be recognized as a master builder or a leader.

This conceptual approach in no way diminishes the very real need for continuing educators to pay careful attention to their adult students or to the institutions that sponsor and nourish continuing education activities. Other contributors to this volume have developed the leaders' important internal opportunities. Clearly, continuing education leaders need to serve adult learners in ways that relate closely to the fundamental mission of the university in order to ensure organizational support and to make lifelong learning a central responsibility of all units in the institution.

This is a solid starting point, and few would contest the educational or the political value of this approach. But such an approach by itself falls short of another leadership challenge. This approach consigns continuing educators to the role of brokering academic resources instead of shaping these resources into new and innovative configurations that can be applied to the changing needs of a new learning society.

Leaders are more than facilitators or effective administrators. Leaders make things happen! Leaders empower other people by enrolling them in visions that inspire them to undertake actions that seem to exceed their normal abilities and expectations of themselves. Brokers do not do that. Managers do not do that. Hence, continuing educators who concentrate only on *doing things right*—whether for adult learners or for the universities they serve—may be rewarded with financial support, with respect, and with the real gratitude of both constituencies. But these continuing educators will have lost the chance to make a more enduring leadership contribution to their institutions and to the communities they serve.

It is my firm conviction that leaders in continuing higher education must concentrate on *doing the right things* rather than doing things right (Bennis, 1984). We must be innovative in relation to the larger learning issues that confront our changing society and that require the transformation of our universities. We must not be satisfied with mission statements that were developed in response to different state and national priorities, different constituencies, and different learning agendas from those that confront us now.

Bennis finds that people are drawn to leaders because they have "a vision, a dream, a set of intentions, an agenda, a frame of reference." In these individuals, he says, we discover "an extraordinary focus of commitment . . . , a compelling vision that can bring people to a place they have not been before through any variety of means. . . . Leaders make their dreams apparent and enroll others in making them happen" (p. 148).

Continuing educators have a great opportunity for true leadership if they aspire to affect the culture of their institutions as well as of their surrounding communities. Bennis tells us that leaders are those "who are the social architects of their organizations and who create and maintain values" (p. 146). Continuing education leaders must rise to this challenge within their own agencies, their universities, and throughout the learning system beyond the academy. To appreciate the magnitude of this challenge and the attraction of this vision, continuing educators must first acquaint themselves with the forces of historical change that lead to new partnerships and interactions between our institutions, to new theories, and to the new type of systems thinking.

The Great Transformation

Derek Bok, president of Harvard and author of *Beyond the Ivory Tower,* has pointed the way for continuing educators to exercise leadership in the external arena. "The cloistered university," says Bok, "could probably only exist at a heavy cost to the quality of professional education, applied research, social criticism, and expert advice" (1982, p. 73). Bok's words provide both the challenge and the chance for continuing educators to forge new partnerships between universities and communities—partnerships that can unify the major institutions of our society in a system of learning.

The paradox, says Lynton in his hallmark study, *The Missing Connection Between Business and the Universities,* is that "the most vital function of the academy requires both involvement and detachment. It can no longer remain aloof, yet it cannot lose its identity and become merely another piece in the societal mosaic. Striking the balance between isolation and assimilation is the great leadership challenge to be faced if higher education is to survive as a force in postindustrial society" (1984, p. 154).

Transformation of the Nation. These growing challenges to higher education have a common refrain: we must become more actively involved in the application of our learning resources to the solution of our nation's social and economic problems. The stimulus is the growing recognition that we are in the throes of a profound economic transformation. The basic outlines of this revolutionary change are now generally accepted by experts from many different disciplines (Bell, 1973, 1979; Botkin, Dimancescu, and State, 1982; Naisbitt, 1982; Toffler, 1980; Bluestone and Harrison, 1982).

Today we stand awkwardly stretched with one foot still in the industrial machine age and the other foot already planted in the new information systems age. It is likely that the strain of our stance will continue to worsen until we complete the transition and step completely into the new age.

Among other things, we are witnessing a dramatic shift in the nature of work. Since 1900 our work force has made a long journey from farms to factories and finally to offices. Many of our economic difficulties in the last decade can be traced to this shift that is shaking the confidence of our educational and industrial communities—both of which are beginning to recognize that insulation from each other has contributed to the current malaise.

On the economic side, we have experienced in the last twenty years a precipitous decline in our productivity, our standard of living, and our share of manufacturing exports. At the same time, our national budget deficit has soared, innovation has lagged, and we have lost our competitive advantage to foreign countries. These developments have been further exacerbated by the deliberate diversion of capital from productive investments to unproductive investment in mergers. Additional capital has been exported abroad on the wings of new technology and communications as a way of avoiding the high cost of American labor. With the resultant closing of many factories and basic industries, we were left with over seven million unemployed workers in 1985. Many millions of these jobs are gone forever, and we now face an alarmingly high level of structural unemployment.

According to one measurement, the new age officially began in 1955 when the number of white-collar workers in service and information jobs exceeded that of blue-collar workers in manufacturing jobs (Porat, 1977). Over 90 percent of the new jobs since 1970 have been generated in the service economy. This entire process of decline and transformation is brilliantly described by Bluestone and Harrison in *The Deindustrialization of America* (1982). By the early eighties there was a growing consensus that we were shifting from a physical-resource-based economy to a knowledge-intensive, human-resource-based economy—a fundamental shift from products to services that required a new strategy (Botkin, Dimancescu, and State, 1982).

External Challenges to the Academy. In the midst of this crisis it is not surprising that American business and industry began to "recognize in higher education a strategic source for research, innovation, and trained workers" (Matthews and Norgaard, 1984, p. 2). These breakdowns in our national economy and the resultant difficulties in our major industries led directly to the first big push to forge new partnerships between business and higher education.

Unfortunately, aside from the successful partnerships that formed in the seventies in Silicon Valley, around Route 128 in Boston, in the Research Triangle in North Carolina, and in Austin, Texas, most universities were slow to respond. The crisis on the bottom line had not yet penetrated to the academy. In 1974, American higher education was coming to the end of twenty years of unparalleled prosperity.

For the most part, the academy ignored the early warning signals that were already in evidence in the world outside the university. Lynton argues that higher education failed to examine the basic assumptions and modes of university growth for two principal reasons. First, it seemed that vast increases in support for basic and applied research would never end, especially in the sciences, engineering, and health areas. Grants became a major measure of institutional quality. Second, says Lynton, the academy thought of itself as its own principal labor market to meet the needs of an expanding university research and development complex. Consequently, undergraduate and graduate education came to be viewed as a preparation for academic and quasi-academic careers. In the words of Lynton, "The discipline became dominant" (1984, pp. 65-66). And although the great transformation taking place in our economy and society was being carefully documented by distinguished scholars and researchers across the country, the academy generally ignored the implications for higher education and continued its "head in the sand" posture into the late seventies.

As we entered the 1980s, however, economic and demographic changes and new governmental policies precipitated a series of crises that struck higher education with a vengeance. There are now many fine studies describing the impact of these events and the response—or lack of it—from American universities. The funding crisis in higher education became more acute as corporations, the federal government, and philanthropic foundations began to shift their priorities. To make matters worse, the extraordinary postwar baby boom came abruptly to an end in 1978 when freshman classes peaked and then began to decline, with a 25 percent drop projected for the years from 1979 to 1994 (Crossland, 1980). While a burgeoning market of older students took up some of the slack, most of these students were part time, with intermittent learning patterns.

Nevertheless, these adults were at least precious enough to universities to bring about innovation in marketing and delivery systems. Continuing education units, off-campus programs, extension divisions, evening and weekend classes, contract education, credit for life experience, and a variety of similar strategies were implemented to lure these adults back to school.

In the words of Clark Kerr, elder statesman and distinguished commentator on higher education, "the road to survival now leads through the marketplace. A new academic revolution is upon us" (Carnegie Council on Policy Studies in Higher Education, 1980, p. 30). Financial pressure, more than anything else, compelled universities to look outside to new constituencies and to look inside to continuing education units and even traditional academic disciplines to find the leaders who could develop these new markets and partnerships. The struggle for "bucks and bodies" began to guide policies, decisions, and, to a modest extent, even some curricula change. Finances came to dominate campus management in ways that would not have been imaginable in the fifties or sixties.

Universities Under Siege. As powerful as the funding crisis was and remains today, it is only one of the external threats forcing educators to look beyond the ivory tower in the eighties. Universities face increased external controls and a rising public demand for accountability (Keller, 1983). Kerr wrote in 1979 that "full autonomy—to the extent it ever existed—is dead. . . . The greatest change in governance now going on is not the rise of student power or faculty power but the rise of public power. The governance of higher education is less and less by higher education. . . . The 'ivory tower' of yore is now becoming a public utility" (1979, p. 19).

A year later, President Harold Enarson of Ohio State University made the same argument in *Change* magazine: "The universities today are under siege. I do not exaggerate. The cumulative weight of federal and state encroachments is crippling the university, sapping morale, and destroying the very quality and accountability they were devised to foster" (1980, p. 9).

Compounding these external threats are internal breakdowns in governance and leadership within the academy itself. Keller's brilliant analysis of the management revolution in American higher education describes the erosion of leadership at both the faculty and upper-administration levels. Few would argue with his observation that there has been a withering away of faculty senates to the point that they have been reduced to ineffective debating societies, seldom concerned with matters of educational policy (Keller, 1983; Kerr, 1982). The focus of faculty members, more often than not, has been on "specialized activities rather than on departmental problems and problems of university-wide significance" (Gross, 1963, p. 71).

Keller is even more scathing in his indictment of the upper echelons of academic administration, where he finds little evidence of "courage, purpose, or leadership" among college and university presidents. Instead, we find "mediators, fund raisers, and genial survivors" (1983, pp. 37-38). What is needed in the new era, says another analyst, is a more "active and instructive" leadership style (Behn, 1980, p. 618). The handwriting is on the wall, says Keller: "Retrenchment, constricting finances, new competition, marketing, and rapid changes in the academic and demographic areas all spell the end of the traditional unobtrusive style of organizational leadership on campuses" (1983, p. 39).

Pressure for Change in the Academy. Meanwhile, as the academy floundered in its newly discovered crises, American business and industry had been working hard to find solutions to their immediate learning problems. Prompted by ongoing financial crises and economic transformation, corporations developed a formidable learning enterprise outside of higher education. As the nation shifted toward a service economy, corporate America launched an unprecedented investment in human resource development that has been pegged by the most recent study in 1986 at an annual figure of $210 billion—more than twice the amount spent each year by all our 3,100 colleges and universities (Carnevale, 1986).

It is astonishing to think how quickly this new adult learning enterprise emerged and how large it became before higher education finally began to pay some attention to it in the early eighties. Not surprisingly, the rapid growth of corporate education paralleled the emergence of the new industries and technologies of the information age. This coincided with a national perception that our educational institutions, elementary and secondary schools as well as higher education, were unable to meet their responsibilities to produce a labor force that "enters employment with real competence and maintains effectiveness through lifelong education" (Lynton, 1984, p. 68). The external challenge to our educational institutions was becoming clear: the nation's colleges, universities, and schools needed to come out of their isolation and assist with the national transformation of our economy.

According to the excellent work by Matthews and Norgaard, *Managing the Partnership Between Higher Education and Industry*, there is now evidence that higher education is "beginning to pull itself out of its own depression, look to the future, and freshly evaluate its mission. . . . Ever since the birth of the great European universities in the Middle Ages, the mission of education has been quite separate from that of business, commerce, and industry. Surprisingly, the industrial revolution did little to change the essential nature of our educational system. The current technological revolution demands that higher education institutions recognize that training and research have broad economic implications" (1984, p. 62).

While advocating the critical need to break down the barriers between universities and business, Lynton is less sanguine about the academy's capacity to reform itself in ways that will accelerate the process. The "center of the university," says Lynton, "continues to be driven by internal values and priorities that have changed little or not at all" since the 1930s (1984, p. 64). Despite the enormous external pressures for change, despite a recent rash of mostly short-term business-university partnerships, and despite the dramatic growth of adult and continuing education programs, there is little evidence that higher education is examining the need for internal restructuring or curricular reform in order to reshape its product to meet the new national priorities. According to both

Kerr (1982) and Lynton, the traditional research university has changed very little "despite the fact that education has evolved from being for the few and the young to being for the many of all ages" (Lynton, 1984, p. 64). Our universities must face up to a very clear and important choice, Lynton says. Are our higher education institutions going to be "defined by *what* they teach, regardless of the nature of the student body, or are they to be characterized by *whom* they teach?" (1984, p. 73).

University presidents and leaders in continuing education who wish to bring their institutions out of isolation and into productive partnerships with outside organizations must understand that we are dealing in one commodity—learning—and that we are delivering it to many different audiences in many different ways. Another important piece of the challenge to end institutional isolation is to recast our thinking in terms of systems and then to consider all the opportunities for external leadership and partnerships that are possible within an integrated learning system.

Understanding the Learning System

Most of us would accept the common description of the age we are leaving as the machine age or the age of the industrial revolution. And while there is not yet unanimity on the essential characteristics of the new age, there is widespread agreement that something fundamental is happening, that a new paradigm or world view is coming into focus. Every age emerges slowly in bits and pieces out of the previous period until a new view of nature is generally accepted by the scientific community. There are now a growing number of scientists and philosophers who agree that the most satisfying view of the postindustrial world is that of a systems age (Ackoff, 1981; Singer, 1959; Rosenblueth and Wiener, 1950; Niebuhr, 1984).

One of the most persuasive cases for this view is found in the breakthrough study by Ackoff entitled *Creating the Corporate Future* (1984). Regrettably, there is not sufficient space in this chapter to do justice to Ackoff's provocative and convincing analysis of the basic elements in the emerging systems age paradigm. But we can illustrate the difference between machine age thinking and systems age thinking by looking at two different explanations of a university. A machine age thinker, says Ackoff, would explain a university by disassembling it into ever smaller elements from "university to college, from college to department, and from department to faculty, students, and subject matter" (1984, p. 17). This type of thinker would define these latter elements and then aggregate them into a definition of a department, then of a college, and finally of a university.

In contrast, a systems age thinker "would begin by identifying a system containing the university; for example, the educational system. Then such a thinker would define the objectives and functions of the educational system and do so with respect to the still larger social system that contains it. Finally, he or she would explain or define the university in terms of its roles and functions in the educational system" (Ackoff, 1984, p. 17). While machine age thinking is concerned only with the interaction of the parts of the thing to be explained, "systems thinking is occupied with the interactions of that thing with other things in the environment and with the environment itself" (p. 17).

Systems age thinking strikes me as the "right thing" for continuing educators—the right vision, and the right way to define their leadership role between the academy and the marketplace. I believe that this is our central challenge as developers of the new age. Leadership will come to those continuing educators who involve themselves in the search for solutions to the new problems that challenge our society, our universities, and all our institutions that have a stake in a brighter and smarter future. Instead of looking for solutions from within and working our way out from the interior, in the systems age we look outside for solutions and work our way in. And when "we focus on organizations," says Ackoff, "we are concerned with three levels of purpose: the purposes of the system, of its parts, and of the system of which it is a part, the suprasystem" (1984, p. 23). In this context, environmental scanning and strategic planning as a way to strengthen continuing education leadership become a practical necessity.

The most convincing argument for the application of a systems approach to learning has been advanced by Niebuhr in his outstanding work, *Revitalizing American Learning* (1984). Systems thinking, says Niebuhr, is now commonly applied to many aspects of our lives. We think of an economic system, systems of defense and governance, an international system, and ecosystems, to name just a few.

In each of these areas, the planning for solutions proceeds systematically from a "treatment of the whole to the interaction of the parts, and then finally to the parts themselves" (Ackoff, 1984, p. 52). But in matters of learning and education, machine age thinking still dominates our approach to the problems we face. Despite the magnitude of our economic transformation and our deepening learning crisis, we persist in dealing with the parts independently of the whole. We are still "fixated at the institutional level in terms of human learning," says Niebuhr (1984, p. 31). We have failed to see our schools and colleges as a part of a learning system that requires linkages and systems thinking between all our institutions. Echoing Niebuhr, Gagliano said that our learning crisis is "so great and so grave that it cannot be met by schools alone." To make the transition to the new information age, our society needs to recognize that learning is paramount to the development of all economic, communal, and personal goals. We need to recognize that our learning system consists of all our institutions. Family, community, church, school, university, workplace, and media are all interdependent and interactive institutions in the system (Niebuhr, 1984).

There is no question that continuing educators can apply this new world view to strengthen their leadership position inside and outside their institutions. Indeed, since no one else seems to be driving the bus, as Niebuhr is so fond of saying, continuing educators in every public and private institution can seize the wheel and assume the responsibility for steering the system. The formation of partnerships takes on new meaning in the context of this emerging paradigm.

Similarly, when developing continuing education programs and negotiating with partners in the learning system, the continuing education leader will do well to remember that growth and development are not the same thing. The former has to do with increase in size, in volume, in number. Development, however, focuses on the quality of life and large purposes rather than on the bottom line or on the standard of living (Ackoff, 1984). Continuing education leaders will strengthen their communities and their institutions with meaningful partnerships only if they understand them as a series of market transactions and a calculated set of strategic plans to improve the organization or the economy for some broader social purpose.

Naturally, firms and external organizations will be attracted initially to specific agreements with the expectation of some short-term outcomes. But, according to Ackoff, top corporate leaders are now moving more rapidly than academicians to the broader long-term view of planning and development. Indeed, the systems approach is already being implemented in the planning of the corporate world while the academy follows behind (Ackoff, 1984).

Building the Major Partnerships

There is no simple or single approach to the construction of partnerships, the development of networks, or the creation of linkages with individuals and organizations external to the university. Leaders must rely on their own individual strengths and instincts to find the right thing to do and the right way to do it.

Bringing partnerships to life is not an easy task. But though difficult and challenging, the process is frequently more important than some of the intended outcomes. The leadership plan, at least for the development of grand strategy, begins with recognition of the learning system. The essential movement flows from the outside to the inside. The linkage process within an interactive, interdependent system is not linear, according to a 1982 National Science Foundation report: "it is circular, interactive, and sometimes discontinuous. . . . It is, more importantly, an exercise in mutuality where understanding is more important than contracting; where personal contacts outweigh administrative mechanisms; and where ostensible purposes shelter undefined and even more valuable priorities" (National Science Foundation, 1982, p. 23). Bridges are difficult to engineer and to build, but good bridges can carry many things not originally intended for them.

As noted earlier, continuing educators can find a leadership role in basically three types of agreements that link academic to external institutions: research, technology transfer, and human resource development (HRD). Most partnerships engineered by continuing educators have been in the latter category of HRD—education and training.

Within this conceptual framework, the more typical level of interaction to date has led to the establishment of campus-based research centers, the exchange of scientists between higher education and industry, contracts for in-house training, industrial liaison programs, and other agreements that are similarly characterized by limited, short-term objectives. The most ambitious and largest number of these agreements have been made between top universities and Fortune 500 companies. And with few exceptions, these arrangements have been implemented within the institutional framework and have not resulted in any fundamental organizational changes on either side.

There are growing signs, however, that we are now moving toward the higher level of partnerships—the major partnerships of the kind I am describing in this chapter. These partnerships have several common characteristics: They usually involve complex formal agreements, they take a broad view of scientific and human resource development, and they eventually require organizational adjustments on both sides (Johnson, 1984).

While continuing educators are positioned for leadership in all these types of activity, their greatest opportunity lies in the development of the larger and more ambitious partnerships with outside organizations and community groups. Because these kinds of partnerships involve complex arrangements, they usually require the leadership of someone with broad understanding of all university resources, someone with solid experience in the application of knowledge, and someone with practical understanding of the needs of business, government, and other institutions. Most of all, these partnerships require someone who is expert in designing learning solutions for the complex problems facing individuals and organizations in the throes of rapid technological and economic change. Finally, because these major partnerships usually require the involvement of the highest leaders from both the university and the external organizations, the continuing educator has a special opportunity to demonstrate leadership and to focus attention on the larger meaning of the partnership.

Metropolitan Council for Lifelong Learning. Almost immediately after I became dean of Metropolitan College at the University of New Orleans in 1980, I set about to develop a major partnership with leaders from business, industry, labor, government, religious, and higher education groups. This initiative resulted in the creation of the Metropolitan Council for Lifelong Learning, whose broad purposes were threefold: (1) to assist key university officials and myself in our effort to develop a community-based strategy to address adult learning needs; (2) to focus attention on lifelong learning and training as resources that are crucial to the economic, social, political, and cultural development of the region; and (3) to provide a means of forging productive partnerships between the university and all the mainstream institutions in the community. Figure 1 illustrates the structure of the Metropolitan Council for Lifelong Learning.

Since December 1980, the board of directors has grown to more than seventy people. The chancellor, the vice-chancellors for academic affairs and development, and several key faculty members of the University of New Orleans serve as ex officio members along with a blue-ribbon membership that includes chief executive officers, the mayor, and the presidents of the most important civic and nonprofit organizations in New Orleans. Recently, the council added six program development board committees, each comprised of four university faculty and four community members. Both these latter groups are asked to apply their common academic and professional knowledge to help meet the special needs of adults. They are also asked to recommend to the board of directors any programs or partnerships that might address a specific learning need or advance in some way the economic development and quality of life of the city.

The Metropolitan Council for Lifelong Learning provides at least one example of how the conceptual framework presented

Figure 1. The Metropolitan Council for Lifelong Learning.

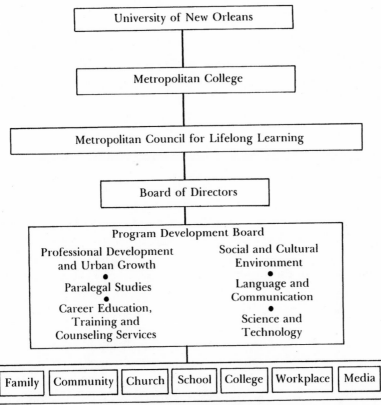

The Human Learning System

in this chapter can be put into action. After five years, some council members are beginning to see themselves as part of the learning system. And, in its advisory role to the university and the Metropolitan College, the council process works according to systems thinking. Beginning with the whole, meaning recognition of the learning system, the advisory process works from the outside in. This process is gradually being extended to other institutions in the learning system. Our long-term strategy is to cause business, labor, school, media, government, church, and nonprofit groups to become aware of their place and responsibility in the learning system as well as to define their own learning agendas. Obviously, continuing educators are perfectly positioned within the system to orchestrate the process.

Every business and community leader who invests time and money in such a partnership is making a public commitment to the need for lifelong learning. Increasingly, civic-minded leaders are looking for more effective ways to leverage public- and private-sector resources to improve economic development. And through partnerships such as this council, leaders from the university and the community can find a public means of giving value and importance to the creation of a learning ethic.

In addition to these broad benefits, several specific projects and grants have resulted directly or indirectly from council support: a Records Management Conference; forums on the future of the city; relocation of the University of New Orleans's Downtown Center in the heart of the busines district; state legislative authorization for the development of an Institute for Continuing Education and Employment Research; award of a substantial Job-Training Partnership Act grant to retrain displaced professional workers; and a business-education newspaper that is circulated twice a year to 50,000 businessmen and women in New Orleans. Moreover, in the spring of 1986, the council sponsored a two-day business-higher education conference. The latter event brought national experts to New Orleans to challenge our city's leadership to develop new partnerships that will accelerate the development of our economic and educational resources alike.

Practical Advice. The Metropolitan Council for Lifelong Learning is but one example of the many kinds of partnerships available to continuing educators. A growing body of literature describes other innovative partnerships that have many different goals and benefits. Continuing education leaders moving into this external arena will want to learn as much as possible about the bricks and mortar of those partnerships that appear most relevant to their own institutions.

My approach has been to focus on the practical methods for giving meaning to these emerging partnerships. For those continuing educators who seek to strengthen their leadership through such external activity, I can make several practical suggestions:

1. Continuing education leaders must begin by becoming authorities on the individual learning needs of adults as well as on the human resource needs of government, business, industry, and other institutions in the external markets to be served.

2. Continuing education leaders must secure institutional support for partnerships, including financial resources, a recognized administrative home, and separate policies and procedures designed to nourish the external alliances.

3. Continuing education leaders should seek partnerships and external relations with the purpose of finding specific solutions to specific problems.

4. Continuing education leaders who deal with leaders outside the university in business, government, or other organizations must think and act as leaders themselves. They must develop a strong conceptual understanding of the important trends that influence the learning enterprise in higher education as well as in the local and national economy.

5. Continuing education leaders must learn how to translate their strategic vision of partnerships and the learning system into benefits that mesh short-term, concrete objectives with the long-term, more purposeful goals of development.

6. Continuing education leaders should share their vision as often as possible on every public or private occasion and at every opportunity within the continuing education unit and the parent organization.

7. Continuing education leaders must learn that systems management in the modern organization requires the chief executive officer, dean, or director to function at the periphery rather than at the center of the organization or continuing education agency.

8. Continuing education leaders must recognize that commitment to partnerships and external leadership activity is a risky business. Since important partnerships are highly visible and involve the highest levels of leadership both on and off

campus, the outcomes are watched closely. Large amounts of energy, patience, courage, and hard work are all necessary.

9. Continuing education leaders should always give careful attention to the meaning of partnerships between the university and its external environment.

10. Continuing education leaders should always incorporate partnerships and external activities into their strategic planning process.

Future Course for Continuing Education Leaders

What will the role of the continuing educator be in the university of tomorrow? Continuing educators who see themselves as leaders in a learning system will play a decisive role in bringing their universities into the mainstream of the learning enterprise, whose broad currents are now carrying us ever more steadily into the new information age. To help guide their institutions through these turbulent waters, continuing educators will need to become skillful and courageous navigators.

In charting their course, continuing education leaders will have to convince their faculty, as well as the leaders of business, government, and industry, that lifelong learning, far from being a marginal activity, is indispensable to individual and community development. I believe that this effort will inevitably lead to increasingly important partnerships and new academic programs that will in turn create new markets for the university's programs. This, in turn, will gradually transform the relation between higher education and its external constituencies.

The result, says Lynton, will be "an institution no longer isolated but indeed so closely intertwined with society as to no longer have clear boundaries in time, in location, or even in membership" (1984, p. 153). The extended academic community envisioned in the 1982 MIT Report has all the characteristics of an interactive learning system, says Lynton. There will be great movement of individuals "between the campus and the workplace, both as students and as instructors." This will result in a sharing of authority over curriculum, as well as in a growing need to utilize and disseminate knowledge rapidly, with more faculty involved in "applied research, technical assistance, and public information" (Lynton, 1984, p. 153). The lesson for higher education and continuing education leaders is clear. The academy will have to adjust its mission and many of its traditional learning activities in order to meet the needs of a new economy.

The twin issues of learning and economic development are sure to dominate national policy and debate for the remainder of this century. The convergence of these two issues offers a great leadership opportunity for continuing educators. Leadership will accrue to the experts, to those who are recognized for their understanding of the dynamic changes confronting our society, to those who can build the major partnerships linking higher education to our institutions, and to those who can frame these partnerships around the vision of the emerging systems age.

Continuing education leaders must take advantage of their advantages. We have few peers in the application of knowledge to the solution of our nation's most pressing social and economic problems. While we must continue our successful efforts to extend our learning resources to adult learners by every traditional and nontraditional means at our disposal, we must commit equal energy to building the major partnerships that can tie the components of the learning system closer together. This will get our institutions and our people to the future a little faster. As continuing educators, we have never had a better opportunity for leadership in this century; if we walk away from this opportunity, we will never get a similar one.

Our challenge is to develop strategic plans for transforming the Protestant work ethic into a learning ethic. Armed with the vision of a learning society, continuing educators can lead the movement to take the learning resources and the learning ethic of the academy beyond the ivory tower into every corner of the society that we serve.

It was Max Weber, the nineteenth-century German sociologist, who first described how the Protestant work ethic gave birth to the spirit of capitalism in the great revolutionary transformation we call the Protestant Reformation. In a powerful metaphor, Weber wrote, "Christian asceticism, at first fleeing from the world into solitude, had already ruled the world which it had renounced from the monastery and through the Church. . . . Now it strode into the marketplace of life, slammed the door of the monastery behind it, and undertook to penetrate just that daily routine of life . . ." (Weber, [1904] 1958, p. 154). Now, as we approach the information age of the twenty-first century, our challenge will be to build a Society of Learners who will champion the liberating power of continuous lifelong learning to those beyond the academy.

The purpose of learning is to free people. As they stride into the marketplace of life, continuing education leaders can carry this message to people everywhere. It is a vision that is as powerful as it is true.

Developing a Strategic Marketing Plan

MARY LINDENSTEIN WALSHOK

The concept of marketing has become an important one in the not-for-profit world. Long a central concept in the management of for-profit enterprises, it began to gain attention in the not-for-profit sector with the publication of Kotler's *Marketing for Nonprofit Organizations* (1982). Kotler's conceptualization of marketing was sufficiently broad that its applicability to cultural, health, and educational services became readily apparent. In the last decade of increasing competition for members, clients, and students, leaders in the not-for-profit sector have come to rely increasingly on marketing activities and marketing strategies as integral parts of their broader strategic planning (Montana, 1978; Andreasen, 1981; Kotler, 1984b; Kotler, 1985a). In this chapter marketing will be analyzed in a way that is pertinent to the educational leader interested in adult and continuing education. In addition, a set of guidelines for integrating marketing into the organization's planning process will be introduced.

Kotler (1984b) notes that marketing involves establishing an exchange between organizations and the publics they serve. There are two important assumptions to note in analyzing the concept of marketing for adult and continuing education. The first is that the research and teaching activities of educational institutions serve vital needs and interests in the larger sponsoring society. Thus such institutions are not isolated ivory towers. The second is that mechanisms must be established to allow two-way communication between the educational institution and the larger society. With these assumptions in mind it is possible to elaborate on Kotler's work.

Marketing, like other aspects of strategic planning, is first and foremost an orientation. It is an attitude about how an organization should function in its larger environment (Rados, 1981). This orientation is characterized by the notion of publics or what Mitroff (1983) calls *stakeholders*. These are constituencies, interest groups—however you wish to label them—that legitimately make claims on the institution for services. The institution has a responsibility to be responsive to these publics and, even more precisely, to have a clear understanding of the specific needs and publics it is serving. Kotler emphasizes that this orientation should be an integral part of the institution's planning and should include mechanisms for periodically evaluating the satisfaction of the publics being served (Kotler, 1982; Kotler, 1984b; Kotler, 1985a).

What exactly is a public? In Kotler's work a public is described as a distinctive group of people or organizations that have actual or potential interest in or impact on the organization. Publics can be divided into groups demographically and in terms of special interests, which means they can be *segmented*. In the marketing orientation there is no such thing as the "general public." There are many comprehensive publics, such as youth and seniors, men and women. There are also more narrowly defined publics such as black professional women or teachers of high school science.

What defines a public is a set of specific socioeconomic characteristics or interests. The publics for an organization vary in the extent to which they are direct or indirect beneficiaries of an organization's services or activities. In addition, they vary in the extent to which they have a stake or interest in the organization's activities, even though they may not be direct beneficiaries of the organization's services. This is why it is important to consider "interest in" or "impact on" the organization when identifying publics (Schoner and Uhl, 1975; Kotler, 1982; Weiers, 1984; Robertson, Zielinski, and Ward, 1984).

This distinction between direct and indirect is important because, as will be shown later in this chapter, the direct beneficiaries of a program or service are not the only interest groups or publics with a stake in a service being provided (Porter,

1980). The failure on the part of many continuing educators to inventory comprehensively their various publics in the program-planning and delivery process can sometimes have disastrous consequences, since they must be able to serve the needs of selected adult student constituencies in a way that simultaneously supports the values and interests of the faculty and the institution. This is no easy challenge.

Marketing is an exchange relationship that contains an intrinsic assumption that the raison d'etre for the organization is to serve the needs of specific publics or constituencies. Such an orientation will be characterized by responsiveness, clarity of purpose, and evaluation. All these are of necessity central activities of the managerial process. Marketing should not be confined to a "department" that is responsible for one-way communication or "sales" to various constituencies (Aaker and Myers, 1982; Kinnear and Taylor, 1983; Webster, 1984). Rather marketing should be a central part of strategic planning, of determining goals and objectives, and it should also provide criteria for evaluating organizational performance. The accuracy with which it adjusts, refines, or refocuses its effort, on the basis of regular feedback from its constituencies, is a formal, ongoing process affecting all sectors of the organization.

The need to understand marketing and to use marketing techniques effectively thus becomes the responsibility of everyone in the organization, not just of the marketing department, because planning, implementing, and program review take place through-out the organization. Therefore the ability to secure and exchange views with various constituencies becomes an essential profes-sional skill for all members of the organization. Central to such skill is knowing how to define the constituencies with whom an exchange relationship is desired and appropriate in relation to the organization's mission and resources. One must know how to communicate with constituencies as a way of learning their needs and interests. This is an integral part of program planning. It includes knowing how to adapt organizational resources and capacities to constituent needs (Walshok, 1985). What follows is a series of suggestions about how to accomplish the following goals as a leader in continuing higher education:

1. Clarifying your mission and identifying your constituencies.
2. Implementing an ongoing exchange process with important stakeholders through dialogue and planning.
3. Communicating, promoting, and evaluating success with targeted constituencies.

Matching the Parties in the Exchange Process

The first stage of any strategic marketing effort is that of clarifying mission and identifying constituencies. There is a temptation among continuing education leaders to think of their organization's mission in terms that are either too broad or too narrow. One often hears a statement such as, "Our role is to provide educational services to adults not otherwise served by the university." This kind of mission statement is too broad in that it implies that adults represent a large, undifferentiated public with common educational needs. Adults, much more than children and teen-agers, bring different histories, capacities, motivations, and characteristics to the learning experience. Their needs must be met within the context of a highly sophisticated sense of socioeconomic and social psychological differentiation.

The mission statement quoted above is also too narrow in that it fails adequately to incorporate the mission of the larger parent organization within which the continuing education program resides. It fails to articulate clearly how the continuing education enterprise enhances the parent institution's mission and thus complements the broader goals, objectives, and constituencies that drive the total organization.

A first step for the continuing education leader who is developing a more sophisticated approach to marketing is to begin with an examination of his or her immediate context. This is generally the parent institution and the various constituencies and needs it serves both within its walls and in its surrounding environment. The commitment made to adult learners and specific adult learning constituencies will flow from, or at least be framed by, these larger systems of accountability.

A conventional marketing person would describe this process as clarifying what business you are in or spelling out what services or benefits you can offer to specific constituencies. In a continuing education enterprise, this means defining the particular educational services you are best equipped to provide to given adult constituencies.

But to do so, you must take a long, hard look at what the parent organization does and what it is known for, the sorts of societal needs it is committed to serving, and then review how what you do fits with the parent organization's mission. It means clearly describing whom you currently serve or might potentially serve and assessing where you stand in relation to other providers of continuing education in your area. Each of these issues needs to be addressed separately. In addition, each can be posed as a question for which qualitative and quantitative data must be gathered. Once these issues have been clarified, it is possible to define a unit's strategic academic position. This includes deciding on what it is uniquely capable of offering to clearly targeted constituencies. What follows are some points to consider when attempting to address these issues in the process of clarifying the organization's mission and key constituencies.

For What Is the Parent Organization Best Known? If the parent organization is best known for research and scholarship, in what specific fields is it preeminent? To what larger social ends are its achievements in research and scholarship pertinent? Such societal ends might be the improvement of agriculture, the health sciences, or economic forecasting.

If the institution is best known for curriculum offerings, what is the range of its disciplines? How much prestige do its degrees have in the eyes of peers, employers, and graduate and professional schools? What are the demographic characteristics of students in degree programs? Are they chiefly full-time or part-time, residential or commuter students? What are the enrollment trends across disciplines? Is there a difference in enrollment trends in liberal arts and professional or vocational offerings?

If the institution is best known for public service activities, what do these include? Do they include health care, employment counseling, free public lectures, or concerts? To what extent are faculty involved in such community activities as lecturing, volunteer service, and expert advising or private consulting? What is the extent of their collaboration with off-campus groups in research, teaching, or special-service programs? Are campus leaders involved in community activities?

What Societal Needs and Constituencies Does the Parent Organization Serve? For example, who makes up the primary student population of the campus? Are admission requirements open or selective? Are there provisions for special-need constituencies such as Hispanics, full-time or part-time students, undergraduate or graduate students? How does the campus define its teaching mission? Is it interested in preparing future leaders and educating the future labor force or in preparing students for graduate and professional study? How does the campus articulate and implement its public service charge? Through its existing program of undergraduate and graduate teaching? Through dissemination of research findings by faculty consulting? Or through units with a special mission, such as the alumni office or the continuing education office?

With What Educational Services and Constituencies Is the Continuing Education Unit Identified? It is important to define in broad terms the extent to which continuing education is perceived as a serious academic enterprise. Thus, it is necessary to ask to what extent continuing education activities are central to the social and economic life of the community? How are they related to the research, teaching, and public service activities of the college or university? To what extent does continuing education represent a chance for adults to get basic education or advanced learning?

In seeking answers to these questions, it is important to determine how the unit is seen by its own faculty and staff. This should be accomplished by internal discussions of the strengths and weaknesses of the continuing education unit, along with an analysis of the obstacles it faces and the opportunities open to it. One way to gain such information is to interview faculty and administrators. Views of former and presently enrolled students can be sampled through survey questionnaires and course evaluations. Random surveys of potential students are also useful, as are the views of key people from local businesses and industries, the professions, and voluntary associations.

What Steps Can the Continuing Education Unit Take to Better Describe the Educational Needs in Its Community? It is important to assess the overall demand for adult educational services and determine the continuing education unit's strategic market position in relation to other providers. This will help to establish the unit's strategic market position. Thus it is important to analyze what sources of aggregate population and economic data are available. This analysis is a first step in obtaining an accurate assessment of the immediate socioeconomic environment. The information here might include census and labor data, as well as indicators of trends in economic development. It might include population trends that take into account such factors as age, family size, migration patterns, residential data, educational attainment, and occupational distribution of the local population.

Other steps important in determining educational needs in the community include identifying what government programs are in place to help economic and employment development. What kinds of private capitalization are taking place? What product or service areas are at the top of the list? How much money is involved, and how many people will be affected by this capitalization? What is the demographic profile of the institution's service area, including residential and industrial zones; that is, what are the educational attainments, occupational characteristics, and income levels of residents? And, most importantly, what are the major motivators for education in the community?

A further question is, how much education and what kinds are required for entering, maintaining, and advancing in particular jobs? At a minimum this should be known for all major work or employment spheres in the community. Data bearing on this question should be categorized and listed according to such job titles as farmer, manager, small-business person, professional person, technician, and other major occupational groupings found in the community. This analysis should also address what credentialing, licensing, or relicensing requirements exist for employment or service or for practicing in specific business and professional fields.

One should also identify the key business and professional organizations in the community and then find out what spokespeople in these organizations identify as important educational needs. What new social and economic developments are on the horizon in the community? When these developments have been identified, it is possible to begin translating them into education or training needs.

There are other questions to ask. For example, what are the normative and cultural motivators in the community? What are some of the traditions, sources of status, and life-style priorities that influence educational decisions? How mobile geographically and socioeconomically is the community? How does this affect the character and quality of education sought by students? What other institutions and organizations are providing education for adults in the community? What place does education occupy in people's priorities? How do people in the community already spend their discretionary time and money? Do they spend it on arts and culture or on outdoor recreation? Do they read, go to concerts, and attend art galleries, or do they prefer family, personal development, social, and religious activities?

It is important to find out how people use and distribute their time across a typical day or week. When this is known, it is possible to determine when they would be most likely to want to attend educational activities. You should also determine how much people are willing to pay for given products, services, and activities. It then becomes possible to address the issue of how educational fees and tuition at your institution compare with those of other providers of services and activities. What is the rationale in the consumer's mind for any fee discrepancies?

How Do the Current and Potential Services and Constituencies for the Continuing Education Unit Fit with Those of the Parent Organization? In this area it is important to consider whether or not the continuing education unit disseminates knowledge that is comparable in substance and level with that of the college or university as a whole. Are adult constituencies served in ways comparable to those enjoyed by the full-time student body in terms of educational interests, capacities, and values? Does the continuing education instructional staff reflect levels of achievement and leadership similar to those of full-time faculty?

Do continuing education students come from social, occupational, political, and cultural sectors that reflect the core emphasis of the larger campus? Do the nature and substance of the continuing education program enhance, enrich, and extend the goals and objectives of the larger campus or do they compete with, detract from, or even undermine them?

It is imperative that the continuing education leader address all these issues as comprehensively as possible as a first step in the development of a strategic marketing plan. At the end of this first stage of mission analysis the organization should have a clear sense of how it is perceived, how it wishes to be perceived, and whom it wishes to serve. Marketing specialists refer to this as defining a marketing niche.

Implementing an Ongoing Exchange Process

Having arrived at a consensus as to the organization's strategic academic position, the continuing education leader is ready to move to the second major stage of marketing. This stage requires putting in place professional staff, as well as institutional mechanisms and financial resources, to support ongoing dialogue with constituencies. This ongoing dialogue represents the heart of the marketing model.

At a minimum, such a dialogue should take place on the following three levels: (1) within the continuing education enterprise, (2) between the continuing education unit and the parent organization, and (3) between the professional staff in continuing education and the various constituencies that the organization is committed to serving. The commitment to this ongoing dialogue has profound implications for the type of professional skills and background that the continuing education leader must have. In addition, it has important implications for the type of systems that the organization must have in place to support the process of dialogue and to be able to adapt, often rapidly and innovatively, to emerging opportunities in the larger environment as these are discovered in the dialogue process.

The continuing educator must work to understand specific disciplines such as history, engineering, and psychology. Such a leader's job description and performance measures must include membership on advisory committees, attendance at discipline-focused seminars and meetings, and reading and writing about the specific constituencies for whose educational needs she or he is responsible. The organization has to allow time and resources for professionals to participate in such interactions through memberships, travel, and the hosting of lunches for advisory boards. It must also allow time for professional development for staff members.

The effective continuing education leader in this proposed model keeps himself or herself informed about developments in basic research and scholarship, about changing demands in the adult marketplace as a result of social and economic shifts, and about changes in educational delivery systems. Such a person must be able to understand the information being communicated by faculty and other relevant intellectuals, by journals, and by the larger environment. She or he must have developed process skills as a way of eliciting information from various sources. The person must then be able to facilitate interaction and listen to what is being communicated directly and indirectly. She or he must also have expert planning and organizing skills and be able to monitor performance and adjust plans as necessary.

Finally such a planner must have an enormous tolerance for ambiguity and uncertainty. The process of listening to diverse constituencies and monitoring environmental trends often yields contradictory perspectives. If care is not taken, this can lead to high-risk projects with uncertain outcomes. A marketing orientation, regrettably, does not simplify the job. In fact, it complicates the job. However, in a world of rapid technological and social change, taking a marketing approach may be the only way for a continuing education enterprise to remain current and competitive.

There are a number of obvious and effective ways of keeping current and in touch with the constituencies one is committed to serving. First, there is no substitute for personal contact. This may involve one-to-one communication in the form of mixed group consultations and advisory committees, that represent leadership among key constituencies, along with a regular and careful reading of local business, political, and social news. Personal participation in local professional interest groups or in community volunteer activities often results in connections and insights not to be found elsewhere.

The watchword is broad outreach that is diverse and conducted on a regular basis. This is what is popularly termed *networking*. For the marketing-oriented continuing education leader, the majority of networking time should be with constituencies—the users of knowledge. A smaller portion of time should be spent networking with other professional continuing educators. Thus the needs of adult learners in Detroit can be quite different from those of adult learners in San Diego. A professional with a marketing orientation will know how to learn about, assess, and connect with those needs in either location by engaging in this critical ongoing dialogue with the constituencies served by the institution for whom she or he works.

Using these various interactions, framed by the more standardized environmental data gathered in stage one, it is possible to generate specific ideas about valid programming opportunities, about on-campus and community people who are qualified and interested in teaching, about alternative sources of funding for new program ideas, and about the best vehicles or communications strategies to employ with a given constituency on a given topic. This information, balanced against the realistic resources of the continuing education unit, gives rise to a marketing plan that includes the following elements:

- The audience for a program and its likely size.
- The benefits that the audience will derive from that program.
- When, where, and at what price the program should be offered.
- How best to communicate with the audience targeted for a given program.

What is critical here is that instead of "selling" a program, the marketing-oriented planner delivers a service in response to a clearly articulated need. This is accomplished through program design, promotion, and endorsements (Lenz, 1980; Walshok, 1985).

Above and beyond providing specific program ideas and information invaluable to program promotion and delivery, this approach to networking and ongoing dialogue can build broad-based support for the continuing education enterprise within both the organization and the community. A program that not only solicits input but actively incorporates that input at various stages of program development and implementation creates stakeholders—people who want to assure the success of the program as much as the continuing education professional does. A program that reflects the values of the larger institution and simultaneously responds to the needs of the larger society becomes an invaluable public service activity that the parent organization can enthusiastically support.

It is important to underscore that this orientation does not support the knee-jerk attitude that says, "If the public wants it, it must be okay." The orientation being advocated here builds from the central mission of the organization and addresses the needs of constituencies that can be best served in the light of that mission. The continuing education leader who can successfully move between her or his organization and the larger society outside becomes a critical part of an organization's leadership team. Such a person can be the best possible advocate for the needs of the adult learner and thus justify the validity of continuing higher education as a major activity of the campus.

Communicating, Promoting, and Evaluating Success

Even with good input from, and key support in, the communities to which programs are directed, there remains a third critical stage in setting up a strategic marketing plan. This is the development of a systematic promotional and public relations strategy, along with tracking techniques for evaluating the effectiveness of specific promotional strategies. Most people typically associate this set of activities with marketing. However, the point of this chapter has been to demonstrate that what some people think of as "the whole ball of wax" represents only about a third of what is involved in effective marketing—and the least significant third at that.

No amount of promotion can save an ill-conceived, untargeted program for which there is strong competition. In contrast, a well-planned, targeted program can always benefit from a carefully thought-out promotional and public relations strategy. In fact, if such an effort is properly orchestrated, it should promote not only the individual program but also the entire continuing education enterprise in the eyes of the constituencies it is designed to reach.

Communication and promotional strategies need to be thought of in the broadest possible terms. They should be planned with a concern for how they fit with the image of the larger enterprise. In addition, they must be planned with a sensitivity to the need for a unifying image for all continuing education activities. Such strategies should also result in a clear return on investment. Ad hoc brochures developed at a program planner's desk, random ads in the newspapers, and press releases from a variety of sources all may ultimately undermine the carefully developed dialogues with relevant constituencies.

The consumer and the media require clearly stated information about educational opportunities. Such information must be communicated in a way that reflects the values of the institution and in a way that helps various constituencies understand the potential benefits of the programs. Thought, planning, and professionalism are all necessary to achieve this.

Communication and promotional efforts can take a variety of forms. The suitability of these is dictated by the nature of the program, as well as by the size and character of the constituency for which it is intended. Sometimes new programs can be promoted in a very low-key, narrowly focused way because they are for a small, targeted audience. But sometimes such programs may merit advertising or inclusion in a general catalogue because of the contributions they can make to the overall image and positioning of the continuing education unit as a whole.

Every program promotional effort should be planned with a sensitivity to the need for maintaining or increasing enrollments as well as for enhancing the overall efforts of the continuing education unit in relation to a variety of constituencies, including the campus community. The key techniques for accomplishing this include direct mail publications such as catalogues, brochures, newsletters, and special letters or invitations. They also include publicity and media relations, public relations, paid advertising, telemarketing, and personal representation. One of the critical roles of the continuing education leader is evaluating what vehicles and what kinds of messages are best suited to an individ-

ual program in relation to the overall institution. What follows are
some brief descriptions of the various vehicles available and some
ideas about the conditions under which they can be appropriately
used.

Direct Mail. Direct mail is by far the most popular format
for promotion. Its popularity derives from its efficiency. A
promotional piece usually generates a large response relative to the
amount it costs to design, produce, and mail it. For many
constituencies, the only major promotional piece produced in a
semester may be a catalogue. For larger operations, quarterly
catalogues may be augmented by a variety of brochures on
programs for such specific constituencies as electrical engineers,
high school English teachers, or emergency-room nurses. With the
possible exception of course catalogues, which are deliberately
comprehensive and are mailed out in large quantities, highly
targeted direct mail pieces are the best promotional method. At the
same time, direct mail strategies require a quite large mailing list
or a very specialized smaller list in order to be effective. It is
possible to purchase such mailing lists for promotional purposes.
Thanks in part to affordable personal computers, continuing
education units increasingly build and maintain their own
mailing lists.

Direct mail strategies require a reasonably sophisticated
understanding of market segments and relatively thoughtful
preplanning in order to be effective. The costs of producing direct
mail pieces can be kept low because under current regulations
nonprofit organizations can take advantage of bulk mail rates.
Direct mail pieces can also be designed to look expensive if such a
look is necessary or desirable for a given audience. But such
mailings are highly impersonal and often go unread. Because of
this they may be ill suited to certain kinds of constituencies and
programs.

Paid Advertising. This represents a second increasingly
popular promotional technique in continuing education circles.
Advertising is less expensive than direct mail, but it is also less
targeted. This is particularly true of newspaper advertising. An
advertisement in a newspaper with a circulation of 250,000 may
cost $800. However, a direct mail piece may cost $8,000. The

important issue here, of course, is the rate of return on the advertising investment. Very large continuing education programs in densely populated urban centers use advertising extensively to promote specific events and course offerings. They usually send those who respond to an advertisement a copy of the catalogue or relevant brochures. Therefore this type of advertising is a way to build a unit's mailing list for future direct mailings.

Advertising can be highly controlled and carefully orchestrated so as to communicate institutional messages in ways that will build an effective new image. Advertising can increase awareness of the institution in the mind of the general public as well as express the institution's philosophy and style in a coherent and persistent way. Advertising, when it is used in this manner, contributes in positive, effective ways to institutional positioning in relation to other providers of educational programs. Educational advertising typically relies on daily and weekly newspapers, but advertising can also be highly effective in specialized magazines and trade and professional publications or in such publications as concert programs and public television guides because of the uniformity of their readership.

Some institutions also utilize paid radio and television advertising. Even outdoor billboards may be used to stimulate interest in programs. The appropriateness of any kind of paid advertising requires a clear sense of what you want to achieve and how much you are willing to spend, along with a careful analysis of the potential effects of this kind of advertising on the image and credibility of the institution. Physicians and Harvard University do not advertise their services in Sunday newspaper supplements, although they clearly have their own methods of promoting themselves.

Publicity and Media Relations as Free Promotion. It is possible to enjoy free promotion and publicity through carefully cultivating the media and deliberately establishing effective relationships with them. Universities have long had public information offices to respond to inquiries by the press and various constituent groups. Publicity, however, implies a more proactive relationship with the media and constituent groups. It includes such activities as the deliberate preparation of news releases, orchestration of press conferences and interviews, development of story ideas, solicitation of media coverage, and preparation of public service and calendar announcements. All these represent the unified communication strategy being advocated in this chapter.

The goal of such a deliberately planned communications strategy is to put the spotlight on particular programs. News releases and notices are often more effective in engaging a reader, viewer, or listener than is an advertisement or a piece of direct mail. The return on investment for this kind of publicity is very difficult to track. If this type of communications strategy is desired, as is the case in many large continuing education organizations, it will be necessary to have adequate staff to do the job of establishing effective media relations. Getting items into the press, as well as responding to press inquiries and story opportunities, often requires more than one full-time professional.

Well-managed media relations can greatly enhance an institution's reputation. Personal relationships with media representatives and a good sense of what is considered interesting or newsworthy can result in attention and visibility far in excess of what an advertising budget can buy. Some examples of newsworthy items that can be used to enhance the overall publicity efforts of the institution's image are sending out news releases when new staff are hired or new programs are developed. For example, policy conferences sponsored by the continuing education unit and seminars reporting on cutting-edge research in a new field represent activities for which news releases or media coverage can produce free publicity.

Use of Special Events to Showcase Continuing Education. Special events are often used by a business to showcase a product, bring attention to their enterprise, develop a new constituency, or thank an existing one. Such events can also be strategically used by educators for similar purposes. Free career-counseling days, open houses, and free public lecture series are ways to showcase services and attract constituencies. Such events can also aid in developing mailing lists for future programs or in introducing a highly targeted group to a particular program. An example of the latter would be a luncheon or reception for corporate leaders as a way of bringing an executive education program to their attention. The advantage of special events is that they can be tailored to the style of the constituency you want to reach. They allow for personal interaction and, properly done, they can have a unique impact and quality of memorableness. However, the continuing education leader must have a sophisticated understanding of constituency interests and an internal staff possessed of the time and skill to ensure the success of such events.

Organizational Versus Individual Constituencies for Continuing Education. The constituency for continuing higher education is often an organization rather than an individual or group of individuals. Personal representation can be a highly effective way of introducing a program to institutional clients such as hospitals, software companies, and school districts. To have a skilled professional make what amounts to a sales call is often the best way to describe and explain complex programs, their benefits to the user, and how they compare with what is available from other providers. Much more information can be communicated through this personal approach than through print. In addition, such an approach enables the continuing education leader to personally answer any questions that clients may have. A properly prepared representative who is a member of the permanent continuing education staff can also be a goodwill ambassador for the entire college or university. In fact, personal representation is often an underutilized communication strategy in continuing higher education.

Taking a less formal approach, the continuing education leader may simply attend special meetings of such groups as the local Chamber of Commerce. It is also important for him or her to give speeches to groups such as Rotary, Junior League, or the hospital auxiliary. Such activities are important to good public relations, but their purpose is to build awareness and knowledge of some aspect of the continuing education enterprise or the institution as a whole. It is usually inappropriate to use such contexts for making sales or signing up students.

Telemarketing. Telemarketing, or phone sales, is included here because it is an increasingly used promotional strategy among such groups as alumni associations and performing arts companies. Telemarketing may be useful to continuing educators because it allows them to target communication in a personal and detailed manner. But telemarketing also can be intrusive and may be experienced as pressured selling if not properly orchestrated.

Evaluating Effectiveness of Alternative Promotional Strategies. The promotional strategies described in this chapter need to be evaluated against a variety of criteria, each of which could be the subject of a separate chapter in a marketing book. A strategic market-planning process should establish the educational goals of a program in relation to the interests and values of the market segments for which that program is intended. The unique position one is seeking to establish should emerge out of the planning process and should logically suggest promotional techniques that are both appropriate and potentially effective.

There is a temptation among professionals in the promotional field to rely on tried and true direct mail approaches or on formulas that, under certain circumstances, may be neither appropriate nor effective. There is an equally strong temptation among amateurs to want to see their name in lights. As a result, they will often press for expensive paid advertisements or heavy media coverage. Such approaches should be avoided unless an extensive market analysis indicates that this is an effective strategy.

Instead the promotion strategy must be driven by a sophisticated understanding of program content, audience preferences, how to get the attention and interest of given constituencies, and what you hope to achieve through the promotion. For example, in some cases you may simply want to achieve visibility. In other cases you may want to secure paid enrollees. The ongoing dialogues described earlier can help you to identify how best to promote given programs to specific groups.

Finally, you can evaluate the effectiveness of any of these promotional techniques by tracking results. This involves logging phone inquiries in response to advertisements, news stories, or radio spots. It means coding enrollment forms in brochures and catalogues so that you can count how many registrants they actually produce. Other effective tracking techniques involve asking enrollees who register by phone or in person how they learned about the program. Course evaluation forms can ask the same question.

The number of such responses, when divided into the costs of the particular promotion budget of a program, will give some indication of the average cost of delivering an enrollment. The average cost should be well below the amount of revenue that an enrollment generates. For example, responses to an ad may indicate that each $75 enrollment produced by a newspaper advertisement costs the organization $12, which is an acceptable ratio. But if it cost, say, $40 to secure a registration, you might have to question the viability of newpaper advertisements.

A continuing education leader has to determine acceptable ranges and percentages of total income to allocate to promotion. Even this will vary from program to program as well as over the life of programs. New activities and programs may require a higher initial investment in promotion to achieve the visibility and market position needed for long-term success. Here again, the knowledge gained about the marketplace in the early planning stages should give the leader a good sense of approach, timelines, and levels of investment appropriate to any given circumstance.

This chapter has emphasized the broad concept of what marketing is and how it can benefit the educational enterprise. It has emphasized that marketing is an ongoing exchange relationship between the educational unit and the specific market segments or constituencies it is committed to serving. The ongoing character of this exchange requires continual dialogue and feedback on questions of staffing, planning, management, and promotion.

The continuing education leader who can master marketing at both the conceptual and managerial levels can look forward to successful academic programs and financial stability. In addition, such a leader will be able to demonstrate that she or he is serving society well by delivering the best resources available to targeted groups whose input has been a critical part of the program development and evaluation process.

✤ 10 ✤

Using Evaluation to Monitor Plans and Assess Results

MARGARET E. HOLT

The ability to design, conduct, interpret, and utilize evaluations is an important skill for strategic planning and effective leadership. Well-constructed evaluations can provide important data for the ongoing process of environmental scanning mentioned by many of the other authors in this volume. Evaluations can be designed to collect the kind of data necessary for making better decisions related to continuing education programming. This, in turn, provides a way for organizations to engage in the process of self-renewal that is critical to meeting the rapidly changing needs of the constituencies served by continuing education.

Well-constructed evaluations can examine feelings and reactions of client groups, levels and degrees of knowledge, behavior and performance, and occasionally more global societal or communal changes. These are often referred to as indirect benefits of evaluations. Leaders find they must constantly attend to and review the ongoing debates about the worthiness and cost-effectiveness of many types of evaluations. They must avoid succumbing to fads or fashions in assessment procedures. For example, Deshler (1984) argues that the use of summative or impact evaluations is on the decline. He feels that evaluation is now primarily used for accountability and is most appropriate when used for well-developed, mature programs. In the same year that Deshler noted the decline in the use of summative evaluations, however, a dean of a large college of education in the U.S. stated: "We are witnessing a shift in society about education from a preoccupation with inputs to a preoccupation with outputs."

Sorting through such confusion is a high-level skill that separates leaders from managers. Managers concentrate on short-term, more immediate assessments of their operations. Leaders combine their understanding of what was, what is, and what is to be in selecting and implementing evaluations. For example, Cleveland (1985) notes that effective leadership demands a tolerance for paradox and ambiguity. This is the reality of the world for the leader who uses strategic planning as an integral part of enhancing his or her leadership style.

Leaders in continuing education create visions for their organizations from a wide variety of evaluation methods. It is not possible to prescribe a universal plan or formula for the use of evaluations in continuing education operations because the nature and needs of each organization are unique. Therefore this chapter will consider the following three topics as they relate to leadership responsibility for evaluation in a continuing education organization: (1) matching the organizational culture and needs to an evaluation plan, (2) evaluation as an integral part of strategic scanning and planning, and (3) using evaluation to bring visibility to the leader's vision.

Evaluating Organizational Culture

The concept of organizational culture, also called corporate culture or the organizational unconscious, refers to the unspoken and unwritten norms that fashion and direct organization life. In Chapter Six, Terrence Deal presents a comprehensive overview of planning for effective organizational cultures in continuing education. John Schmidt in Chapter Three and James Votruba in Chapter Eleven emphasize the need to develop an appropriate fit between continuing education programming and the culture of the parent organization. Michael Offerman, in Chapter Five, demonstrates the need for values clarification and how this impacts on programming and the culture of the organization. Developing and monitoring an organizational culture that is compatible with a continuing education's parent organization are important parts of strategic planning and effective leadership.

Deal and Kennedy (1982) speak of "deeply ingrained beliefs," "values," "legends," "heroes," and "standards of behavior" when describing organizational culture. Luce (1984) observes that a common factor among the many definitions of corporate culture is the emphasis on behavior, rituals, sagas, myths, and stories. These help to transmit the knowledge of the organization's culture to its members. Turnstall (1983) presents a very similar picture in defining organizational culture. He emphasizes that culture defines acceptable ways of doing business in the organization.

Most organizations can present employees with a manual of standard operating procedures (SOPs) but no manuals exist for standard operating norms (SONs). Allen and Dyer (1980) further complicate the challenge to understand an organization's culture by observing that although it is powerful and is important in influencing people's lives, it is unconscious.

A leader must fully understand his or her organization's culture. However, this kind of understanding is not easy to come by. The informal communication grapevine, for example, is not readily delineated. If asked to describe the organizational culture on paper, each employee would probably produce a different description. Observers of organizations suggest that some cultures are strong and some weak, some healthy and some unhealthy. Wilkins and Ouchi (1983) even argue that many organizations neither have nor need distinct cultures. They contend, however, that certain types of organizations will be more efficient if they generate a strong culture. Continuing education organizations fall into this category. As Luce (1984) notes, when interactions among organizational members are ambiguous, a well-defined and distinct culture can promote effectiveness and efficiency in problem solving.

Transactions between individuals in continuing education operations clearly fit into such categories as ambiguous, complex, and interdependent. In addition to the internal interdependence of various divisions, continuing education employees provide services for outside clientele who often wish to take part in decisions about the content and delivery of services. Further, the faculty members who directly deliver the services become another external factor to take into account. In some corporations, the development of a product involves a patterned, phased, ordered series of activities. Continuing education is not so systematized. Program ideas spring forth internally and externally. Units and divisions do not function according to rigid formulas. A mixture of organizational members may become involved in a particular program, depending on where the ideas were generated, the availability of staff, and the expertise required. Arrangements are complex and are influenced by various interest groups and the amount of funding available. Continuing education leaders and staff must enjoy maximum flexibility from one activity to another. Recall the earlier quotation from Cleveland in which he states that one of the characteristics of executive leadership is a talent for ambiguity. Anyone who has ever worked in continuing education will testify to the need to develop a high tolerance for ambiguity in order to be effective in daily problem solving.

Advantages of a Cultural Audit to Leaders. Analyzing organizational culture enables leaders to see if there is much discrepancy between SOPs and SONs. If there are discrepancies, what is their significance? Is the culture strong or weak? Is it healthy or unhealthy? Does the assessment of culture suggest the need for organizational interventions and change? One caveat exists. Attempts to change culture carry considerable risks. Further, there are not many prototype organizations to be studied in which such changes have been attempted. Most organizations are reluctant to report failures (Luce, 1984).

Nonetheless, a staff evaluation of organizational culture is an effective starting place for continuing education leaders. This is an integral part of the management audit described by Robert Simerly in Chapter Four, as well as of Offerman's values clarification process presented in Chapter Five. In combination, these approaches form important steps in the strategic planning process.

Methods for Conducting a Cultural Audit. Leaders and selected other staff members in the organization can design "belief questionnaires" tailored specifically to their situation. Such questionnaires can contribute to an overall assessment of the culture as well as be fine tuned to collect data on particular details about organizational life. Luce (1984) proposes an informal series of questions that could initiate a study of an organization's culture. She notes that we come to understand an organization's culture by asking staff to identify significant events in the organization's history, their impressions and views of the organization's mission, the way they learned the systems for doing their jobs, and how work is prioritized by leadership. What is learned by asking questions on such matters may or may not be congruent with the organization's stated or written philosophy. Nonetheless, the content of these collected responses would present the staff's perception of organizational culture—that is, their interpretation of how things work.

A more formal evaluation of the organization's culture can be accomplished by using the Human Resources Institute's Cultural Audit (1983) and/or the Norms Diagnostic Index (Allen and Dyer, 1980). The latter contains thirty-eight items covering seven important organizational issues: performance facilitation, job involvement, training, leader-subordinate interaction, policies and procedures, confrontation, and supportive climate. Thirteen additional statements concern pay, communication, work, and benefits.

Other means for evaluating organizational culture can include such ethnographic data collection strategies as observations, interviews, and career histories. Ethnography is most commonly used by the social sciences for the study of cultures, socialization, institutionalization, and sociocultural behavior. An entire ethnographic strategy can be employed or else a selected few collection techniques can be used. The decision regarding the scope of the study will be dependent on the basic objectives adopted. They recommend the design of a comprehensive ethnographic investigation if the objective of the evaluation is to recognize multiple descriptors of culture, including such areas as artifacts, descriptions of organizational environments, analysis of behavioral patterns, and identification of shared beliefs. In addition, they suggest the use of selected ethnographic collection techniques, such as nonparticipant observations, to complement the more standard quantitative evaluations.

Leaders who initiate evaluation activities by conducting both informal and formal assessments of the anthropological and sociological environment within their organizations can confidently base the formulation of more specialized evaluations on findings from these cultural audits. If reorganization is needed, it will be justified and not conducted just for the sake of reorganizing.

Often it is tempting for administrators new to an organization to begin an immediate and vigorous reorganization. However, much of the structure and process operating within an organization is often worth preserving. Sudden reorganization may create more negative fallout and reduce productivity. As Petronius Arbiter observed in the first century A.D., "We trained hard—but it seems that every time we were beginning to form up into teams, we would be reorganized. I was to learn later in life that we tend to meet any new situation by reorganizing; and a wonderful method it can be for creating the illusion of progress while producing confusion, inefficiency, and demoralization" (Dickson, 1980).

Evaluating Organizational Structures, Systems, and Strategies. Continuing education organizations are like snowflakes. No two are alike. Although most are components of larger organizations, their administrative and organizational relationships vary tremendously. An evaluation of structure most frequently will begin with a review of the organizational chart for the continuing education unit as well as for the parent organization in which it resides.

An organization's formal structure is often graphically represented on a chart. The chart illustrates the way that tasks are divided and integrated according to positions and job descriptions. Charts also delineate the chain of command, communication networks, and work-flow systems. Although charts present a formal structure of relationships, Kast and Rosenzweig (1979) observe that interactions do not always take place within these formal arrangements.

Leaders and their teams will frequently review the structure of their organizations and determine if line and staff are properly arranged to facilitate goals and objectives based on a collective vision for the operation. Although changes in structure can never be implemented without extensive and intensive considerations, leaders recognize that the chart is not cast in stone. Certainly, periodic comparisons of how this chart reflects life in the organization and how things really happen will be priority items in the leadership's ongoing evaluations.

Since most continuing education organizations attempt both to anticipate and to respond to societal changes in their programming, it is commonplace for structural shifts to occur at departmental and other unit levels. Moreover, position and job descriptions will often require review and adjustment. Discrepancies indicated by the earlier cultural audit can assist leaders in making structural adjustments.

Another important item on the evaluation agenda for a continuing education leader is a study of the organization's systems. Simerly, Schmidt, Mueller, Walshok, and Votruba all emphasize in their chapters a systems approach to strategic planning and effective leadership. Systems approaches emphasize how the parts of the system and subsystem function in relation to inputs, processes, and outputs. Schoderbek, Schoderbek, and Kefalas (1985) have identified three major organizational inputs— people, materials and equipment, and money. These inputs are processed and result in three important outputs—products (goods and services), waste, and pollution. Therefore a leader's systems analysis will involve an examination of these three functions— inputting, processing, and outputting.

When a leader studies an organization, initial impressions are weighed against cumulative observations, conversations, and measurable data. Early in the assessment comes an identification and analysis of the organization's mission. By combining existing knowledge of the organization with the unique and new data obtained from a cultural audit, the leader gradually begins to build a vision for the future. To realize this vision, the leader will deploy a strategy. The strategy will contain decisions about reduction, stabilization, and growth for various facets of the organizational fabric.

Four environments must be addressed in formulating and evaluating a strategy for organizational management and leadership: (1) external socioeconomic conditions, (2) institutional conditions, (3) structural conditions, and (4) internal cultural conditions.

The organization is subject to a plethora of factors in its external environment that must be incorporated into the evaluation plan. Examples of such factors are local, state, and national economic conditions, population demographics, proximity and programming of competing organizations, political pressures and realities, and opportunities for multiinstitutional and agency partnerships. The external environment is, perhaps, the most dynamic and unpredictable of the four environments to be assessed.

The institutional environment is the official and formal setting in which the continuing education organization resides. In order to evaluate effectively the conditions in the parent organization, it is necessary to assess the mission of the institution and the role played by continuing education in achieving the overall mission. This includes an analysis of the parent organization's formal and informal perception of continuing education and its relationship to other units in the institution. The leader needs to evaluate the level of support from the parent institution and have a clear understanding of the priority placed by that institution on the continuing education organization. As Votruba notes in Chapter Eleven, continuing education will achieve centrality to the degree that it is seen as directly contributing to the mission and goals of the parent organization.

The structural environment is the formal environment imposed by rules and procedures, specified lines of communication, and officially designated tasks and duties. Evaluating the structural environment involves a thorough assessment of the official guidelines and regulations of the organization to determine their contribution to efficiency and productivity.

Evaluation of the cultural environment was discussed at length earlier in this chapter. It will, of course, be helpful for the leader to determine if the internal culture is healthy and strong. In addition, a determination needs to be made regarding the fit of this environment with the other three environments described above.

An examination of these four environments as components of a strategy for growth, stabilization, or reduction provides the major components for strategic evaluation. The chart in Figure 1

**Figure 1. Variables and Environments Helpful in Developing
a Cultural Audit.**

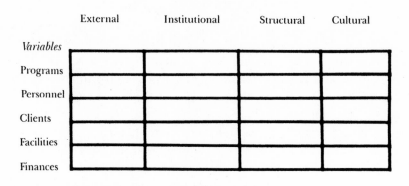

Organizational Environments

	External	Institutional	Structural	Cultural
Variables				
Programs				
Personnel				
Clients				
Facilities				
Finances				

Strategies to Consider Using in Each Cell
1. Reduction
2. Stabilization
3. Growth

illustrates the variables and environments helpful for the development of a cultural audit that is a critical part of strategic planning.

Using the grid to guide strategy formulation, a leader can analyze each cell to determine the appropriate strategy to use—reduction, stability, or growth. Once a leader has completed an audit and evaluated structures, systems, and strategies, he or she will be prepared to conduct a full management audit and diagnosis of the organization such as that suggested by Simerly in Chapter Four. This will enable the leader and staff to determine if and where changes should be initiated.

Intervening in Organizations. A small boy once asked, "Where do parades go?" A similar question can be asked about most evaluation findings. Most reports simply describe the recommendations that resulted from evaluation studies. Not much literature can be found describing what interventions or changes were planned on the basis of findings from evaluations. Occasionally action plans are derived from studies meant to be reviewed periodically as a means of monitoring changes and assessing improvements. However, these plans frequently are forgotten when the organization shifts its attention to more immediate concerns. Leadership becomes most effective when evaluation findings are not allowed to evaporate but instead are incorporated into the strategic planning system.

Leaders who intervene as a result of issues identified in evaluations begin developing strategies to orient their staffs toward change. As a part of this process, they also need to help provide everyone involved in changes with the needed knowledge, skills, and support. In addition, it is important to develop successful reward systems for engaging in change.

It is imperative that participants in an evaluation be made aware that the organization's leadership has taken the evaluation's findings under consideration. Leaders need to develop specific plans for conveying their intentions to act or not act on the evaluation findings. If evaluations are perceived to be nothing more than exercises, the respondents will eventually participate in them accordingly. The very process of evaluation, when appropriately managed, can be a beneficial intervention. The best evaluation processes demonstrate that leaders care about their organizations. Throughout the evaluation process, good leaders attempt to learn as much as possible about the people and operations with the goal of improving both of them.

Perhaps some evaluations will produce a Hawthorne effect; that is, performance and productivity will improve because staff members sense that someone is watching and caring. Good. The lesson for leaders here is: Keep watching and caring. Rosen's (1983) review of participants in one federal training program found that individuals were pleased to be contacted following training sessions. Staff met with them to talk about the implementation of their action plans. The procedure encouraged motivation to change and provided a way to assess change.

Designing, Conducting, and Interpreting Evaluations

Leaders who value the role of evaluations recognize that organizational assessments are most successful if they are underway constantly. Evaluations that are afterthoughts are of little value. Effective leaders learn the strengths and weaknesses of a range of methods—what to evaluate, how to evaluate to find out what they need to know, how to analyze findings, and, most importantly, what to do with the information found. They recognize the variety of domains they must consider when evaluating. These include attitudes, knowledge and information, performance, and societal and cultural changes.

The affective and cognitive types of evaluation are most common, probably because they are more easily designed, conducted, and interpreted. Performance and cultural change analyses, often called follow-up studies, are conducted less frequently and are generally more complicated, expensive, and difficult to interpret. Nonetheless, extrapolations from these latter types of studies are highly valuable for leadership. Of course, the best evaluation plans attempt to correlate affective, cognitive, and behavioral findings. However, caution must be advised in weighing affective and cognitive attitudinal findings too heavily. It is only an assumption that improved attitudes and competence will lead to improved performance. In fact, several studies have demonstrated an absence of correlation here (Del Bueno, 1976; Fielding, 1978; Glamser, 1981; Nemon, 1980; Smola, 1981).

Unfortunately, there are few models of evaluation plans designed to examine the full spectrum of audiences anticipated to experience changes from a particular program. But one such study involved a first-year assessment of Pennsylvania's Customized Job Training Program, conducted in 1983 (Nagy and Gregory, 1984). The key people and groups evaluated included clients (trainees), businesses and industries, local education agencies, local communities, and the commonwealth itself. The design of these evaluations, available in the written assessment, provides a useful illustration of methods that can be used to gain multiple perspectives on the same program. It is important to recognize that the perceptions of employees, sponsors, faculty, external service providers, and clients may not be congruent on certain issues. Evaluations that detect incongruencies among groups or individuals are valuable tools in determining flaws in the system under scrutiny. Misconceptions can be studied and decisions for action delineated on the basis of interpretations and judgments about these incongruencies.

Who should plan and design evaluations for a continuing education organization? A workable team of individuals representing all internal and external facets of the operation likely to be most directly affected by findings from a study should be used as a planning committee. The purpose of the committee should be to share information. Its members can assist the leader in the design, instrument selection, piloting, implementation, interpretation, and intervention phases of an evaluation process. Involving committee members in this way gives them an important stake in the results of the evaluation. Such a team can thus be useful in implementing the ideas for change that may result from the evaluation.

Issues such as the timing of evaluations, anonymity, and selection of quantitative and qualitative methods and procedures (for example, questionnaires, interviews, "opinionnaires," surveys, participant and nonparticipant observations, document analysis, audits, and case studies) can be resolved by this team of planners. Sudman and Bradburn's (1982) book, *Asking Questions,* is invaluable in its discussion of these and related issues when it has been decided that questionnaires are the best method for evaluation. In addition to guidance on such matters, they also provide detailed illustrations of questionnaire/survey instruments.

Utilizing Evaluations for Decision Making and Contingency Planning. Evaluations can provide leaders with valid reasons to continue, change, or terminate projects and programs. Information derived from evaluations can be used to compare a given organization to similar organizations, perhaps by system, state, region, or nationally. These comparisons are more easily conducted from quantitative evaluations, such as assessments of financial strategies and budgeting practices, although qualitative comparisons should be made when parallel information can be secured.

It is one thing to conduct an evaluation. It is something else entirely to use the findings for making decisions. Yet recommendations for program, personnel, and budget changes are more likely to receive attention and action when they are based on reliable evaluation data. Leaders consistently note that the continuing education environment is volatile and unpredictable. Often there is the fear that other social institutions are "getting into the business" and creating new competition. Funding can go up and down like a roller coaster, depending on general economic variables. Training and continuing education needs fluctuate constantly as a result of new technological developments. Separating momentary whims and fads from less risky, stable ventures requires sensitive evaluative procedures that constantly scan the environment.

If evaluations are ongoing, a leader will be fully prepared to act sensibly and fairly when sudden legislative or policy changes require reductions in spending or the setting of new directions. Decisions can be based on more knowns than unknowns. Accusations of poorly thought-out and subjective decision making can be diminished. The leader who has effectively monitored internal and external environments can explain a contingency plan based on identifiable and describable facts and conditions. Because a cultural evaluation is intact alongside the structural, systemic, and strategic evaluations, the leader is able to effectively anticipate and manage problems in the informal environment as decisions are made and courses of action altered.

Adjusting the Organization's Course. Staff support, interaction, and ongoing information need to be provided when change is underway. This helps give assurance to people. Staff often feel awkward, stressed, and generally uncomfortable with new methods, techniques, and technologies. Overt psychological support designed to demonstrate a genuine caring for staff is vital for long-range adoption of change. Lewin's (1958) studies in the late 1940s and 1950s on how individuals most effectively accommodate change remain worthy of consideration. He found that an organizational group rather than just individuals need to commit themselves to a particular change in order for it to succeed. Then a process that involves "unfreezing" of the old ways of doing things needs to be introduced. After the change has been made, time needs to be provided for "refreezing," that is, for adapting to the new behavior.

Organizations are dynamic operations, which means that decision making based upon ongoing monitoring of the internal and external environments is a prerequisite for survival. Evaluations are a primary monitoring and scanning tool. Findings may indicate the need for changes, assess impacts of continuing particular activities, and reinforce present strategies.

It is important to acclimate staff to evaluations. Explanations are helpful so that staff can better understand the purpose of evaluations, the procedures to be employed, the nature of their involvement, and potential outcomes. Oral presentations about evaluations with the employees directly affected, complemented with written descriptions of the process, are important to clarify and validate evaluation activities. Although findings from certain evaluations of personnel must respect individual rights, most other assessments should be available to everyone and should be openly discussed. If deficiencies and problems in the organization are felt and owned by people who view themselves as a team, staff members are most likely to work collectively toward solutions. A consistent and effective leader realizes that shortcomings revealed by evaluations do not devalue either the leader or staff. Rather such findings mean, "*We* have a challenge." There is nothing to be gained in shooting the messenger.

Kanter (1977) noticed in her interview study of organizational operations that effective leaders maximize their direct contact with staff. This is exceedingly important when reporting evaluation findings and after they are presented. Leaders assume responsibility for interpreting and acting on the findings at every level of their organizations and need to be directly available to respond to criticisms and questions from their staff. Staff want and need to know the good, the bad, and the ugly.

Sound evaluations enhance a leader's credibility. A careful reporting of evaluation findings needs to be made internally first to those most directly associated with the assessments, since organizational members may be embarrassed if outsiders have the inside scoop. When decisions are reported either internally or externally on the basis of "judgmental data," the leader should be extremely clear as to whether the judgments are based on absolute or relative standards. Absolute standards are developed for a specific purpose such as to determine acceptable levels of quality. Relative standards are created by comparing one program to other programs (Stake, 1970).

Evaluations, unfortunately, do not always conclude with positive findings. Why should they? They are constructed to measure and assess processes and people. Both are imperfect. Weaknesses, deficiencies, and flaws are as likely to surface as are strengths, efficiencies, and triumphs. Leaders must be aware of the potential for a negative backlash from evaluations if findings are not presented sensitively and cautiously. Evaluations involve risks. Evaluation results may be simultaneously positive and negative. Here the leader needs to become a role model who demonstrates strength of character by wanting to know the "truth" and what to do with it.

Written reports of evaluations are advised for both internal and external communication. Such reports should include an abstract or summary of the evaluation, background information, and a description of the evaluation process, along with its findings, conclusions, and recommendations. Information from evaluations can be presented in graphs and tables as well as in written reports. The main considerations for determining which format to use are the audience that will receive the report and the actions that will likely be generated by the findings. It is helpful if guidelines are developed for highlighting the key findings. Short sentences and paragraphs will make for more attentive reading. The most significant findings will have the greatest impact if they come at the beginning of the report, with auxiliary and supportive documentation conveniently arranged in appendixes.

Focusing Direction and Pacing the Organization with Evaluation Support. Bennis and Nanus (1985), in describing four leadership qualities they observed in a study of ninety American leaders, focus first on what they call management of attention. The leader, they suggest, is skilled at communicating intentions or a vision. This vision is not the outcome of crystal-ball gazing or some religious or mystical experience. Rather, it results from the leader's sense of what the organization's directions, goals, or outcomes should be. Evaluation findings can play an important role in shaping such a vision. When evaluations are conducted sometime after the initiation of new practices and programs the people evaluated are likely to identify needed changes or new procedures. Therefore, evaluations can determine if the organization is on course or off course and, if off, what is needed to reestablish direction.

By monitoring the four environments (external, institutional, structural, and cultural) simultaneously, a leader is better able to pace the work of the operation. Internal and external bottlenecks can be identified and circumvented or confronted depending on the political and practical feasibility of such actions. Evaluations can identify moments at which an activity or program can be initiated.

Shaping the Organization's Future: Leaders and Creative Evaluations

Proactive evaluations can anticipate and thereby help to prevent problems. Reactive evaluations, those developed as a result of organizational mishaps, are generally ineffective in determining precise causes of problems and are usually conducted too late to correct dysfunctions. At best, reactive evaluations provide some insight into whether preestablished objectives have been achieved. Sometimes an organization's view of itself is myopic, making it necessary to turn to external evaluators or auditors. For example, a continuing education leader may think that his or her organization is collaborating successfully with external groups when in fact it is not. An external examiner may be able to point out the gap between goals and actual performance.

Creative evaluation sometimes includes impromptu interviewing during coffee breaks, during individual and group debriefings, or while traveling to and from off-site programs with staff. Staff who trust and feel comfortable with their leaders may be more candid in these settings than in formal ones.

As budgets and schedules permit, staff can be encouraged to visit other continuing education organizations to make first-hand observations of and inquiries about the management of activities similar to their own. These comparisons provide an exemplary means of evaluating the situation back home. Prior to arranging for such visits, those who will represent the organization should meet with home staff to gain assistance in shaping inquiries and observations. Further, if those to be visited can be told in advance the type of information that the home staff is seeking, they can be ready to respond more effectively to concerns and deliver information more congruently to the needs of the visitors.

By evaluating staff members, programs and activities, the organizational culture, and the external and institutional environment, as well as structures, systems, and strategies, leaders find themselves able to transmit their vision to others. Evaluations initiated by leaders demonstrate their expectations to employees. They are proven and viable mechanisms for clarifying what a leader has concluded is most important for the organization.

Sound evaluation procedures that balance both formal and informal methods of assessment strengthen leadership in an organization. Findings from evaluations provide a logical and creditable foundation for decision making and strategic planning. Social scientists have sounded and resounded the alert that the public has become highly distrustful of its most traditional institutions. Accountability and confidence must be restored if our social institutions are to maintain their vitality. The analysis and utilization of well-constructed evaluation plans and procedures can be important activities for increasing accountability in continuing education. Leaders know better than anyone else the mission and effectiveness of their organizations. Developing strategic plans to communicate this to the multiple publics served by continuing education is an important priority for effective leadership.

✥ 11 ✥

From Marginality to Mainstream:

Strategies for Increasing Internal Support for Continuing Education

JAMES C. VOTRUBA

Think for a moment about the variety of organizational settings in which continuing education agencies can be found: corporations, colleges and universities, schools, hospitals, governmental agencies, museums, churches, and many others. As diverse as these settings are, however, they generally have one characteristic in common. None of them views the continuing education of adults as its primary organizational mission. In most cases, these organizations look upon continuing education as a subordinate activity that is valued to the extent that it contributes to more central organizational purposes. Herein lies an unavoidable two-pronged challenge for continuing education leaders. They must guide their agencies to serve their adult student constituency while they also work to build and maintain support within their own parent organizations on whom their very existence depends. It is this process of building internal organizational support that is the subject here.

My approach to building organizational support for continuing education is guided by several assumptions that I make about how organizations function and what they value. The first of these is that organizations seek above all else to maintain their own survival and well-being (Katz and Kahn, 1978). All aspects of organizational life are intended to serve this most important of purposes. While traditions, policies, procedures, and products are all important, they achieve their importance in terms of their contribution to the organization's continued viability. In short, every element of an organization serves as a means to the ultimate organizational objective of continued existence and well-being. This is true for every subunit within an organization, each of which may also have goals or ends of its own. For example, a continuing education agency that is part of a larger parent organization will define its essential purpose as serving adult learning needs. However, the larger parent organization will evaluate the serving of these needs in terms of its contribution to the organization's own survival and well-being.

Dynamics of Organizational Survival and Adaptation

Organizational survival and well-being are accomplished by means of continual adaptation to external environmental change (March and Simon, 1958; Roeber, 1973; Katz and Kahn, 1978; Pfeffer and Salancik, 1978; Drucker, 1980; Keller, 1983). Shifts in such areas as consumer demands, lifestyle patterns, economic conditions, demographic trends, or state and federal laws and regulations can prompt major adaptations in the organization itself. Accordingly, a primary responsibility of an organization's top management is to monitor the organization's external environment and interpret changes that may represent organizational threats or opportunities. The ultimate test of success in any organization is how wisely and how quickly it is able to respond to these external threats and opportunities. For example, in recent years hospitals have had to adapt to changes in third-party payments. Airlines have had to adapt to deregulation. Universities and colleges have had to adapt to declining birthrates and shifting migration patterns. Computer companies have had to adapt to new technologies. And auto makers have had to adapt to increased foreign competition.

If top management wishes to establish a dynamic organization capable of adapting to the external pressures of the marketplace, constant monitoring and environmental scanning is required. This is true in every organization, inluding those in which continuing education agencies function. Keller (1983) argues that strategic planning concentrates on the fate of the organization above all else. Top management in all organizations develops priorities on the basis of their perception of what it will take to guarantee the organization's continued vitality.

If the primary objective of all organizations is to survive and prosper through constant adaptation, then subunits within the organization, including the continuing education agency, will achieve organizational support and centrality to the extent that they are seen as contributing to this fundamental organizational priority. Continuing education administrators can frequently be heard bemoaning their organizational marginality as if this condition were somehow unique to them. This simply is not the case. Continuing education agencies are not treated as organizationally marginal *because* they are continuing education agencies. Rather, their relative degree of centrality or marginality is based on the perceived contribution that they make to broader institutional purposes. This is true not only for continuing education but for every other organizational subunit as well.

Top management in all organizations supports those subunits that are perceived to be most important in meeting the organization's current priorities. Furthermore, the status of organizational subunits tends to rise and fall as forces in the organization's external environment shift, causing changes in organizational priorities to occur. For example, today in many colleges and universities, the admissions office has achieved increased centrality and receives more abundant resources than in the past because of the increasingly heated competition for the best students from a steadily shrinking pool. The engineering and physical science disciplines have become more crucial to institutional survival than the social sciences, as student interests and employment opportunities have shifted in recent years. The point is that organizational support is given to those subunits that are perceived to be serving essential organizational priorities.

Thus the challenge for continuing education leaders, as for the leaders of all other organizational subunits, seems clear. They must relate their activities to the essential priorities of their parent organization if they are to achieve organizational support and centrality. If this is true, then continuing education agencies serve two fundamental and equally important constituencies. They serve adult students, on whom they depend for their credit and noncredit enrollments, and they also serve their parent organization, which they depend on for staffing, budget, program approval, and, ultimately, their existence. To lose touch with either constituency is to court disaster. There are numerous examples of continuing education programs that lost touch with their adult students and were eventually destroyed by the competition of the marketplace. However, there are also numerous examples of programs that successfully served adults but operated at such a distance from their parent organizations that they gradually lost support and were either eliminated or altered beyond recognition. In such cases, other organizational units generally picked up those functions that had been assigned to continuing education.

Our continuing education field has done an excellent job of describing the process of serving adult learner needs. Today, there are hundreds of exciting books and articles that offer insights into needs assessment, program development, marketing, administration, and evaluation. However, there is far less information available to help leaders link their continuing education priorities to the priorities of their parent organization. This process requires the development of special knowledge, of skills, and of approaches that are rooted in the assumptions that I have just discussed.

We turn now to an example of how continuing education programs and professional skills can be used to support broader organizational priorities.

Five Challenges Facing Continuing Higher Education

In his seminal book *Academic Strategy: The Management Revolution in American Higher Education,* Keller writes, "Every meeting of campus presidents these days is choked with exchanges about financial constriction, declining enrollments, and survival" (1983, p. 3.). Indeed, experts predict that up to 30 percent of America's colleges and universities will either close or merge by 1995. There is consensus among students of higher education that the task of managing colleges and universities today is far more complex than ever before (Cameron, 1984). In large part this is due to the increasing complexity and turbulence of the external environment combined with the fact that colleges and universities have less slack for dealing with environmental pressures.

The result is that college and university presidents face a bewildering array of forces that must be constantly monitored and assessed in term of institutional impact. These forces include changing state and federal funding policies, shifts in birthrates and population migration patterns, changes in economic conditions at the local, state, and regional level, shifting employment patterns, and the increasingly aggressive behavior of other educational providers. Cameron (1984) suggests that the challenge for higher education administrators will be to ensure institutional strength and adaptability in a postindustrial environment characterized by turbulence, information overload, rapid-fire events, and increasingly complex and interrelated problems that must be addressed. The challenge to campus administrators is further heightened by the loosely coupled nature of the institutions themselves (Weick, 1976). Departmental units resist changes imposed from above, as well as efforts to involve them in the overall institutional planning process. The result is that institutional planning is often difficult to accomplish. No wonder so many college presidents report that the rewards of the job are far outweighed by the difficulties and stress.

Many of the challenges that currently confront higher education, however, also offer unique opportunities for continuing education initiative. Let us examine several of them.

Challenge One. Higher education is currently faced with the challenge of shifting demographics and a changing student population. States such as New York and Pennsylvania have experienced a 30 percent decline in their secondary school population, and this same precipitous drop can be seen in many other states in the Midwest and Northeast (Hodgkinson, 1985). At the same time, populations are growing in the Sun Belt states. Today, the most rapidly growing population of college students consists of adult part-time learners (Cross, 1985). The enrollment of part-time students between twenty-five and thirty-four years of age increased by 27 percent in the past five years. For those over thirty-five, the increase was 44 percent. More than one-third of all college students are now twenty-five or older, and nearly 75 percent of these attend college part-time. Between 1982 and 1992, the National Center for Education Statistics (1985) projects a 15 percent drop in the number of full-time college students.

Higher education's current struggle to adapt to larger numbers of adult and part-time learners offers extraordinary opportunities for continuing education leadership. Recruitment and retention of able adult learners require new approaches to educational marketing as well as new curricular and instructional approaches. These students also require a broad range of new student support services. No one on campus can better understand the adult learner than continuing education staff members. They can assist their campuses to develop sophisticated marketing strategies based on their knowledge of what motivates adults to attend college. They can assist deans, department heads, and faculty to adapt their curricula as well as their teaching styles to accommodate the interests and needs of adult learners. They can work with the campus to reorient student support services such as the counseling office, academic advising, and the career development center, to better serve the needs of this new student population. They can recommend and help design new support services, such as the day-care facilities that are needed by many adult learners. To the extent that a college or university views the education of adults as an important strategy to help guarantee its future, continuing education leaders can take part in guiding this transition and generate greater institutional support in the process.

Challenge Two. A second major challenge confronting colleges and universities is the problem of insufficient resources to support the campus mission. There is little doubt that the federal era is over for higher education. As a consequence, states are being increasingly pressed to pick up the slack in funding. But this comes at a time when competition for funds at the state level has never been more intense. The result is that higher education leaders must become more and more aggressive in the fight to obtain funds if they are even to maintain the status quo. And, in fact, both public and private higher education can expect very little increased financial support for the foreseeable future. The challenge will be to generate alternative income sources that can be used to augment insufficient state allocations.

Self-generated resources will become increasingly important to fund faculty professional travel, finance curriculum development, support junior faculty research, pay for student and faculty receptions, and generally support those activities that enhance the quality of academic life. On the campuses of both public and private institutions, deans and department heads are being pressed to become more efficient managers and more aggressive and creative educational entrepreneurs. These are activities that most academics are ill prepared to pursue. As a consequence, continuing education leaders are presented with another opportunity to link their programs and skills to an important institutional agenda.

Continuing education professionals are trained by both education and experience to be educational entrepreneurs in the best sense of the term. The world of needs assessment, program development, marketing, pricing, budget building, contract writing, and program evaluation is familiar territory for continuing educators. Often, however, these activities strike fear in the hearts of academics. Generally speaking, academics are not trained to be student or market sensitive. Rather, they are educated in graduate school to be discipline or subject centered, and it is this orientation that they bring with them when they become administrators. Continuing educators have the skills that many deans and department chairs need. By working closely with academic administrators, continuing education leaders can help them explore new areas for both credit and noncredit programs and then develop strategic plans for taking advantage of these areas. In doing so, the continuing education agency will become an essential partner in responding to one of the most important challenges facing campuses in the 1980s.

Challenge Three. A third major challenge confronting higher education is what Keller (1983) calls the "faculty conundrum." Nothing is so important to colleges and universities as the strength and vitality of their faculties. In the 1960s, thousands of new faculty members were hired to teach the hordes of baby boom students who flocked to our campuses. Today, these same faculty are twenty years older, and many have been on the same campus for their entire professional lives. Some estimates suggest that by 1990, 35 percent of faculty members will be fifty-five or older.

Eighty percent will be tenured. Most will have little opportunity for mobility. Given these circumstances, how does a campus maintain the morale of faculty members and provide them with opportunities for renewal and continuing growth?

Again, continuing education has a role to play in confronting this difficult institutional challenge. Historically, collegiate continuing education has represented a testing ground for new approaches in higher education. New curricula, new courses, new instructional methods, and the use of new technologies have all had their genesis in continuing education, and the same should hold true today. Continuing education holds out an opportunity for faculty renewal by exposing them to new types of students who bring different needs and expectations to the classroom. New instructional formats and teaching modes can be explored in both noncredit and credit areas. Those continuing education agencies that generate excess income can establish faculty development grants that encourage faculty to become involved with adult learners. The point is that continuing education can represent an important element in the renewal of campus faculty.

Challenge Four. Certainly one of the largest and most complex challenges facing higher education is to apply its research, teaching, and service capabilities to the economic revitalization of the nation. Higher education's public support has historically depended upon the extent to which it is perceived to be serving the public interest. Today, in Washington, D.C., and in state capitals throughout the nation, public policy makers are struggling with ways to revitalize our economy so that we can compete effectively in the world marketplace. Higher education is being called upon to contribute to this effort. In one large Midwestern industrial state, the governor has charged the state university to become a full partner in forging the state's economic recovery. The university's role will involve helping to educate a modern work force, developing and transferring new technologies, assisting in the development of new economic legislation, and collaborating with other agencies and institutions to improve education, health care, transportation, and other quality of life indices that help attract new business and industry. Gordon Mueller provides a comprehensive analysis of these ideas in

Chapter Eight in describing a systems approach that can be used for linking continuing education to community development and economic impact. Higher education cannot afford to walk away from this challenge. The strength of its response will help determine its level of public support for the remainder of this century.

Higher education's contribution to economic revitalization will rest in large measure on its ability to offer both interdisciplinary and applied programs. It will require the creative assessment of educational needs based on the projected work force demands of the future. It will require the development of new, preservice and in-service educational programs that draw from a variety of disciplines and professional fields. It will require new approaches to instructional delivery, including the use of advanced technology and self-directed learning formats. It will require new conceptual and operational approaches to technology transfer and new collaborative relationships with business and industry. It will require the formation of interdisciplinary teams of scholars and practitioners to analyze the multitude of complex and interrelated issues that influence economic renewal. It will require that academics develop a new set of educational values and attitudes beginning with the needs of the learner. It will require short-cutting the often cumbersome bureaucracy of the campus in order to provide creative and quick responses to educational needs. These are not traditional strengths of most colleges and universities, but they are the skills that help define the continuing education profession. Higher education's challenge to contribute to economic revitalization offers continuing education leaders a special opportunity to apply their knowledge and skills to an issue that touches the entire institution.

Challenge Five. A related challenge facing higher education is the increasing pressure to build public support, particularly at the state level (Jonson, 1984). This challenge has become greater as the federal government has reduced its commitment, thus increasing higher education's dependence on state revenues at a time when there is a proliferation of competing demands for these resources. Academic leaders are fond of talking about the importance of their institution's work for the future of humankind.

Governors and state legislators, however, are more heavily influenced by the tangible contributions that an institution can make to the state. At budget hearings, legislators want to know what colleges and universities are doing to alleviate the problems of their districts. This pressure to demonstrate tangible contributions to the state provides another opportunity for continuing education leaders to assist their institutions and thereby strengthen their own roles. For example, the continuing education agency can produce an annual report that specifies the institution's statewide impact. Such a report might break down enrollments and special public service activities by legislative district. It might stress projects that have special appeal for key governmental leaders.

Continuing education leaders have a special opportunity to provide their campus chief executive officer with data that can be used to demonstrate the commitment and contribution of the campus to the state. They can, for example, collect and assemble data on continuing education and public service activities. In addition, continuing education leaders can work with their campus executives to develop programs that help inform the public policy process. For many years, the Southern Regional Education Board has conducted annual legislative work conferences for legislators and their staff from sixteen Southern states. These conferences have been designed to help inform public policy makers about issues facing higher education and to influence legislation to address them. There is no reason why this same process cannot be employed by continuing educators.

I have touched on several major issues that confront higher education and the opportunities that they present for strategic planning and effective continuing education leadership. Specific issues will, of course, vary from campus to campus. The point is that continuing education leaders who seek to build campus support can do so by linking their programs and priorities to the challenges confronting the larger institution. In so doing, they can become important players in helping to ensure the stability and vitality of their campus in a time of substantial stress and uncertainty.

These examples have focused on higher education, but the setting could just as easily have been corporations, hospitals, schools, government agencies, churches, or other kinds of organizations in which continuing education is a subunit. In all settings the challenge is the same—to build continuing education support by linking its agenda to the priorities that drive the larger organization as it continually attempts to adapt to its external environment.

Implications for Strategic Planning

The assumption that continuing education agencies must serve both the needs of their adult learners and the needs of their parent organization has important implications for the planning process. Traditional approaches to planning suffer from several shortcomings. First, they often assume a rational world in which plans can be based solely on logic. Second, they often take place in a vacuum, with little or no attention to the external forces that are likely to shape an organization's direction. Third, the planning process often becomes so lengthy and complicated that it loses much of its meaning. Fourth, planning too often takes place apart from the process of decision making. Finally, in traditional planning approaches, the process too often becomes more important than the results. How often have long-range plans for continuing education been produced, celebrated, and then left on the shelf to collect dust as administrators return to the real world in which decisions must constantly be made in response to everyday crises.

In recent years, the concept of strategic planning has been used to emphasize that most key factors that shape an organization's long-range destiny occur in the external environment. The central focus of strategic planning is developing a good fit between the organization's activities and the demands of the surrounding environment. Strategic planning places major emphasis on flexibility, adaptability, and quick response to external environmental changes. It involves key organizational decision makers in continually assessing changes in the external world that may present new hazards or opportunities (Cyert, 1983). Strategic planning is a continual process, not an event. It is also a state of mind that creates in decision makers a particular sensitivity to those forces in the surrounding world that are likely to influence their destiny.

While they may not always call it "strategic planning," many continuing education agencies engage in such planning as it relates to the constantly changing world of adult learning needs. Indeed, most continuing educators are continually assessing programmatic opportunities or threats that result from changes in their external world. Nevertheless, there is little evidence that continuing educators apply this same strategic process to their interaction with their parent organizations. For the continuing education agency, strategic planning means maintaining a strong fit between its activities and the needs of both the adult learner market and the parent organization. Strategic planning can help identify initiatives that serve both worlds.

Importance of Environmental Scanning. The process of strategic planning depends upon the availability of accurate and relevant data from the organization's environment. Hearn and Heydinger (1985) suggest that the ideal organization scans its environment in general, selects certain key environmental issues, trends, and domains for concentrated tracking, and feeds useful information into its ongoing strategic decision making. This process of environmental scanning can take many forms, some more comprehensive than others. Tichy (1983) describes "radar scanning" as a quick overview of the organization's environment to identify potential hazards and opportunities. This kind of scanning can be a regular component of continuing education staff meetings in which staff take twenty to thirty minutes to identify quickly or update developments that they feel may have implications for the organization. Using this scanning process regularly will help sensitize continuing education staff to the importance of monitoring their environment.

For the continuing education agency, environmental scanning must include both the parent organization and the adult learner market. Thus environmental scanning might identify developments such as new learner needs; new initiatives by other educational providers; new economic, political, and demographic trends; new funding opportunities; state and federal policy shifts in regard to education; campus enrollment trends; changes in faculty promotion and tenure guidelines; new administrative and faculty appointments; new priorities and trends in particular academic units; and general assessments of campus mood and morale. Radar scanning provides a powerful tool for focusing on the total environment and utilizing intuition and instinct, as well as data, to extrapolate meaning for continuing education.

While radar scanning provides a quick overview of the organization's environment, the next step is to sort out those issues, trends, and domains that are deserving of in-depth attention. This process of focused diagnosis sometimes leads to the formation of problem-solving teams that are assigned responsibility for developing a strategy to address significant environmental hazards or opportunities. For example, soon after arriving as dean of General Studies and Professional Education at the State University of New York at Binghamton in 1983, my staff and I were scanning several sectors of the environment that influence our recruitment of adult students. We looked at New York's demographic trends, and we identified increased recruitment efforts by other institutions in what we had defined as our primary recruitment market. While we were not at that time experiencing enrollment problems, we determined that the shrinking student pool was going to increase the competition and that we needed to anticipate this development or risk a decline in our enrollment. A problem-solving team was assembled to look at our current market segmentation, potential new student markets, the marketing approaches of our competitors, and the reasons that students enroll in our programs. The result was a new and more aggressive marketing strategy that fit the new conditions that we had found. This same problem-solving process can be used in any organization for any major environmental hazard or opportunity that scanning uncovers.

Utilizing Integrative Thinking. Strategic planning is more likely to occur in organizations that encourage what Kanter (1983) refers to as "integrative thinking." Integrative thinking is the willingness to move beyond conventional wisdom, to synthesize ideas from a variety of sources, to see change as opportunity, and to see problems integratively and in relation to larger worlds.

Integrative thinking involves thinking holistically, not in small segments. It involves making connections between your particular organization and the complex external world on which it depends. Integrative thinking is not likely to occur in organizations that are highly segmented and enjoy little or no interaction among divisions.

This kind of thinking requires the support of an integrative organizational culture and structure. For continuing education agencies this means that staff be given regular opportunities to move beyond their particular responsibilities and think more globally. Regular exercises in environmental scanning can provide such an opportunity. In addition, it must be clear that the agency values integrative thinking and problem solving and rewards it in performance appraisals. Integrative organizations reduce conflict and isolation between subunits. They create mechanisms for the effective exchange of information and ideas, ensure that multiple perspectives are considered in the decision-making process, and reinforce the values of collegiality and collective problem solving. Above all, integrative organizations stay in touch with their environments and use the information thereby gained in the strategic planning process.

Integrating Strategic Planning and Effective Leadership. While there is no universally agreed on definition for that illusive concept *leadership,* most people would agree that leaders are important to all forms of human progress. Cronin (1984) suggests that leaders are individuals who create options and opportunities. They clarify problems and choices and build morale and inspire action. Leaders provide a vision of a better organization, community, or society. Leaders have the indispensable characteristics of self-confidence, optimism, and idealism that allow them to mobilize others to undertake demanding tasks.

Leaders serve to empower others so that they too can become leaders. Leaders are people who believe so much in themselves and their purposes that they persist in their objectives in spite of the difficulties they confront. Leaders possess a breadth of understanding that allows them to fashion strategies based on a coherent view of the world. They act today in ways that are consistent with a studied view of the future. They are men and women of vision who can link that vision to the reality of everyday decision making. Leaders of this kind do not necessarily occupy positions of formal power in organizations or society. They can emerge anywhere there is a need or an opportunity for them.

To build internal organizational support for continuing education requires leadership of a particular sort. The strength and vitality of any continuing education agency rest on its ability to serve both the needs of adult learners and the needs of its parent organization. If this is true, then it follows that continuing education leaders must understand and be able to relate to both of these worlds and recognize where they intersect.

I am often impressed by how much continuing education leaders know about serving adult learning needs and how little they know about their own parent organization. Understanding one's parent organization comes from studying it and being a part of it. What is its history? Why has it evolved into its present form? What are its traditions? What characterizes its culture and values? What is its reward system? How does it function? Who are the informal as well as formal organizational leaders? How are decisions made? Who is involved in making them? What are the organization's priorities and needs? What are the most immediate problems confronting key decision makers? One learns the answers to these questions by being part of the organization, not by sitting on the sidelines. Continuing education leaders must take every opportunity to participate in the life of their parent organization.

Knowledge of the parent organization must include insight into the external forces that are shaping its future. Top managers in any organization spend much of their time managing the interface between the organization and its external environment. They are what Katz and Kahn (1978) call "boundary spanners" and what Schön (1971) calls "external linkers." The external orientation of the continuing education enterprise provides an opportunity for its leaders to assist leaders of the parent organization in this boundary-spanning process. By continually assessing shifts and trends in the external environment and their implications for the parent organization, continuing education leaders can help other organizational leaders shape a view of the organization's future and the role of continuing education in helping to achieve it. In this sense, continuing education leaders have the opportunity to become leaders in the larger organizational setting.

Building Internal Organizational Support

Beyond development of this knowledge base, there are several principles that I would recommend to continuing education leaders who want to build internal organizational support for continuing education:

First, involve your parent organization in the development of your programmatic priorities. Identify informal and formal leaders and involve them in your planning process. Develop in them a sense of ownership of your mission.

Second, always relate your continuing education mission to that of the broader organization. Show how your mission addresses the priorities and needs of your parent organization. Show how your mission is compatible with the larger organization's traditions and values. Indeed, wrap your initiatives in these traditions and values.

Third, when trying to gain the support of a particular group or individual, approach them from the perspective of their world, not yours. Demonstrate how their support can help accomplish some of their objectives as well as your own.

Fourth, market yourself internally. Make it clear to other units within the larger organization, as well as to the leadership of the organization itself, that continuing education can make unique contributions to the institution.

Fifth, take every opportunity to create and support a continuing education staff and organizational climate characterized by integrative thinking and the constant flow of new ideas. Utilize staff in environmental scanning to help anticipate the future. Spend money on staff development that fosters breadth of thinking and familiarity with the worlds in which your continuing education agency must function.

Finally, create a sense of vision. Do not underestimate your ability to contribute creative responses to the threats and opportunities that confront your parent organization. By contributing to the development of creative responses to pressing organizational needs, you will help shape the organization's future and continuing education's place in it.

Achieving Success in Strategic Planning:

A Practical Road Map for Continuing Education Leaders

ROBERT G. SIMERLY

This book has examined ways to enhance leadership effectiveness through strategic planning. The contributing authors are all practitioner-scholars in the field of continuing education and training and development. All of them have developed a strong conceptual base to guide their daily planning activities and decision making. Their insights are based on their successes and failures in constantly testing theory in relation to the actual daily problems they face in their leadership roles.

An analysis of the ideas presented by these authors reveals that the following twelve issues are important in developing a practical road map for strategic planning and effective leadership:

1. *How can we function effectively as leaders in organizational climates of increasing ambiguity, complexity, diversity, uncertainty, and decentralization?* In the future, leaders will have to cope with increased complexity. They will have to deal with increasingly diverse publics. They will have to deal with increased levels of ambiguity and uncertainty in daily problem solving and decision making. They will have to give away power through decentralization of decision making. Meeting these challenges will demand new sets of assumptions as a basis for developing new leadership skills (Boyatzis, 1982; Kanter, 1983; Fiedler and Chemers, 1984; Geneen and Moscow, 1984; Drucker, 1985).

Traditional models of the leader as hero are not adequate for the challenge facing today's leaders. Leaders in the future will increasingly have to give up heroic models of leadership and the assumptions underlying them. Instead they will have to become developers of people and of problem-solving teams. They will need to concentrate on coaching and counseling in order to help staff members define for themselves a concept of continual professional development and self-renewal.

Bennis and Nanus (1985) have identified four skills necessary to strengthen organizational leadership: (1) creating focus and gaining attention through vision, (2) creating meaning through communication, (3) developing trust through positioning, and (4) developing self through positive self-regard. Thus effective leaders move beyond the administrative aspects of their roles and become statespersons for the organizations they represent. In this statesperson role they create a consensus for visions that require dynamic organizational cultures. They are attuned to the importance of establishing procedures to ensure the continued development and self-renewal of people. Such leaders are future oriented, and yet they are also oriented toward producing results today.

A unifying theme of all the chapters in this volume is that it is essential for continuing education leaders to engage in strategic long-range planning, the development of dynamic organizational cultures, and the management of conflict. All the contributing authors emphasize the importance of developing these skills if leaders are to become organizational statespersons.

2. *How can we engage in systems analysis and environmental scanning as an effective method for strengthening leadership?* Today's literature places an important emphasis on using systems approaches to strengthen organizational leadership (Cohen and Cohen, 1984; Bradford and Cohen, 1984; Argyris, Putnam, and Smith, 1985; Bennis, Benne, and Chin, 1985; Pennings and Associates, 1985).

Kast and Rosenzweig (1979) provide an excellent discussion of the history of systems analysis. It first began to be used after the Second World War with the building of the Polaris submarine. Later it was used by the Ford Motor Company in building the highly successful Mustang automobile in 1964. Thus industry first began to use systems analysis as a mechanical tool for breaking down complex jobs into their component parts so that deadlines could be established for the completion of each component part.

Von Bertalanffy (1950, 1952) introduced the concept of systems analysis in physics and biology. From the physical and biological sciences, systems analysis thinking migrated to the social sciences so that by the 1970s organizational writers were using systems analysis as a method for organizational analysis. During the 1980s, systems analysis has become a concept commonly used by behavioral scientists in tackling complex problems that are characterized by high levels of ambiguity and uncertainty (Tannenbaum, Margulies, Massarik, and Associates, 1985).

The contributing authors all emphasize the necessity for leaders to engage in systems analysis and environmental scanning in order to become effective in picking up the subtle cues that affect problem solving and decision making. For example, in Chapter Nine, Mary Walshok demonstrates that systems analysis and environmental scanning are prerequisites for developing a strategic marketing plan. Gordon Mueller in Chapter Eight explains how the creation of advisory councils can assist in these efforts. Margaret Holt, James Votruba, Michael Offerman, and John Schmidt all use systems analysis and environmental scanning as integral parts of their analysis of continuing education leadership.

3. *How can we create dynamic organizations that emphasize the needs of the individual and the organization?* The traditional mechanistic model of organizations in the industrial era has been replaced by organizational models more appropriate to a cybernetic era in which access to information becomes knowledge that in turn translates into power to accomplish tasks. Increased decentralization of decision making to individuals and teams of people who have the knowledge necessary to make the best possible decisions is a reality in today's complex organizations. Traditional models of work that consider individuals primarily in mechanistic or economic terms have been replaced by organizational effectiveness models that emphasize the importance of creating a working environment in which the needs of both individuals and organization can be met. No longer are these needs

seen as conflicting or mutually exclusive (Argyris, 1964; Schein, 1978; Lippitt, 1982).

4. *How can we understand and utilize the complexities of power and authority so that we can be more effective in our leadership roles?* Reaching consensus on criteria for the use of power and influence within organizations is an important issue (Schein, 1985). Groups give people the ability to use power and influence to achieve goals. However, they can also take away this power and influence and render individuals ineffective. Understanding how groups use power and influence is central to strategic planning and effective leadership because leaders spend so much of their time managing these dynamics in getting work done (Kennedy, 1984; Kotter, 1985).

Increasingly, leaders in today's organizations have to rely on their skills at persuasion rather than on the exercise of formal authority. Mary Parker Follett, one of the early organizational theorists, called this the *law of the situation* (Follett, 1941). It was her thesis that the person with the most expertise in relation to a particular problem should be the leader of the team attempting to solve that problem, regardless of what formal leadership position the person held in the organization. Theobald (1963) refers to this as *sapential authority*. Toffler (1971) uses the term *adhocracy* to explain this same idea. An adhocracy is a temporary work group that is formed to do a specific job. Such a work group is led by the person with the most expertise, and after the task has been accomplished, the work group or adhocracy is disbanded.

Power is the ability to get things done in an organization. Authority is the formal mechanism by which the organization bestows on an individual the responsibility for supervision. An old organizational adage says that you can delegate authority but you cannot delegate power. Power to get things done does not necessarily depend on the possession of formal authority. Rather it depends on expertise, persuasion, and having individuals and work groups give you the right, or power, to engage in leadership (Winter, 1973; Yankelovich, 1981). Barnard (1938) called this the act of *upward delegation*. Tarr (1985) has illustrated how these upward delegation principles operate in a continuing education organization.

Because of the increasingly sophisticated nature of the work force, people want to take an active part in defining goals and objectives for the organization and in achieving these goals and objectives. With this increased level of competence has come an increased ability to solve problems at all organizational levels. Therefore more and more people have been empowered to get work done and accept responsibility for problem solving. The result is that leaders in today's complex organizations can only be successful if they allow people at all levels to *delegate upwards*, to use Barnard's term. This diminishes the use of formal authority as a compliance mechanism and increases the use of informal persuasion and expertise as the primary source of power (McCall, 1978; Pfeffer, 1981; Powers and Powers, 1983; and Yankelovich, 1983). Leadership styles in organizations must be geared to these changing concepts of power and authority. As Schmidt demonstrates in Chapter Three, effective leaders must concentrate on building bridges, not walls, in all their daily contacts.

5. *How can we manage conflict for productive organizational results?* Chapter Seven, entitled "Managing Organizational Conflict: An Important Process in Strategic Planning," provides an excellent summary of the function of conflict in organizations. Cooperation and competition are concepts at opposite ends of a continuum. However, cooperation and competition are also two sides of the same coin when it comes to analyzing organizational issues. They both exist simultaneously within all group problem-solving situations. They form parts of the *problematique* or *gestalt* of problem solving. Conflict accompanies all organizational change. When managed for productive results, such conflict is transformed into the energy required by individuals to make changes in the organization (Robert, 1982; Blake and Mouton, 1984).

Effective conflict managers constantly examine the assumptions and values from which they operate. They engage in the type of introspection that enables them to reach an accommodation with their self-identity, their individual needs, and the needs of the organization. Effective conflict managers establish flexible behavior patterns that lead them to view leadership in situational terms. This approach emphasizes the development of a wide repertoire of skills. As a first step in each new situation, these managers engage in systems analysis and environmental scanning in order to access the complex variables affecting the situation. The next step is to use their repertoire of leadership skills and choose a set of responses and behaviors that are appropriate to the dynamics affecting the task (Hersey and Blanchard, 1977).

Francis Trusty's chapter on conflict management identifies the following nine skills as important for continuing education leaders: (1) the ability to listen; (2) the ability to provide both positive and negative feedback as an integral part of problem solving; (3) the ability to conceptualize as a way of depersonalizing conflict situations; (4) the ability to analyze the nature of conflict; (5) the ability to confront people and problems in ways that reduce defensiveness and concentrate on problem solving; (6) the ability to remain flexible and resourceful in considering alternative strategies and decisions; (7) the ability to accept the arguments of another person and see the world from his or her point of view; (8) the ability to use formal procedures such as negotiation, compromise, grievance procedures, and arbitration; and (9) the ability to use such techniques as the nominal group process and the Delphi technique to solicit alternative points of view during problem solving.

6. *How can we enhance our ability to manage agreement and reach consensus?* Cooperation is necessary if an organization is to achieve its goals. And yet when people cooperate on tasks conflict often results. The management of these conflicts for productive results is an important leadership issue. And of equal importance to the issue of conflict management is the ability to manage agreement and reach consensus. While much research has been done on conflict management, we are just beginning to address the necessity for becoming skillful at managing agreement and reaching consensus. This is an important leadership skill that increasingly will be required for continuing education leaders if they are to assume the role of statespersons for their organizations.

We have much to learn about the management of agreement because many of our leadership models encourage the assumption that organizational problem solving is always built on a zero-sum game of scarce resources (Botkin, Dimancescu, State, and McClellan, 1982). This encourages win-lose situations. However, the possibility for increasing win-win situations is enhanced when agreement rather than disagreement is emphasized. This usually necessitates an entirely new set of assumptions on the part of the leader. The *gestalt* or *problematique* is to create situations in which people can constantly engage in organizational renewal by creating new resources rather than spending undue time squabbling over the distribution of the existing scarce resources.

Organizational resources do not always have to be part of a zero-sum game that emphasizes that the glass is half empty. Rather the management of agreement and consensus building emphasizes the fact that the glass is half full and that through creative, cooperative problem solving new ways can be found to enlarge and renew the organization's resources. As Schmidt demonstrates in Chapter Three, strategic long-range planning is an effective way to build bridges of agreement with internal and external constituencies.

7. *How can we encourage people and our organizations to engage in constant self-renewal?* In today's fast-paced world, where the rate of change is constantly accelerating, people and organizations need to develop effective methods that will ensure their ability to engage in constant self-renewal. This ability to create structures, processes, and environments that encourage self-renewal is an important leadership skill (Gardner, 1981). Self-renewing organizations create an internal dynamic and vitality that enables individuals and the organization to meet their needs. In fact, accommodation patterns in such organizations make it possible to view these two sets of needs as compatible rather than opposing (Golembiewski, 1972; Lippitt, 1982; Lippitt, Langseth, and Mossop, 1985; Boyatzis, 1982; Bradford and Cohen, 1984).

Several of the authors have directly addressed this issue. In Chapter Five Offerman examines the leader's role in influencing continuing education programming. By taking part in this program development role rather than simply administering policy developed by others, leaders can achieve the kind of self-renewal that comes from constantly defining new goals and directions within the organization. Chapter Four shows how the organization can build in a structure and process for this self-renewal through periodically conducting a management audit of the health of the organization. The chapter presents a practical, easy-to-use model for conducting such a management audit. Decision rules and guidelines are identified to assist in implementing the model.

Walshok's chapter on developing a strategic marketing plan also deals with the concept of organizational self-renewal. She shows how the organization, by constantly fine tuning its marketing plan, can automatically build in a self-renewal process. Marketing plans have an important impact on the entire organization.

8. *How can we understand more effectively the impact organizational culture has on people, policies, and decisions?* We are increasingly coming to understand the importance of culture on the effectiveness of the organization (Peters and Waterman, 1982; Deal and Kennedy, 1982; Grove, 1983; Bolman and Deal, 1984; Schein, 1985). A central theme that emerges from current research on organizational culture is that effective leadership requires the successful management of cultural change within the organization (Lippitt, 1982; Lippitt, Langseth, and Mossop, 1985; Kilmann, Saxton, Serpa, and Associates, 1985). Thus effective leaders need to become behavioral scientists who are lifelong students of organizational culture and change. This involves giving time and attention to developing methods for changing culture in ways apppropriate to the needs and the tasks of the organization.

Terrence Deal's chapter, entitled "Planning for Effective Organizational Cultures," analyzes these ideas in detail. He concludes that those who administer continuing education organizations will need to bring new leadership skills to their jobs in the decade ahead. He has identified the following three questions as important for consideration and analyzes each in detail: (1) How can leaders shape both the identity and image of continuing education? (2) How can conflict between the cultures of traditional and continuing education within the same institution be managed? (3) What are some specific leadership strategies that can be considered in building culture and tradition under nontraditional conditions?

Building on ideas from the book *Corporate Cultures* (1982) that he and Allan Kennedy wrote, Deal has developed a useful typology of corporate cultures. These are the "macho" culture, the "bet-your-company" culture, the "work hard/play hard culture," and the "process" culture. Macho cultures thrive in an environment of high risk and usually get almost instant feedback from the environment. Bet-your-company cultures arise in an environment of high risk and slow feedback. Often such organizations wait for years before they can obtain reliable feedback on their successes and failures. Work hard/play hard cultures develop in an atmosphere of low risk and quick feedback. An important value to them is action. Process cultures work most effectively in an environment of low risk/slow feedback. Such organizations put their energy into managing details and not making mistakes. Understanding these types of organizations and how they use feedback to help establish their cultures can assist continuing educators to be more effective in understanding and analyzing the cultural dynamics that affect their own organizations.

In addition to considering examples that illustrate the difference between administration and leadership, Deal identifies nine activities important to creating and maintaining dynamic organizational cultures. These are: (1) surveying the environment, mapping its movement, and figuring out what it will take to succeed; (2) trying new things; (3) articulating core values; (4) anointing and celebrating cultural heroes; (5) amplifying and underscoring cultural rituals; (6) convening and giving special attention to cultural ceremonies; (7) telling vivid stories; (8) working the cultural network; and (9) spending time working on symbolic issues (Ackoff, 1984; Harris, 1985; Bellman, 1986).

9. *How can we use knowledge of group dynamics to enhance strategic planning and effective leadership?* Since organizations get work done through mobilizing groups of people, it is important for leaders to understand the major dynamics that are of concern to groups. All organizational work groups deal with two basic issues simultaneously: (1) accomplishing the task at hand and (2) creating satisfactory social-emotional relationships among group members (Halpin, 1966; Bales, 1970; Zander, 1982; London, 1985). Effective leaders understand this dual nature of

group interaction because these task and maintenance dynamics act as powerful and influential forces with the group.

Schein (1985) has identified the following as major task and maintenance issues that all groups face as they cónduct their daily work: (1) developing a common language and set of conceptual categories for organizing information, (2) reaching consensus on group boundaries and the criteria for inclusion in the group, (3) reaching consensus on criteria for the use of power and influence within the group, (4) reaching consensus on criteria for friendship and intimacy within the group, and (5) reaching consensus on the criteria for giving out rewards and punishments. A collection of individuals does not become a high-performance group until they find ways to manage the dynamics involved in these issues. Therefore an important issue facing leaders in the future will be to work with groups in ways that enable them to address these issues.

10. *How can we demonstrate the value and effectiveness of our continuing education organizations to the multiple publics we serve?* Today's publics want accountability from their organizations. People value all aspects of education, and they want their institutions to take the lead in demonstrating exactly what consumer benefits are being produced (Kaufman and Stone, 1983; Kilmann, 1984; and Drucker, 1985). In Chapter Ten, Holt describes ways to achieve institutional accountability. First, she emphasizes the need to match the evaluation plan in appropriate ways to the existing organizational culture. Second, she illustrates the importance for building systems analysis and environmental scanning into the evaluation plan. Third, she considers ways in which evaluation can be used for bringing visibility to the leader's overall vision.

We are now beginning to develop more formal ways to engage in management audits as a way of increasing our public accountability. For example, Chapter Four describes in detail how to undertake an internal management audit. In addition, Holt suggests use of the Human Resources Institute's Cultural Audit or the Norms Diagnostic Index. This latter instrument covers such organizational issues as job involvement, leader-subordinate interaction, building supportive climates, and how people confront problems. Other methods of creating accountability include ethnographic data collection, interviews with people, observations, and assembling career histories.

Holt also suggests four areas in which to gather data to demonstrate accountability: (1) internal cultural conditions, (2) external socioeconomic conditions, (3) institutional climate, and (4) the organization's structure. She sets forth a grid useful for evaluating these four environments in relation to the organization's programs, personnel, clients, facilities, and finances.

11. *How can we engage in effective strategic long-range planning?* Strategic long-range planning is essential to maintaining the vitality of organizations and ensuring that they can adapt to changing external conditions (Craig, 1978; Hopkins and Massey, 1981; Mitroff, 1983; Keller, 1983; Pfeiffer, Goodstein, and Nolan, 1985). In Chapter Eleven, Votruba analyzes a number of ways to engage in strategic long-range planning. In addition, he notes the importance of coming to terms with basic assumptions about organizations before engaging in such a process. Using the research from Katz, Kahn, and Adams (1980), he illustrates within a continuing education context two basic assumptions about organizations: (1) organizations always seek to maintain their own survival and well-being, and (2) organizational survival and well-being are accomplished through the process of continual adaptation to change in the internal environment.

Votruba then goes on to develop the argument that top management in any type of organization will always develop priorities that are based on their view of what it will take to guarantee the organization's survival and continued vitality. He notes, "If the primary objective of all organizations is to survive and prosper through constant adaptation, then subunits within the organization, including the continuing education agency, will achieve organizational support and centrality to the extent that they are seen as contributing to this fundamental organizational priority."

The message to continuing education leaders is clear. If institutional leaders see continuing education as marginal, it is because they perceive that continuing education is not contributing in vital ways to the overall institutional mission. In such instances, continuing education leaders will have to develop specific plans to change the perceptions of people before they will be able to move the continuing education unit from a position of marginality to one of centrality.

Votruba offers six major suggestions for leaders to consider in moving continuing education to a more central position within their institutions: (1) involve the parent organization in the development of your continuing education program priorities rather than trying to make these decisions without advice and input, (2) always relate the continuing education mission to the broad mission of the parent organization, (3) approach people from the point of view of their world or perspective when trying to gain their support, (4) engage in appropriate internal marketing efforts to let others know how you can assist them in achieving the broad mission of the institution, (5) establish a continuing education organizational climate that encourages staff renewal, and (6) create a sense of vision for continuing education.

12. *How can we build bridges, not walls, with the internal and external constituencies that we serve?* In Chapter Three, Schmidt presents a wide variety of specific ways in which leaders can build bridges rather than walls. Through an extensive analysis of the literature, he has identified six important actions critical to leadership success: (1) analyzing the environment to identify important trends and their implications for the continuing education unit; (2) examining institutional problems, strengths, weaknesses, and windows of opportunity; (3) clarifying the mission, values, and traditions that are important to the institution; (4) matching the organization's mission to the strengths of the continuing education unit in ways that enhance opportunities for increased centrality for continuing education; (5) engaging in the design of strategic alternatives; and (6) choosing from these alternatives.

Schmidt emphasizes the need to engage in strategic long-range planning in order to become as effective as possible in these six areas. He concurs with Knox (1979) that planning is the primary means through which leaders can directly deal with the fact that continuing education often is not viewed as central to the mission of the institution. Strategic planning can provide a forum for clarifying this relationship. This, in turn, will encourage the building of bridges, not walls, with the parent organization. During the planning process assumptions can be clarified and agreed on, data related to accountability and the production of services can be examined, the relationship of continuing education to the parent organization can be examined, and new agreements for cooperative endeavors can be established (Steiner, 1979; Steiner and Miner, 1982; Ohmae, 1982; Morrison, Renfro, and Boucher, 1984).

All the chapters in this volume have addressed the important issue of building organizational success for continuing education programs. Leaders can be most effective in accomplishing this if they conceptualize their role as that of statespersons. Statespersons make clear distinctions between administration and leadership. While both of these are important roles, the leadership role concentrates on creating a vision for the organization, giving meaning to work, and developing trust by positioning continuing education activities so that they come to be seen as actively contributing to the attainment of institutional goals. Through strategic planning, therefore, leaders can achieve centrality by demonstrating that continuing education activities contribute to the central mission of the institution. This is the leadership challenge facing continuing education statespersons.

✛ ✛ ✛

References

Aaker, D. A., and Myers, J. A. *Advertising Management.* Englewood Cliffs, N. J.: Prentice-Hall, 1982.

Abelson, P. H. "Differing Values in Academia and Industry." *Science,* 1982, *217,* 1095.

Ackoff, R. L. *Creating the Corporate Future.* New York: Wiley, 1984.

Adizes, I. *How to Solve the Mismanagement Crisis.* Los Angeles: MDOR Institute, 1979.

Alexander Hamilton Institute. *Conflict Management: Vital Skill for the Successful Executive.* New York: Alexander Hamilton Institute, 1983.

Allen, L. A. *Making Managerial Planning More Effective.* New York: McGraw-Hill, 1982.

Allen, R. F., and Dyer, F. J. "A Tool for Tapping the Organizational Unconscious." *Personnel Journal,* 1980, *59* (3), 192–198.

Alm, K., Buhler-Miko, M., and Smith, K. B. *A Future-Creating Paradigm: A Guide to Long-Range Planning for the Future.* Washington, D.C.: American Association of State Colleges and Universities, 1978.

Anderson, R. E., and Kasl, E. S. *The Costs and Financing of Adult Education and Training.* Lexington, Mass.: Lexington Books, 1982.

Andreasen, A. R. *Mythological Barriers to the Use of Marketing Research by Small and Nonprofit Organizations.* Urbana: College of Commerce and Business Administration, University of Illinois, 1981.

Apps, J. W. *Improving Practice in Continuing Education: Modern Approaches for Understanding the Field and Determining Priorities.* San Francisco: Jossey-Bass, 1985.

215

Argyris, C. *Integrating the Individual and the Organization.* New York: Wiley, 1964.

Argyris, C. *Reasoning, Learning, and Action: Individual and Organizational.* San Francisco: Jossey-Bass, 1982.

Argyris, C., Putnam, R., and Smith, D. M. *Action Science: Concepts, Methods, and Skills for Research and Intervention.* San Francisco: Jossey-Bass, 1985.

Argyris, C., and Schön, D. *Theory in Practice: Increasing Professional Effectiveness.* San Francisco: Jossey-Bass, 1974.

Argyris, C., and Schön, D. A. *Organizational Learning: A Theory of Action Perspective.* Reading, Mass.: Addison-Wesley, 1978.

Ashby, E. "The Case for Ivory Towers." Paper delivered at International Conference on Higher Education in Tomorrow's World, University of Michigan, Ann Arbor, Apr. 1967. Cited by D. Bok, *Beyond the Ivory Tower: Social Responsibilities of the Modern University.* Cambridge, Mass.: Harvard University Press, 1982.

Asher, W., and Overholt, W. *Strategic Planning and Forecasting.* New York: Wiley, 1983.

Astin, A. W., and Scherrei, R. A. *Maximizing Leadership Effectiveness: Impact of Administrative Style on Faculty and Students.* San Francisco: Jossey-Bass, 1980.

Azaroff, L. V. "Industry-University Collaboration: How to Make It Work." *Research Management,* 1982, *25,* 31–34.

Bacharach, S. B., and Lawler, E. J. *Power and Politics in Organizations: The Social Psychology of Conflict, Coalitions, and Bargaining.* San Francisco: Jossey-Bass, 1980.

Bales, R. F. *Personality and Interpersonal Behavior.* New York: Holt, Rinehart & Winston, 1970.

Barnard, C. I. *The Functions of the Executive.* Cambridge, Mass.: Harvard University Press, 1938.

Battenburg, J. R. "Forging Links Between Industry and the Academic World." *SRA Journal,* 1980, Winter, 5–11.

Bean, J. P., and Kuh, G. D. "A Typology of Planning Problems." *Journal of Higher Education,* 1984, *55,* 35–55.

Beck, A. C., and Hillmer, E. D. *Positive Management Practices: Bringing Out the Best in Organizations and People.* San Francisco: Jossey-Bass, 1986.

Behn, R. "Leadership for Cutback Management: The Use of Corporate Strategy." *Public Administration Review,* 1980, *40,* 613-20.

Behn, R. D., and Vaupel, J. *Quick Analysis for Busy Decision Makers.* New York: Basic Books, 1982.

Bell, D. *The Coming of Post-Industrial Society: A Venture in Social Forecasting.* New York: Basic Books, 1973.

Bell, D. "Communications Technology—For Better or for Worse." *Harvard Business Review,*1979, May/June, p. 20.

Bellman, G. M. *The Quest for Staff Leadership.* Glenview, Ill.: Scott, Foresman, 1986.

Bennis, W. *Changing Organizations: Essays on the Development and Evolution of Human Organization.* New York: McGraw-Hill, 1966.

Bennis, W. "Who Sank the Yellow Submarine?" In J. V. Baldridge and T. E. Deal (eds.), *Managing Change in Educational Organizations.* Berkeley, Calif.: McCutchan, 1975.

Bennis, W. *The Unconscious Conspiracy: Why Leaders Can't Lead.* New York: AMACOM, 1976.

Bennis, W. "The 4 Competencies of Leadership." *Training and Development Journal,* 1984, *38* (8), 14-19.

Bennis, W. G., Benne, K. D., and Chin, R. *The Planning of Change.* New York: Holt, Rinehart & Winston, 1985.

Bennis, W., and Nanus, B. *Leaders: The Strategies for Taking Charge.* New York: Harper & Row, 1985.

Bercovitch, J. *Social Conflicts and Third Parties: Strategies of Conflict Resolution.* Boulder, Colo.: Westview Press, 1984.

Blake, R. R., and Mouton, J. S. *The Managerial Grid: Key Orientations for Achieving Production Through People.* Houston, Tex.: Gulf, 1964.

Blake, R. R., and Mouton, J. S. "Out of the Past: How to Use Your Organization's History to Shape a Better Future." *Training and Development Journal,* 1983, *37* (2), 58-65.

Blake, R. R., and Mouton, J. S. *Solving Costly Organizational Conflicts: Achieving Intergroup Trust, Cooperation, and Teamwork.* San Francisco: Jossey-Bass, 1984.

Blake, R. R., Mouton, J. S., and Williams, M. S. *The Academic Administrator Grid.* Jossey-Bass, 1981.

Bluestone, B., and Harrison, B. *The Deindustrialization of America.* New York: Basic Books, 1982.

Bok, D. *Beyond the Ivory Tower: Social Responsibilities of the Modern University.* Cambridge, Mass.: Harvard University Press, 1982.

Bolman, L. G., and Deal, T. E. *Modern Approaches to Understanding and Managing Organizations.* San Francisco: Jossey-Bass, 1984.

Botkin, J., Dimancescu, D., and State, R., with McClellan, J. *Global Stakes: The Future of High Technology in America.* Cambridge, Mass.: Ballinger, 1982.

Boulding, K. E. *A Primer on Social Dynamics: History as Dialectics and Development.* New York: Free Press, 1970.

Boyatzis, R. E. *The Competent Manager: A Model for Effective Performance.* New York: Wiley, 1982.

Boyer, E. Commencement address at National Institute on the Management of Lifelong Learning, Harvard University, Aug. 1979.

Bradford, D. L., and Cohen, A. R. *Managing for Excellence: The Guide to Developing High Performance in Contemporary Organizations.* New York: Wiley, 1984.

Brodsky, N. H., Kaufman, H. G., and Tooker, J. D. *University/ Industry Cooperation: A Preliminary Analysis of Existing Mechanisms and Their Relationship to the Innovation Process.* New York: Center for Science and Technology Policy, Graduate School of Public Administration, New York University, 1980.

Brown, L. D. *Managing Conflict at Organizational Interfaces.* Reading, Mass.: Addison-Wesley, 1983.

Brubacher, J. S., and Rudy, W. *Higher Education in Transition.* New York: Harper & Row, 1968.

Bruce, J. D., Silbert, W. M., Smullin, L. D., and Fano, R. M. *Lifelong Cooperative Education.* Report of the Centennial Study Committee. Cambridge, Mass: MIT Press, 1982.

Bryant, B. I., Chesler, M. A., and Crowfoot, J. E. "Barometers of Conflict," *Educational Leadership,* Oct. 1975, pp. 17-20.

Cameron, K. S. "Organizational Change in Higher Education." *Journal of Higher Education,* Mar./Apr. 1984, 122-144.

Cameron, K. S., and Whetten, D. A. (eds.). *Organizational Effectiveness: A Comparison of Multiple Models.* New York: Academic Press, 1983.

Campbell, T. L. "Extension Academic Quality: Some Observations on Sharing Responsibility." *Continuum,* 1982, *46* (4), 10-16.

Carlson, R. O. "Environmental Constraints and Organizational Consequences: The Public School and Its Clients." In J. V. Baldridge and T. E. Deal (eds.), *Managing Change in Educational Organizations.* Berkeley, Calif.: McCutchan, 1975.

Carnegie Council on Policy Studies in Higher Education. *Three Thousand Futures: The Next Twenty Years for Higher Education.* San Francisco: Jossey-Bass, 1980.

Carnegie Foundation for the Advancement of Teaching, The. *Missions of the College Curriculum: A Contemporary Review with Suggestions.* San Francisco: Jossey-Bass, 1977.

Carnevale, A. P. "The Learning Enterprise." *Training and Development Journal,* 1986, *40,* 18-26.

Chickering, A. W., and Associates. *The Modern American College: Responding to the New Realities of Diverse Students and a Changing Society.* San Francisco: Jossey-Bass, 1981.

Clark, B. R. "The Organizational Saga in Higher Education." In J. V. Baldridge and T. E. Deal (eds.), *Managing Change in Educational Organizations.* Berkeley, Calif.: McCutchan, 1975.

Cleveland, H. *The Knowledge Executive: Leadership in an Information Society.* New York: Dutton, 1985.

Cohen, W. A., and Cohen, N. *Top Executive Performance: 11 Keys to Success and Power.* New York: Wiley, 1984.

Collins, M. "Some Further Thoughts on Principles of Good Practice in Continuing Education." *Lifelong Learning,* 1985, *8* (8), 12-28.

Comfort, R. W. "Integration: The Fusing of Tradition with Uniqueness." *Continuum,* 1981, *46* (1), 21-24.

Commission on Higher Education and the Adult Learner. *Adult Learners: Key to the Nation's Future.* Columbia, Md.: Commission on Higher Education and the Adult Learner, 1984.

Cope, R. G. *Strategic Policy Planning: A Guide for College and*

University Administrators. Littleton, Colo.: Ireland Educational Corporation, 1978.

Cope, R. G. *Strategic Planning, Management, and Decision Making.* AAHE-ERIC Higher Education Research Report no. 9. Washington, D.C.: American Association for Higher Education, 1981.

Corporate Classrooms: The Learning Business. New York: Carnegie Foundation for the Advancement of Teaching, 1985.

Coser, L. A. *The Functions of Social Conflict.* New York: Free Press, 1956.

Council on the Continuing Education Unit. *Principles of Good Practice in Continuing Education.* Silver Springs, Md.: Council on the Continuing Education Unit, 1984.

Craig, D. P. *Hip Pocket Guide to Planning and Evaluation.* San Diego: University Associates, 1978.

Cronin, T. E. "Thinking and Learning About Leadership." *Presidential Studies Quarterly,* 1984, *14* (1).

Cross, K. P. *Adults as Learners: Increasing Participation and Facilitating Learning.* San Francisco: Jossey-Bass, 1981.

Cross, K. P. "The Changing Role of Higher Education in the Learning Society." *Continuum,* 1985, 49, (2), 101–110.

Crossland, F. "Learning to Cope with a Downward Slope." *Change,* 1980, *12,* 18, 20–25.

Culliton, B. J. "Academe and Industry Debate Partnerships." *Science,* 1983, *219,* 150–151.

Cunningham, P. M. "Contradictions in the Practice of Nontraditional Continuing Education." In S. B. Merriam (ed.), *Linking Philosophy and Practice.* New Directions for Continuing Education, no. 15. San Francisco: Jossey-Bass, 1982.

Cyert, R. M. "Foreword." In G. Keller (ed.), *Academic Strategy: The Management Revolution in American Higher Education.* Baltimore: Johns Hopkins University Press, 1983.

Cyert, R. M. "Academic Leadership." *Continuum,* 1985, *49* (2), 123–128.

Dahl, R. A. "The Concept of Power." *Behavioral Science,* 1957, *2,* 201–218.

Deal, T. E., and Kennedy, A. A. *Corporate Cultures: The Rites and*

Rituals of Corporate Life. Reading, Mass.: Addison-Wesley, 1982.

Declerq, G. V. "A Third Look at the Two Cultures: The New Economic Responsibility of the University." *International Journal of Institutional Management in Higher Education,* 1981, *5*, 237-252.

Del Bueno, D. J. "An Empirical Evaluation of the Relationship Between Continuing Education and Nursing Behavior." Unpublished doctoral dissertation, Columbia University, 1976.

Derr, C. B. "Conflict Resolution in Organizations: Views from the Field of Educational Administration." *Public Administration Review,* 1972, *5,* 495-501.

Deshler, D. "An Alternative Approach to Evaluation in Continuing Education." In D. Desher (ed.), *Evaluation for Program Improvement.* New Directions for Continuing Education, no. 24. San Francisco: Jossey-Bass, 1984.

Deutsch, M. *The Resolution of Conflict: Constructive and Destructive Processes.* New Haven, Conn.: Yale University Press, 1973.

Dickson, P. *The Official Explanation.* New York: Dell, 1980.

Diebold, J. *Making the Future Work: Unleashing Our Powers of Innovation for the Decades Ahead.* New York: Simon & Schuster, 1984.

Dill, D. D. "The Structure of the Academic Profession: Toward a Definition of Ethical Issues." *Journal of Higher Education,* 1982, *53,* (3), 243-381.

Drucker, P. F. *Managing in Turbulent Times.* New York: Harper & Row, 1980.

Drucker, P. F. *Innovation and Entrepreneurship.* New York: Harper & Row, 1985.

Duke, J. T. *Conflict and Power in Social Life.* Provo, Utah: Brigham Young University Press, 1976.

Edgerton, R. "A College Education Up to Beating the Japanese." *AAHE Bulletin,* 1983, *35,* 3-7.

Education Commission of the States, Task Force on Education for Economic Growth. *Action for Excellence.* Denver, Colo.: Education Commission of the States, 1983.

Elias, J. L. "The Theory-Practice Split." In S. B. Merriam (ed.), *Linking Philosophy and Practice.* New Directions for Continuing Education, no. 15. San Francisco: Jossey-Bass, 1982.

Enarson, J. J. "Quality and Accountability: Are We Destroying What We Want to Preserve?" *Change,* 1980, *13,* 7–10.

Erikson, E. H. *Youth: Change and Challenge.* New York: Basic Books, 1963.

Etzioni, A. *An Immodest Agenda: Rebuilding America Before the Twenty-First Century.* New York: McGraw-Hill, 1983.

Fenwick, D. C. (ed.). *Directory of Campus-Business Linkages.* New York: Macmillan, 1983.

Fiedler, F. E., and Chemers, M. M. *Improving Leadership Effectiveness.* New York: Wiley, 1984.

Fielding, D. W. "Performance Evaluation of a Program in Pharmacy Continuing Education." Unpublished doctoral dissertation, University of British Columbia, 1978.

Filley, A. C. *Interpersonal Conflict Resolution.* Glenview, Ill.: Scott, Foresman, 1975.

Flanagan, G. J., and Smith, F. B. "What's the Bottom Line?: Continuing Educators Discuss Priorities and Values." In S. B. Merriam (ed.), *Linking Philosophy and Practice.* New Directions for Continuing Education, no. 15. San Francisco: Jossey-Bass, 1982.

Folberg, J., and Taylor, A. *Mediation: A Comprehensive Guide to Resolving Conflicts Without Litigation.* San Francisco: Jossey-Bass, 1984.

Follett, M. P. *Dynamic Administration: The Collected Papers of Mary Parker Follett* (edited by H. C. Metcalf and L. Urwick). New York: Harper & Row, 1941.

Forrester, J. W. "Innovation and the Economic Long Wave." *Management Review,* 1979, *68,* 16–24.

Fowler, D. R. "University-Industry Research Relationship." *Research Management,* 1984, *27,* 35–41.

Gardner, J. W. *Self-Renewal.* New York: Norton, 1981.

Gavert, R. V. "Business and Academe: An Emerging Partnership." *Change,* 1983, *15,* 23–28.

Geneen, H., and Moscow, A. *Managing.* New York: Doubleday, 1984.

General Accounting Office. *The Federal Role in Fostering University-Industry Cooperation.* Washington, D.C.: General Accounting Office, 1983.

Glamser, F. D. "The Impact of Preretirement Programs on the Retirement Experience." *Journal of Gerontology,* 1981, *36,* 244–250.

Glasser, W. *The Identity Society.* New York: Harper & Row, 1972.

Goetz, J. P., and LeCompte, M. D. *Ethnography and Qualitative Design in Educational Research.* Orlando, Fla.: Academic Press, 1984.

Gold, G. G. "Toward Business-Higher Education Alliances." In G. Gold (ed.), *Business and Higher Education: Toward New Alliances.* New Directions for Experiential Learning, no. 13. San Francisco: Jossey-Bass, 1981.

Golembiewski, R. T. *Renewing Organizations: The Laboratory Approach to Planned Change.* Itasca, Ill.: Peacock, 1972.

Gros Louis, K.R.R. "Making a Beginning: Adult Learners and the 21st Century University." *Continuum,* 1985, *49* (2), 118–122.

Gross, N. "Organizational Lag in American Universities." *Harvard Educational Review,* 1963, *33,* 58–73.

Grove, A. S. *High Output Management.* New York: Random House, 1983.

Halpin, A. W. *Theory and Research in Administration.* New York: Macmillan, 1966.

Hamilton, W. B. "The Research Triangle of North Carolina: A Study of Leadership for the Common Wealth." *South Atlantic Quarterly,* 1966, *65,* 255–278.

Harris, P. R. *Management in Transition.* San Francisco: Jossey-Bass, 1985.

Hearn, J. C., and Heydinger, R. B. "Scanning the University's External Environment: Objectives, Constraints, and Possibilities." *Journal of Higher Education,* 1985, *56,* 419–445.

Hefferlin, J. L. *Dynamics of Academic Reform.* San Francisco: Jossey-Bass, 1969.

Heilizer, F. "Conjunction and Disjunctive Conflict: A Theory of Need Conflict." *Journal of Abnormal and Social Psychology,* 1964, *68,* 21–37.

Hersey, P., and Blanchard, K. H. *Management of Organizational Behavior: Utilizing Human Resources.* Englewood Cliffs, N. J.: Prentice-Hall, 1977.

Hickson, D. J., Butler, R. J., Cray, D., Mallory, G. R., and Wilson, D. C. *Top Decisions: Strategic Decision Making in Organizations.* San Francisco: Jossey-Bass, 1986.

Hodgkinson, H. L. "The Changing Face of Tomorrow's Students." *Change,* 1985, May/June, 38–39.

Hollowood, J. R. *College and University Strategic Planning: A Methodological Approach.* Cambridge, Mass.: Arthur D. Little, 1979.

Hopkins, D.S.P., and Massey, W. F. *Planning Models for Colleges and Universities.* Stanford, Calif.: Stanford University Press, 1981.

Human Resources Institute Cultural Audit. Morristown, N.J.: Human Resources Institute, 1983.

Illich, I. D. *Deschooling of Society.* New York: Harper & Row, 1971.

Jackman, M.J.G., and Mahoney, J. R. *Shoulders to the Wheel: Energy-Related College/Business Cooperative Agreements.* Washington, D.C.: American Association of Community and Junior Colleges, 1982.

Jandt, F. E., and Gillette, P. *Win-Win Negotiation: Turning Conflict into Agreement.* New York: Wiley, 1985.

Janov, J. E. "Gone Is the Corporate Doberman." *Training and Development Journal,* 1985, *39* (7), 46–49.

Jedamus, P., Peterson, M. W., and Associates. *Improving Academic Management: A Handbook of Planning and Institutional Research.* San Francisco: Jossey-Bass, 1980.

Johnson, E. C., and Tornatzky, L. G. "Academia and Industrial Innovation." In G. G. Gold (ed.), *Business and Higher Education: Toward New Alliances.* New Directions for Experiential Learning, no. 13. San Francisco: Jossey-Bass, 1981.

Johnson, L. G. *The High-Technology Connection: Academic/Industrial Cooperation for Economic Growth.* ASHE-ERIC Higher Education Research Report no. 6. Washington, D.C.: Association for the Study of Higher Education, 1984.

"Joint Ventures Between Business and Higher Education: Human Resource Evaluation." *Report of the Conference Hosted by Arthur Anderson and Company and Northwestern University.* St. Charles, Ill.: Arthur Anderson, 1984.

Jonson, R. W. "Small Colleges Cope with the Eighties." *Journal of Higher Education,* Mar./Apr., 1984, 171–183.

Kanter, R. M. *Men and Women of the Corporation.* New York: Basic Books, 1977.

Kanter, R. M. *The Change Masters: Innovation and Entrepreneurship in the American Corporation.* New York: Simon & Schuster, 1983.

Kaplan, R. E. "Creativity in the Everyday Business of Managing." *Issues and Observations,* 1983, *3,* (2), 1–5.

Kast, F. E., and Rosenzweig, J. E. *Organization and Management: A Systems and Contingency Approach.* New York: McGraw-Hill, 1979.

Katz, D., and Kahn, R. *The Social Psychology of Organizations.* (2nd ed.) New York: Wiley, 1978.

Katz, D., Kahn, R. L., and Adams, J. S. (eds.). *The Study of Organizations: Findings from Field and Laboratory.* San Francisco: Jossey-Bass, 1980.

Kaufman, R., and Stone, B. *Planning for Organizational Success: A Practical Guide.* New York: Wiley, 1983.

Keane, J. G. "Higher Education: Some Trends Stressing the Need for Strategic Planning." *Continuum,* 1985, *49* (2), 88–100.

Keller, G. *Academic Strategy: The Management Revolution in American Higher Education.* Baltimore: Johns Hopkins University Press, 1983.

Kennedy, M. M. *Powerbase: How to Build It, How to Keep It.* New York: Macmillan, 1984.

Kerr, C. "Administration of Higher Education in an Era of Change and Conflict." In *Conflict, Retrenchment, and Reappraisal: The Administration of Higher Education.* Urbana-Champaign: University of Illinois Press, 1979.

Kerr, C. *The Uses of the University.* (3rd ed.) Cambridge, Mass.: Harvard University Press, 1982.

Kilmann, R. H. *Beyond the Quick Fix: Managing Five Tracks to Organizational Success.* San Francisco: Jossey-Bass, 1984.

Kilmann, R. H., Saxton, M. J., Serpa, R., and Associates. *Gaining Control of the Corporate Culture.* San Francisco: Jossey-Bass, 1985.

Kinnear, T. C., and Taylor, J. R. *Marketing Research.* New York: McGraw-Hill, 1983.

Kirkpatrick, D. L. *How to Manage Change Effectively: Approaches, Methods, and Case Examples.* San Francisco: Jossey-Bass, 1985.

Knox, A. B. (ed.). *Enhancing Proficiencies of Continuing Educators.* New Directions for Continuing Education, no. 1. San Francisco: Jossey-Bass, 1979.

Knox, A. B. "The Continuing Education Agency and Its Parent Organization." In J. C. Votruba (ed.), *Strengthening Internal Support for Continuing Education.* New Directions for Continuing Education, no. 9. San Francisco: Jossey-Bass, 1981.

Knox, A. B. "Priority Setting." In A. B. Knox (ed.), *Leadership Strategies for Meeting New Challenges.* New Directions for Continuing Education, no. 13. San Francisco: Jossey-Bass, 1982.

Knox, A. B. "Strengthening Leadership of Continuing Higher Education." *Continuum,* 1985, *49* (2), 135–139.

Knox, A. B., and Associates. *Developing, Administering, and Evaluating Adult Education.* San Francisco: Jossey-Bass, 1980.

Kotler, P. *Marketing for Nonprofit Organizations.* Englewood Cliffs, N.J.: Prentice-Hall, 1982.

Kotler, P. *Marketing Management: Analysis, Planning, and Control.* Englewood Cliffs, N.J.: Prentice-Hall, 1984a.

Kotler, P. *Principles of Marketing.* Englewood Cliffs, N.J.: Prentice-Hall, 1984b.

Kotler, P. *Strategic Marketing for Educational Institutions.* Englewood Cliffs, N.J.: Prentice-Hall, 1985a.

Kotler, P. *The New Competition.* Englewood Cliffs, N.J.: Prentice-Hall, 1985b.

Kotter, J. P. *Power and Influence: Beyond Formal Authority.* New York: Free Press, 1985.

Kozol, J. *Illiterate America.* New York: Doubleday, 1985.

Lenz, E. *Creating and Marketing Programs in Continuing Education.* New York: McGraw-Hill, 1980.

Lewin, K. "Group Decision and Social Change." In E. E. Maccoby, T. M. Newcomb, and E. L. Hartley (eds.), *Readings in Social Psychology.* New York: Holt, Rinehart & Winston, 1958.

Likert, R., and Likert, J. G. *New Ways of Managing Conflict.* New York: McGraw-Hill, 1976.

Lindquist, J. *Strategies for Change.* Berkeley, Calif.: Pacific Soundings Press, 1978.

Lippitt, G. L. *Visualizing Change: Model Building and the Change Process.* Fairfax, Va.: NTL-Learning Resources Corporation, 1973.

Lippitt, G. L. *Organizational Renewal: A Holistic Approach to Organization Development.* Englewood Cliffs, N.J.: Prentice-Hall, 1982.

Lippitt, G., Langseth, P., and Mossop, J. *Implementing Organizational Change: A Practical Guide to Managing Change Efforts.* San Francisco: Jossey-Bass, 1985.

London, M. *Developing Managers: A Guide to Motivating and Preparing People for Successful Managerial Careers.* San Francisco: Jossey-Bass, 1985.

Lovelock, C. *Services Marketing.* Englewood Cliffs, N.J.: Prentice-Hall, 1984.

Loye, D. *The Leadership Passion: A Psychology of Ideology.* San Francisco: Jossey-Bass, 1977.

Luce, S. R. "Managing Corporate Culture." *Canadian Business Review,* 1984, *11* (1), 40-43.

Lynton, E. A. *The Missing Connection Between Business and the Universities.* New York: Macmillan, 1984.

McCall, M. W., Jr. *Power, Influence, and Authority: The Hazards of Carrying a Sword.* Greensboro, N.C.: Center for Creative Leadership, 1978.

McCarthy, J. (ed.). *Resolving Conflict in Higher Education.* New Directions for Higher Education, no. 32. San Francisco: Jossey-Bass, 1980.

McCorkle, C. O., Jr., and Archibald, S. O. *Management and Leadership in Higher Education: Applying Modern Techniques of Planning, Resource Management, and Evaluation.* San Francisco: Jossey-Bass, 1982.

Machlup, F. *Education and Economic Growth*. Lincoln: University of Nebraska Press, 1970.

March, J. G., and Simon, H. A. *Organizations*. New York: Wiley, 1958.

Mason, R. C. "Managerial Role and Style." In P. D. Langerman and D. H. Smith (eds.), *Managing Adult and Continuing Education Programs and Staff*. Washington, D.C.: National Association for Public Continuing and Adult Education, 1979.

Mason, R. O., and Mitroff, I. I. *Challenging Strategic Planning Assumptions*. New York: Wiley, 1981.

Matthews, J. B., and Norgaard, R. *Managing the Partnership Between Higher Education and Industry*. Boulder, Colo.: National Center for Higher Education Management Systems, 1984.

Mayhew, L. B. *Surviving the Eighties: Strategies and Procedures for Solving Fiscal and Enrollment Problems*. San Francisco: Jossey-Bass, 1979.

Merriam, S. B. "Some Thoughts on the Relationship Between Theory and Practice." In S. B. Merriam (ed.), *Linking Philosophy and Practice*. New Directions for Continuing Education, no. 15. San Francisco: Jossey-Bass, 1982.

Michael, D. N. *On Learning to Plan—and Planning to Learn: The Social Psychology of Changing Toward Future-Responsive Societal Learning*. San Francisco: Jossey-Bass, 1973.

Millett, J. D. *Conflict in Higher Education: State Government Coordination Versus Institutional Independence*. San Francisco: Jossey-Bass, 1984.

Mitroff, I. I. *Stakeholders of the Organizational Mind: Toward a New View of Organizational Policy Making*. San Francisco: Jossey-Bass, 1983.

Montana, P. J. *Marketing for Nonprofit Organizations*. New York: American Management Association, 1978.

Morrison, J. L., Renfro, W. L., and Boucher, W. I. *Futures Research and the Strategic Planning Process: Implications for Higher Education*. ASHE-ERIC Higher Education Report no. 9. Washington, D.C.: Association for Study of Higher Education, 1984.

Mueller, S. "The Post-Gutenburg University." In *Colleges Enter the Information Society.* Current Issues in Higher Education Series, no 1. Washington, D.C.: American Association for Higher Education.

Nagy, M. C., and Gregory, L. W. *Assessment of the First-Year Impact: Pennsylvania's Customized Job-Training Program 1982-1983.* Final Report, Feb. 27, 1984. (ED 247 420)

Naisbitt, J. *Megatrends: Ten New Directions Transforming Our Lives.* New York: Warner Books, 1982.

Nash, M. *Managing Organizational Performance.* San Francisco: Jossey-Bass, 1983.

Nash, M. *Making People Productive: What Really Works in Raising Managerial and Employee Performance.* San Francisco: Jossey-Bass, 1985.

National Center for Education Statistics. *Projections of Educational Statistics to 1992-93.* 2 vols. Washington, D.C.: U.S. Government Printing Office, 1985.

National Commission on Research. *Industry and the Universities: Developing Cooperative Research Relationships in the National Interest.* Pasadena: California Institute of Technology Press, 1980.

National Science Foundation. *University-Industry Research Relationships: Myths, Realities, and Potentials.* Fourteenth Annual Report of the National Science Board. Washington, D.C.: Government Printing Office, 1982.

Nemon, A. "The Effects of a Continuing Education Class on Knowledge of, and Attitudes and Behavior Toward, Deaf Persons." Unpublished doctoral dissertation, University of California, Berkeley, 1980.

Niebuhr, H., Jr. "Strengthening the Human Learning System." *Change,* 1982, *14,* 16-21.

Niebuhr, H., Jr. *Revitalizing American Learning: A New Approach That Just Might Work.* Belmont, Calif.: Wadsworth, 1984.

Northern Illinois University. *Concept Paper: The Lindeman Center for Community Empowerment Through Education.* DeKalb: Northern Illinois University, 1984.

Obershall, A. *Social Conflict and Social Movements.* Englewood Cliffs, N.J.: Prentice-Hall, 1973.

Odiorne, G. S. *The Change Resisters: How They Prevent Progress and What Managers Can Do About Them.* Englewood Cliffs, N.J.: Prentice-Hall, 1981.

Odiorne, G. S. *Strategic Management of Human Resources.* San Francisco: Jossey-Bass, 1984.

Ohmae, K. *The Mind of the Strategist.* New York: McGraw-Hill, 1982.

Parsons, T. "Social Classes and the Class Conflict in the Light of Recent Sociological Theory." *American Economic Review,* 1959, *39,* 16–26.

Peairs, R. H. (ed.). *Avoiding Conflict in Faculty Personnel Practices.* New Directions for Higher Education, no. 7. San Francisco: Jossey-Bass, 1974.

Pennings, J. M., and Associates. *Organizational Strategy and Change: New Views on Formulating and Implementing Strategic Decisions.* San Francisco: Jossey-Bass, 1985.

Peters, J. M., and Associates. *Building an Effective Adult Education Enterprise.* San Francisco: Jossey-Bass, 1980.

Peters, T. J., and Austin, N. *A Passion for Excellence: The Leadership Difference.* New York: Random House, 1985.

Peters, T. J., and Waterman, R. H., Jr. *In Search of Excellence: Lessons from America's Best-Run Companies.* New York: Warner Books, 1982.

Peterson, M. W. "Analyzing Alternative Approaches to Planning." In P. Jedamus, M. W. Peterson, and Associates, *Improving Academic Management: A Handbook of Planning and Institutional Research.* San Francisco: Jossey-Bass, 1980.

Peterson, R. E. "Implications and Consequences for the Future." In R. E. Peterson and Associates, *Lifelong Learning in America.* San Francisco: Jossey-Bass, 1979.

Pfeffer, J. *Power in Organizations.* Boston: Pitman, 1981.

Pfeffer, J., and Salancik, G. R. *The External Control of Organizations.* New York: Harper & Row, 1978.

Pfeiffer, W. J., Goodstein, L. D., and Nolan, T. M. *Understanding Applied Strategic Planning: A Manager's Guide.* San Diego: University Associates, 1985.

Pinchot, G., III. *Intrapreneuring.* New York: Harper & Row, 1985.

Ping, C. J. "Bigger Stake for Business in Higher Education." *Harvard Business Review,* Sept./Oct., 1981, 122–129.

Pondy, L. R. "Organizational Conflict: Concepts and Models." *Administrative Science Quarterly,* 1967, *12,* 296–320.

Porat, M. U. *The Information Economy.* Vol. I. Washington, D.C.: Government Printing Office, 1977.

Porter, M. *Competitive Strategy: Techniques for Analyzing Industries and Competitors,* New York: Free Press, 1980.

Powell, W. W., and Robbins, R. (eds.). *Conflict and Consensus.* New York: Free Press, 1984.

Powers, D. R., and Powers, M. F. *Making Participatory Management Work: Leadership of Consultive Decision Making in Academic Administration.* San Francisco: Jossey-Bass, 1983.

Prager, D. J. "Institutional Change: Impact on Science and Technology in the 80s." *Journal of the Society of Research Administrators,* 1983, *14,* 5–10.

Project on Continuing Higher Education Leadership. *Challenges to Higher Education.* Washington, D.C.: National University Continuing Education Association, 1985.

Pusey, N. *American Higher Education 1945–1970: A Personal Memoir.* Cambridge, Mass.: Harvard University Press, 1978.

Quinn, J. B. *Strategies for Change.* Homewood, Ill.: Irwin, 1980.

Rados, D. L. *Marketing for Nonprofit Organizations.* Boston: Auburn House, 1981.

Rawls, J. A. *A Theory of Justice.* Cambridge, Mass.: Harvard University Press, 1971.

Rhodes, F.H.T. "Reforming Higher Education Will Take More Than Just Tinkering with Curricula." *Chronicle of Higher Education,* May 22, 1985, p. 80.

Robbins, S. P. *Managing Organizational Conflict: A Non-Traditional Approach.* Englewood Cliffs, N.J.: Prentice-Hall, 1974.

Robert, M. *Managing Conflict from the Inside Out.* Austin, Tex.: Learning Concepts, 1981.

Robert, M. *Managing Conflict from the Inside Out.* San Diego: University Associates, 1982.

Robertson, T. S., Zielinski, J., and Ward, S. *Consumer Behavior.* Glenview, Ill.: Scott, Foresman, 1984.

Roeber, R.J.C. *The Organization in a Changing Environment.* Reading, Mass.: Addison-Wesley, 1973.

Rosen, S. "The Participant Action Plan Approach: A Generic Follow-Up Evaluation Method." In R. Salinger and J. Bartlet (eds.), *Evaluating the Impact of Training: A Collection of Federal Agency Evaluation Practices.* Report no. OPM/WDG-83/1. Washington, D.C.: U.S. Office of Personnel Management, Spring, 1983.

Rosenblueth, A., and Wiener, N. "Purposeful and Non-Purposeful Systems." *Philosophy of Science,* 1950, *17,* 318–326.

Rubin, J. Z. (ed.). *Dynamics of Third-Party Intervention.* New York: Praeger, 1981.

Rudolph, F. *Curriculum: A History of the American Undergraduate Course of Study Since 1636.* San Francisco: Jossey-Bass, 1977.

Ryan, J. H. "The Continuing Educator: Change Agent or Prisoner?" *Continuum,* 1985, *49* (2), 129–134.

Sayles, L. R. *Leadership: What Effective Managers Really Do . . . and How They Do It.* New York: McGraw-Hill, 1979.

Schein, E. H. *Career Dynamics: Matching Individual and Organizational Needs.* Reading, Mass.: Addison-Wesley, 1978.

Schein, E. H. *Organizational Culture and Leadership: A Dynamic View.* San Francisco: Jossey-Bass, 1985.

Schellenberg, J. A. *The Science of Conflict.* New York: Oxford University Press, 1982.

Schoderbek, P. P., Schoderbek, C. G., and Kefalas, A. G. *Management Systems.* (3rd ed.) Plano, Tex.: Business Publications, 1985.

Schön, D. A. *Beyond the Stable State.* New York: Norton, 1971.

Schoner, B., and Uhl, K. P. *Marketing Research: Information Systems and Decision Making.* Huntington, N.Y.: Krieger, 1975.

Schuh, G. E. "Revitalizing the Land-Grant University." Paper presented at colloquium of Strategic Management Research Center, University of Minnesota, Sept. 28, 1984.

Selznick, P. *Leadership in Administration: A Sociological Interpretation.* New York: Harper & Row, 1957.

Shirley, R. C., and Volkwein, J. F. "Establishing Academic Program Priorities." *Journal of Higher Education*, 1978, *49*, 472–488.

Shoben, J. E., Jr. "University and Society." In H. L. Hodgkinson and M. B. Bloy, Jr. (eds.), *Identity Crisis in Higher Education*. San Francisco: Jossey-Bass, 1971.

Singarella, T. A., and Sork, T. J. "Questions of Values and Conduct: Ethical Issues for Adult Education." *Adult Education Quarterly*, 1983, *33* (4), 244–251.

Singer, E. A., Jr. *Experience and Reflection*. Philadelphia: University of Pennsylvania Press, 1959.

Smart, C., and Vertinsky, A. "Strategy and the Environment: A Study of Corporate Responses to Crisis." *Strategic Management Journal*, 1984, *5*, 199–213.

Smith, C. G. (ed.). *Conflict Resolution: Contributions of the Behavioral Sciences*. Notre Dame, Ind.: University of Notre Dame Press, 1971.

Smith, D. K. *The Learning Society*. Madison: Wisconsin Idea Commission, 1985.

Smola, J. K. "Evaluation of the Training and Continuing Education for Employment as an Emergency Medical Technician-Ambulance." Unpublished doctoral dissertation, Iowa State University, 1981.

Sparks, H. *Tradition, Transformation, and Tomorrow: The Emerging Role of American Higher Education*. Occasional Papers in Continuing Education, no. 2. Washington, D.C.: National University Continuing Education Association, 1985.

Srivastva, S., and Associates. *Executive Power: How Executives Influence People and Organizations*. San Francisco: Jossey-Bass, 1986.

Stake, R. E. "Objectives, Priorities, and Other Judgmental Data." *Review of Educational Research*, 1970, *40* (2), 181–212.

Steiner, G. A. *Strategic Planning: What Every Manager Must Know*. New York: Free Press, 1979.

Steiner, G. A., and Miner, J. B. *Management Policy and Strategy*. New York: Macmillan, 1982.

Stodgill, R. M. *Handbook of Leadership: A Survey of Theory and Research*. New York: Free Press, 1974.

Strother, G. B., and Klus, J. P. *Administration of Continuing Education.* Belmont, Calif.: Wadsworth, 1982.

Sudman, S. S., and Bradburn, N. M. *Asking Questions: A Practical Guide to Questionnaire Design.* San Francisco: Jossey-Bass, 1982.

Tannenbaum, R., Margulies, N., Massarik, F., and Associates. *Human Systems Development: New Perspectives on People and Organizations.* San Francisco: Jossey-Bass, 1985.

Tarr, D. L. "The Strategic Toughness of Servant-Leadership." *Continuum,* 1985, *49* (3), 163–175.

Theobald, R. *Free Men and Free Markets.* New York: Potter, 1963.

Thomas, J., and Bennis, W. *The Management of Change and Conflict.* New York: Penguin Books, 1972.

Tichy, N. M. *Managing Strategic Change: Technical, Political, and Cultural Dynamics.* New York: Wiley, 1983.

Toffler, A. *Future Shock.* New York: Random House, 1971.

Toffler, A. *The Third Wave.* New York: Morrow, 1980.

Trusty, F. M. "Strategy Development for Managing Selected Educational Conflicts." (Contract no. NIE-P-77-0206.)

Trusty, F. M. *Administering Human Resources: A Behavioral Approach to Educational Administration.* Berkeley, Calif.: McCutchan, 1971.

Trusty, F. M. "Approaches to the Management of Conflict." *The New Era: Journal of the World Education Fellowship,* 1978, *58,* 92–98.

Turner, J. H. *The Structure of Sociological Theory.* Homewood, Ill.: Dorsey Press, 1974.

Turnstall, W. B. "Cultural Transition at AT&T." *Sloan Management Review,* 1983, *25* (1), 15–26.

Uhl, N. P. (ed.). *Using Research for Strategic Planning.* New Directions for Institutional Research, no. 37. San Francisco: Jossey-Bass, 1983.

University of Missouri and Lincoln University. *The State of the State: Missouri's Changing Economy and People.* Columbia, Mo.: Cooperative Extension Service, 1984.

University of Wisconsin—Oshkosh. *Long-Range Plan for the Extension Function.* Nov. 1983. (Draft version.)

Veysey, L. R. *The Emergence of the American University.* Chicago: University of Chicago Press, 1965.

Vicere, A. A. "Creating Order from the Chaos: Academic Integrity in Continuing Professional Education." *Adult Education Quarterly,* 1985, *35* (4), 229–236.

von Bertalanffy, L. "The Theory of Open Systems in Physics and Biology." *Science,* Jan. 13, 1950.

von Bertalanffy, L. *Problems of Life.* New York: Wiley, 1952.

Votruba, J. C. "A Final Note to Continuing Educators Working as Change Agents." In J. C. Votruba (ed.), *Strengthening Internal Support for Continuing Education.* New Directions for Continuing Education, no. 9. San Francisco: Jossey-Bass, 1981.

Vroom, V. H., and Yetton, P. W. *Leadership and Decision Making.* Pittsburgh: University of Pittsburgh Press, 1973.

Walshok, M. L. "Capturing the Adult Market: UCSD's Experience." In *The Admissions Strategist,* no. 3. New York: College Board Publications, 1985.

Walton, R. E. *Interpersonal Peacemaking, Confrontation, and Third-Party Consultation.* Reading, Mass.: Addison-Wesley, 1969.

Walton, R. E., and McKersie, R. B. *A Behavioral Theory of Labor Negotiations.* New York: McGraw-Hill, 1965.

Weber, M. *The Protestant Ethic and the Spirit of Capitalism.* New York: Scribner's, 1958. (Originally published 1904.)

Webster, F. E., Jr. *Industrial Marketing Strategy.* New York: Wiley, 1984.

Weick, K. E. "Educational Organizations as Loosely Coupled Systems." *Administrative Science Quarterly,* 1976, *21,* 1–19.

Weick, K. E. "Managing Change Among Loosely Coupled Elements." In P. S. Goodman and Associates, *Change in Organizations: New Perspectives on Theory, Research, and Practice.* San Francisco: Jossey-Bass, 1982.

Weiers, R. M. *Marketing Research.* Englewood Cliffs, N.J.: Prentice-Hall, 1984.

West, M. L. "The Struggle for Identity." In S. Mudd (ed.), *Conflict Resolution and World Education.* Bloomington, Ind.: Indiana University Press, 1967.

White, T. J., and Reed, J. A. "Leadership." In A. B. Knox and Associates, *Developing, Administering, and Evaluating Adult Education.* San Francisco: Jossey-Bass, 1980.

Wilkins, A. L., and Ouchi, W. G. "Efficient Culture: Exploring the Relationship Between Culture and Organizational Performance." *Administrative Science Quarterly*, 1983, *28*, 468-81.

Winter, D. G. *The Power Motive.* New York: Free Press, 1973.

Wooten, K. C., and White, L. P. "Ethical Problems in the Practice of Organization Development." *Training and Development Journal*, 1983, *37* (4), 16-23.

Yankelovich, D. *New Rules: Searching for Self-Fulfillment in a World Turned Upside Down.* New York: Random House, 1981.

Yankelovich, D., and Associates. *Work and Human Values.* New York: Public Agenda Foundation, 1983.

Zander, A. *Making Groups Effective.* San Francisco: Jossey-Bass, 1982.

❖   ❖   ❖

Name Index

A

Aaker, D. A., 151
Ackoff, R. L., 47, 137–138, 139, 140, 210
Adams, J. S., 212
Adizes, I., 54
Allen, L. A., 12
Allen, R. F., 170, 172
Alm, K., 37
Andreasen, A. R., 149
Apps, J. W., 11
Argyris, C., 3, 53, 203, 205
Ashby, E., 33
Asher, W., 39
Astin, A. W., 52
Austin, N., 1

B

Bales, R. F., 6, 210
Barnard, C. I., 205, 206
Barthelemy, S., 125–126, 128
Bean, J. P., 34, 40
Beck, A. C., 3
Behn, R. D., 23, 70, 135
Bell, D., 131
Bellman, G. M., 3, 210
Benne, K. D., 3, 23, 52, 203
Bennis, W. G., 3, 5, 23, 52, 85, 88, 90, 92, 130, 182, 203
Bercovitch, J., 103, 113
Blake, R. R., 54, 76–77, 103, 104, 105, 206
Blanchard, K. H., 207
Bluestone, B., 131, 132
Bok, D., 32, 34, 131

Bolman, L. G., 3, 52, 92, 209
Botkin, J., 131, 132, 207–208
Boucher, W. I., 35, 38, 39, 214
Boulding, K. E., 103
Boyatzis, R. E., 4, 52, 202, 208
Boyer, E., 31
Bradburn, N. M., 179
Bradford, D. L., 4, 12, 203, 208
Brown, L. D., 103, 105, 106
Brubacher, J. S., 32, 33
Buhler-Miko, M., 37
Butler, R. J., 10, 23

C

Cameron, K. S., 3, 188, 189
Campbell, T. L., 74
Carlson, R. O., 88
Carnevale, A. P., 135
Chemers, M. M., 4, 202
Chin, R., 3, 23, 52, 203
Clark, B. R., 88
Cleveland, H., 3, 10, 12, 169, 171
Cohen, A. R., 4, 12, 203, 208
Cohen, N., 3, 203
Cohen, W. A., 3, 203
Collins, M., 78
Comfort, R. W., 74, 75
Cope, R. G., 35, 36, 41, 44
Coser, L. A., 103, 104
Craig, D. P., 2, 24, 51, 212
Cray, D., 10, 23
Cronin, E. E., 198
Cross, K. P., 80, 189
Crossland, F., 134
Cunningham, P. M., 76
Cyert, R. M., 74, 195

D

Dahl, R. A., 113
Deal, T. E., 3, 6, 52, 87, 92, 93-94,
   169, 170, 209, 210
Del Bueno, D. J., 178
Derr, C. B., 107, 113
Deshler, D., 168
Deutsch, M., 103
Dickson, P., 173
Diebold, J., 33
Dill, D. D., 77
Dimancescu, D., 131, 132, 207-208
Donald, T., 60
Drucker, P. F., 4, 186, 202, 211
Duke, J. T., 103, 104, 105
Dyer, F. J., 170, 172

E

Edgerton, R., 33
Elias, J. L., 75
Enarson, J. J., 134-135
Erikson, E. H., 105

F

Fiedler, F. E., 4, 202
Fielding, D. W., 178
Filley, A. C., 103, 106-107, 108
Fisher, S., 60
Flanagan, G. J., 52
Folberg, J., 106, 114, 115
Follett, M. P., 205
Foxworth, W., 58-59

G

Gagliano, A., 125-126, 128, 139
Gardner, J. W., 24, 208
Geneen, H., 4, 202
Gillette, P., 104, 106, 108, 113
Glamser, F. D., 178
Glasser, W., 105
Gold, G. G., 128
Golembiewski, R. T., 53, 208
Goodstein, L. D., 2, 12, 212
Gregory, L. W., 178
Gros Louis, K.R.R., 74

Gross, N., 135
Grove, A. S., 6, 10, 53, 209

H

Halpin, A. W., 6, 210
Harris, P. R., 210
Harrison, B., 131, 132
Hearn, J. C., 37, 39, 196
Heilizer, F., 105
Hersey, P., 207
Heydinger, R. B., 37, 39, 196
Hickson, D. J., 10, 23
Hillmer, E. D., 3
Hodgkinson, H. L., 189
Hollowood, J. R., 35
Holt, M. E., 168, 204, 211, 212
Hopkins, D.S.P., 23, 51, 212
Hull, J., 56-57

I

Iacocca, L., 91-92

J

Jameson, S., 60-61
Jandt, F. E., 104, 106, 108, 113
Janov, J. E., 72
Jedamus, P., 24
Johnson, L. G., 41, 127, 141
Jonson, R. W., 193

K

Kahn, R., 185, 186, 199, 212
Kanter, R. M., 4, 51, 181, 197, 202
Kaplan, R. E., 53
Kast, F. E., 6, 52, 173, 203
Katz, D., 185, 186, 199, 212
Kaufman, R., 3, 10, 25, 53, 211
Keane, J. G., 74
Kefalas, A. G., 174
Keller, G., 34, 35, 36, 38, 44, 134,
   135, 186, 188, 191, 212
Kennedy, A. A., 6, 52, 92, 93-94,
   170, 209, 210
Kennedy, M. M., 10, 205
Kerr, C., 134, 135, 137

Kilmann, R. H., 10, 92, 209, 211
Kinnear, T. C., 151
Kirkpatrick, D. L., 3, 10
Klus, J. P., 75
Knox, A. B., 36, 70, 74, 84, 213
Kotler, P., 149, 150
Kotter, J. P., 11, 205
Kozol, J., 84
Kuh, G. D., 34, 40

L

Landrieu, M., 126
Langseth, P., 6, 53, 208, 209
Lenz, E., 159
Lewin, K., 180
Likert, J. G., 103
Likert, R., 103
Lippitt, G. L., 6, 51, 53, 205, 208, 209
London, M., 6, 53, 210
Luce, S. R., 170, 171-172
Lynton, E. A., 31, 131, 133, 136, 137, 146-147

M

McCall, M. W., Jr., 206
McCarthy, J., 107
McClellan, J., 207-208
McKersie, R. B., 106
Mallory, G. R., 10, 23
March, J. G., 186
Margulies, N., 1, 204
Mason, R. C., 77
Mason, R. O., 51
Massarik, F., 1, 204
Massey, W. F., 23, 51, 212
Matson, L., 18
Matthews, J. B., 132, 136
Mayhew, L. B., 35
Menton, S., 58
Merriam, S.B., 75
Michael, D. N., 12, 54
Miner, J. B., 3, 12, 51, 214
Mitchell, G., 92, 101
Mitroff, I. I., 8-9, 51, 54, 150, 212
Montana, P. J., 149
Morgan, A., 91

Morrison, J. L., 35, 38, 39, 214
Moscow, A., 4, 202
Mossop, J., 6, 53, 208, 209
Mouton, J. S., 54, 77, 103, 104, 105, 206
Mueller, G. H., 125, 174, 192, 204
Myers, J. A., 151

N

Nagy, M. C., 178
Naisbitt, J., 131
Nanus, B., 5, 90, 92, 182, 203
Nash, M., 11
Nemon, A., 178
Niebuhr, H., Jr., 31, 137, 138-139
Nolan, T. M., 2, 12, 212
Norgaard, R., 132, 136

O

Odiorne, G. S., 3, 11, 54
Offerman, M. J., 71, 169, 171, 204, 208
Ohmae, K., 214
Ouchi, W. G., 170
Overholt, W., 39

P

Parsons, T., 105
Pennings, J. M., 3, 11, 203
Peters, T. J., 1, 6, 70, 71-72, 75, 76, 85, 209
Peterson, M. W., 24, 35
Petronius Arbiter, 173
Pfeffer, J., 186, 206
Pfeiffer, W. J., 2, 12, 212
Pinchot, G., III, 11
Pondy, L. R., 104, 113
Porat, M. U., 132
Porter, M., 150-151
Powers, D. R., 11, 54, 206
Powers, M. F., 11, 54, 206
Putnam, R., 3, 203

Q

Quinn, J. B., 3

R

Rados, D. L., 150
Rawls, J. A., 106
Reed, J. A., 35
Renfro, W. L., 35, 38, 39, 214
Rhodes, F.H.T., 32
Robbins, S. P., 105, 106
Robert, M., 104, 206
Robertson, T. S., 150
Roeber, R.J.C., 186
Rosen, S., 177
Rosenblueth, A., 137
Rosenzweig, J. E., 6, 52, 173, 203
Rubin, J. Z., 112
Rudolph, F., 33
Rudy, W., 32, 33
Ruma, S., 55n
Runyon, M., 92
Ryan, J. H., 76

S

Salancik, G. R., 186
Saxton, M. J., 10, 92, 209
Sayles, L. R., 70
Schein, E. H., 6-7, 52, 92, 205, 209, 211
Schellenberg, J. A., 106, 113
Scherrei, R. A., 52
Schmidt, J. W., 31, 169, 174, 204, 206, 208, 213
Schoderbek, C. G., 174
Schoderbek, P. P., 174
Schön, D. A., 3, 53, 199
Schoner, B., 150
Schuh, G. E., 31, 47
Selznick, P., 71, 75-76, 79
Serpa, R., 10, 92, 209
Shirley, R. C., 44
Shoben, J. E., Jr., 32, 34
Simerly, R. G., 1, 12, 51, 171, 174, 176, 202
Simon, H. A., 186
Singarella, T. A., 77
Singer, E. A., Jr., 137
Smart, C., 40
Smith, C. G., 103
Smith, D. K., 35

Smith, D. M., 3, 203
Smith, F. B., 52
Smith, K. B., 37
Smola, J. K., 178
Sork, T. J., 77
Sparks, H., 73
Srivastva, S., 4
Stake, R. E., 182
State, R., 131, 132, 207-208
Steiner, G. A., 2, 3, 12, 13, 51, 214
Stimpson, J., 62-64, 65-66, 68-69
Stodgill, R. M., 70
Stone, B., 3, 10, 25, 53, 211
Strother, G.B., 75
Sudman, S. S., 179

T

Tannenbaum, R., 1, 204
Tarr, D. L, 205
Taylor, A., 106, 114, 115
Taylor, J. R., 151
Theobald, R., 205
Thomas, F., 19
Tichy, N. M., 3, 12, 51, 196
Toffler, A., 70, 131, 205
Travers, M., 58-59
Trusty, F. M., 103, 104, 207
Turner, J. H., 105
Turnstall, W. B., 170

U

Uhl, K. P., 150
Uhl, N. P., 35

V

Vaupel, J., 23, 70
Vertinsky, A., 40
Veysey, L. R., 32
Vicere, A. A., 72
Volkwein, J. F., 44
von Bertalanffy, L., 204
Votruba, J. C., 75, 169, 174, 175, 185, 204, 212, 213
Vroom, V. H., 64

W

Walshok, M. L., 149, 151, 159, 174, 204, 209
Walton, R. E., 106
Ward, S., 150
Waterman, R. H., Jr., 1, 6, 70, 72, 75, 76, 85, 209
Weber, M., 147–148
Webster, F. E., Jr., 151
Weick, K. E., 189
Weiers, R. M., 150
West, M. L., 105
Westin, W., 62
Whetten, D. A., 3
White, L. P., 78
White, T. J., 35

Wiener, N., 137
Wilcox, E., 63, 65, 66
Wilkins, A. L., 170
Wilson, D. C., 10, 23
Wilson, J., 19
Winter, D. G., 205
Wooten, K. C., 78

Y

Yankelovich, D., 205, 206
Yetton, P. W., 64

Z

Zander, A., 6, 70, 210
Zielinski, J., 150

Subject Index

A

Accountability, issue of, 211–212
Action plan, in strategic planning model, 20–21
Advertising, paid, for promotion, 162–163
Agreement and consensus, leadership for, 207–208
American Association of State Colleges and Universities, 37
Antioch College, culture of, 91
Apple Computer, culture of, 91
Archetypes, creating and maintaining, 9
Audit. *See* Cultural audit; Management audit

B

Boeing, culture of, 94

C

California: business and education partnerships in, 133; community colleges and clients in, 88
Carnegie Council on Policy Studies in Higher Education, 134
Carnegie Foundation for the Advancement of Teaching, 33
Change: and conflict management, 116–117; evaluation for, 180–182; and higher education, 135–137; maintenance balanced with, 52–53; national, 131–132; rewards for, 68–69; values related to, 73–74. *See also* Maintenance/Change Diagnostic Model

Chrysler, culture of, 91–92
Cincinnati, University of, as forerunner, 33
Club of Rome, 9
Commission on Higher Education and the Adult Learner, 78
Community and economic development: analysis of continuing education links with, 125–148; background on, 125–126; and continuing education, 192–193; future for, 146–148; leadership for, 127–131, 145–148; and learning, 127–129, 148; and learning system, 137–140; partnerships for, 140–146; practical advice on, 144–146; and transformations, 131–137; and vision, 129–131
Conceptualization, and conflict management, 117
Conflict: causes of, 105–106; concept of, 103–105; functional and dysfunctional aspects of, 104–105; management of, 27, 103–124
Conflict management: analysis of, 103–124; collaborative, examples of, 109–111; issue of, 206–207; negotiation in, 111–113; organizational, 123; power used for, 113–114; skill evaluation form for, 119–122; skills for, 114–122; strategy selection for, 107–111; summary on, 123–124; win-win approach to, 106–107, 108
Confrontation, and conflict management, 117–118
Constituencies, and marketing, 151, 154, 158, 160, 165

Continuing education: accountability for, 211-212; barriers to strategic planning in, 34-36; bridges and walls for, 31-32, 213-214; building culture of, 98-101; challenges for, 185-214; characteristics of, 88; and clash of cultures, 93-98; code of behavior for, 78-79; and commitment to values of integrity, 84-86; and community and economic development, 125-148; and demographic shifts, 189-190; and economic revitalization, 192-193; faculty conundrum for, 191-192; and fit with parent organization, 156-157; future for, 146-148; integrity in, 79-84; internal diagnosis of, 51-70; internal support for, 200-201; issues of, 89; marginality of, 187; and need for strategic planning, 1-11; organizational support for, 165, 185-201; in partnerships for community and economic development, 140-146; resources dwindling for, 190-191; risk and feedback in, 97; state support for, 193-194; successful strategic planning in, 202-214

Council on the Continuing Education Unit, 78

Cultural audit: advantages of, 171; conducting, 171-173; variables and environments for, 176

Culture. *See* Organizational culture

Customized Job Training Program, 178

D

Dana Corporation, culture of, 92, 101

Decision rules, for Maintenance/Change Diagnostic Model, 64-70

Demography, shifts in, 189-190

Direct mail, for promotion, 162

E

Economic development. *See* Community and economic development.

Environment: analysis of role of, 31-50; background on, 31-34; challenge of, 189; historical relationships with, 32-33; scanning, 36, 49; summary on, 48-50

Environmental scanning: categories in, 36-37; importance of, 36, 49, 196-197; and institutional strengths and weaknesses, 41-47, 49; interdisciplinary committee for, 39-40; and leadership, 8-10, 203-204; methods and sources for, 37-40; for organizational culture, 98-99; pilot screening for, 38; and trend evaluation, 40-41

Ethnography, for cultural audit, 172

Evaluation: analysis of, 168-184; background on, 168-169; for change, 180-182; cultural audit as, 171-173; for decision making, 179-180; designing, conducting, and interpreting, 177-183; for focusing and pacing organizations, 182-183; future for, 183-184; and interventions, 176-177; of organizational culture, 169-177; of organizational structures and systems, 173-176

Exchange process: implementing, 157-160; matching parties in, 152-157

External probability-diffusion matrix, for strategic decisions, 44-46

F

Faculty, implications of, 191-192

Feedback: for conflict management, 115-116; patterns of, 94-96; in strategic planning model, 21-22

Flexibility, and conflict management, 118
Ford Motor Company, systems analysis by, 203

G

GI Bill, 33
Goals: concept of, 17; and strategic decisions, 47; in strategic planning model, 17-20
Groups, task and maintenance dynamics of, 6-8, 210-211

H

Harvard University: and change, 131; culture of, 90, 92-93, 99, 100; and promotion, 163
Higher education: bridges or walls for, 31-32, 213-214; challenges to, 188-195; and change, 135-137; environment related to, historically, 32-33; external challenges to, 132-134; siege of, 134-135; traditional culture of, 96-97
Human Resources Institute, 172, 211

I

IBM, culture of, 90, 95
Ideal modeling, and values clarification, 77
Innovation. *See* Change
Institutions: community orientation of, 87-102; market position of, 43-44; resources of, 42-43; and strategic decisions, 44-47, 49-50; strengths and weaknesses of, 41-47, 49; values assessment for, 44
Integrative thinking, for strategic planning, 197-198
Integrity: commitment to, 79, 84-86; concept of, 71, 72; and ethics, 77; and programming, 79-84
Internal Revenue Service, culture of, 95

J

Job Training Partnership Act, 144

L

Leaders: for agreement and consensus, 207-208; and commitment to integritty, 79; for community and economic development, 127-131, 145-148; concept of, 198; as diagnosticians, 53-54; and evaluation, 177, 180, 181, 183-184; functions of, 4, 198-199; and group dynamics, 6-8, 210-211; learning emphasized by, 127-129, 148; and management of attention, 182; managers distinct from, 90, 130, 169; and marketing, 157-158; and need for strategic planning, 1-11; negotiation by, 111-112; and organizational culture, 6, 90-93, 202-203; and organizational success, 10; power and authority of, 205-206; skills of, 3-6, 85, 203, 207; as statespersons, 214; strategic planning integrated with, 2, 198-200; strategic planning role of, 31-50, 202-214; strategies of, 5; strengthening, 10-11; support for strategic planning by, 27-28; and systems analysis and environmental scanning, 8-10, 203-204; and values clarification, 71, 72-73, 76, 84-86; vision by, 129-131, 169
Learning: and community and economic development, 127-129, 148; system approach for, 137-140
Lindeman Center, and values, 84
Listening, and conflict management, 114-115

M

Maintenance/Change Diagnostic Model: decision rules for, 64-69;

described, 54-64; healthy conditions in, 55-57, 59-61; and strategic planning balance, 52-53; summary on, 69-70; unhealthy conditions in, 57-59, 61-64

Management audit: analysis of, 51-70; background on, 51-52; conducting, 53-64; and data collection, 66-67; decision rules in, 64-69; and ease of achievement, 65-66; for maintenance and change, 53; and rewards for changes, 68-69; in strategic planning model, 14, 51-70; summary on, 69-70

Managers: leaders distinct from, 90, 130, 169; top, support from, 23-24

Marketing: analysis of, 149-167; background on, 149-152; and community needs, 154-156; concept of, 149-150; and constituencies, 151, 154, 158, 160, 165; and educational services, 154; elements, in, 159; evaluation of promotions for, 166-167; and fit of continuing education with parent organization, 156-157; goal and objectives for, 18-19; implementation of, 157-160; and matching parties in exchange, 152-157; networks for, 159; and parent organization's reputation, 153-154; and promotion, 160-167; and social needs, 154

Mary Kay Cosmetics, culture of, 91, 95

Massachusetts, business and education partnerships in, 133

Massachusetts Institute of Technology, report from, 146

Media relations and publicity, free promotion from, 163-164

Metropolitan Council for Lifelong Learning, 142-144

Minnesota, University of, environmental scanning at, 39

Mission statement: guidelines for, 16-17; and marketing, 152, 160; and strategic decisions, 46-47; in strategic planning model, 16-17

Missouri, environmental scanning in, 37

Monitoring system, characteristics of, 25-26

Morrill Act of 1862, 33

N

Nation, changes in, 131-132

National Center for Education Statistics, 190

National Commission on Excellence in Education, 126

National Science Foundation, 140

National Training Labs, 55n

National University Continuing Education Association, 73

Networks: for marketing, 159; for organizational culture, 101

New Orleans, community and economic development in, 126, 128

New Orleans, University of, and partnerships with business, 142, 144

New York City, private adult education in, 98

New York state, demographic shift in, 189

Nissan of America, culture of, 92

Nontraditional programs, characteristics of, 87-89

Norms Diagnostic Index, 172, 211

North Carolina, business and education partnerships in, 133

Northern Illinois University, 84

O

Objectives, in strategic planning model, 17-20

Ohio State University, and siege of universities, 134

Organizational culture: analysis of building, 87-102; audit of, 171-173; background on, 87-90; and ceremonies, 100-101; clash of, 93-98; concept of, 6, 92, 169-170;

of continuing education, 93-101;
and core values, 99; environmental scanning for, 98-99;
evaluation of, 169-177; and heroes, 99-100; identity and image
in, 90-92; impact on, 209-210;
issue of, 202-203; and leadership, 6, 90-93, 202-203; managing, 6; and networks, 101; and
new approaches, 99; risk and
feedback in, 94-96; and rituals,
100; and stories, 101; summary
on, 101-102; and symbolic
issues, 101; types of, 93-95, 210;
and values clarification, 16
Organizational diagnosis. See Management audit
Organizations: adjusting course of,
180-182; background on, 185-
186; continuing education support from 185-201; dynamics of
survival and adaptation by, 186-
188; environments of, 174-176;
focusing and pacing, 182-183;
and individual and group needs,
204-205; internal diagnosis of,
51-70; intervening in, 176-177;
self-renewal for, 208-209; structures and systems of, 173-176;
success of, 10; values clarification for, 71-86

P

Pennsylvania: demographic shift
in, 189; evaluation in, 178
Planning: approaches to, 13; long-
range, steps in, 35; program, and
strategic decision, 47-48, 50; traditional, shortcomings of, 195.
See also Strategic planning
Probability-diffusion matrix: and
environmental scanning, 41-42;
external, 44-46
Problematique, and leadership, 9-
10, 206, 208
Procter & Gamble, culture of, 99
Programming: concept of, 74; integrity and, 79-84; role of values

in, 74-76; and values clarification, 71-86
Project on Continuing Higher Education Leadership, 73, 78
Promotion, and marketing, 160-
167
Publics, and marketing, 150

R

Radar scanning, 196-197
Reality test, in strategic planning
model, 21
Regional Planning Commission,
126
Resourcefulness, and conflict management, 118-119
Resources, dwindling, 190-191
Rewards: for change, in management audit, 68-69; for strategic
planning, 28

S

Scanning. See Environmental
scanning
Segmentation, and marketing, 150
Social needs: and marketing, 154;
and values clarification, 84
Southern Regional Education
Board, 194
Special events, for promotion 164-
165
Stakeholders: concept of, 8; and
marketing, 150, 160; and strategic planning, 8-10
State University of New York at
Binghamton, environmental
scanning at, 197
States, continuing education support by, 193-194
Strategic decision: concept of, 44;
and goals, 47; and institutions,
44-47, 49-50; and program planning, 47-48, 50
Strategic planning: action plan in,
20-21; activities of, 1-2; advantages of, 195-196; applications
of, 71-184; background on, 1-3,

12-14; barriers to, 34-36; challenges to, 185-214; characteristics of, 22-29; committee for, 24-25; and community and economic development, 125-148; concept of, 12-14; conflict management in, 27, 103-124; as continuing process, 28-29; elements in, 13-14; and environmental scanning, 196-197; and evaluation, 168-184; flexibility in, 26-27; goals and objectives in, 17-20; and group dynamics, 6-8; implications for, 195-201; importance of, 34; integrative thinking for, 197-198; issues in, 3-10, 23-29, 202-214; leadership integrated with, 2, 198-200; leadership role in, 31-50, 202-214; long-range, 212-213; maintenance and change balanced in, 52-53; management audit in, 14, 51-70; and marketing, 149-167; mission statement in, 16-17; model for, 14-22; monitoring implementation of, 25-26; need for, 1-11; and organizational culture, 87-102; organizational readiness for, 24; overview of, 1-70; reality test in, 21; rewards for, 28; as rope, 12-13; skills in, 3-6; steps in process of, 12-30; success in, 202-214; summary on, 30; and support by top management, 23-24, 27-28; and systems analysis and environmental scanning, 8-10; time for, 25, 29; values clarification in, 14-16, 71-86

Strengths/weaknesses/opportunities/threats (SWOT) profile, for strategic decisions, 44-45

Systems analysis: and continuing education, 137-138; and leadership, 8-10, 203-204

T

Telemarketing, for promotion, 165-166

Texas, business and education partnerships in, 133

U

United States Air Force, culture of, 99

United States Mediation Service, 111

V

Values clarification: analysis of, 71-86; background on, 71-72; case examples of, 81-84; and change, 73-74; and code of behavior, 78-79; and commitment to integrity, 79, 84-86; for institutions, 44; and leaders, 71, 72-73, 76, 84-86; and opposing tendencies, 76-77; and organizational culture, 16, 99; role of, in programming, 74-76; and social problems, 84; in strategic planning model, 14-16, 71-86

Vision, and community and economic development, 129-131

W

Wagner Labor Relations Act, 111

Wisconsin Cooperative Extension Service, and environmental scanning, 37, 40-41

Wisconsin-Extension, University of, and goals, 47

Wisconsin Idea, 33

Wisconsin, University of, environmental scanning at, 39

X

Xerox, culture of, 95